"*Facing the Wind* is the true story of Bob Rowe, whose horrifying murders of his wife and children will remain forever etched in my mind. . . . [The book] had me tossing at night and racing to finish it by day. It is a rare combination of superb reporting and narrative skill. Over years of effort, Salamon secured access to the most intimate thoughts and writings of nearly all the participants, enabling her to amass a wealth of detail. And she makes the most of it, proving Tom Wolfe's assertion that narrative nonfiction can be every bit as important as fiction in exploring the most important issues of our lives and times. *Facing the Wind* raises profound questions: of guilt, retribution, justice, redemption, and absolution. There are no easy answers. It is not a book that can be read and forgotten."

—*The New York Times Book Review*

"[*Facing the Wind*] tests our beliefs about punishment, retribution and even murder itself. . . . When author Julie Salamon explains what drew her to the story of the Rowes, she writes movingly of 'the fragility of ordinary expectations, the fine line between happy families and tragic ones.' "

—*The Washington Post*

"Salamon doesn't shy away from the larger questions, both personal and institutional . . ."

—*The New Yorker*

"Salamon's book is an achievement in reporting. She presents an honest mix of findings while posing questions so hard they may not be answerable."

—New York *Daily News*

"Happily for the reader, Ms. Salamon is a fine reporter whose intellectual curiosity leads her into some fascinating digressions. . . . In tackling the issue of personal heroism, *Facing the Wind* brings home the point that while certain of life's difficulties can be fought and conquered, others must simply be borne with dignity."

—*The New York Times*

"This true-crime story reaches beyond the relatively narrow focus of the genre to ask painful and provocative questions about guilt and forgiveness. . . . This expertly crafted account is informed by diligent research and interviews . . ."

—*Publishers Weekly* (starred)

"A suspenseful, well-researched account . . . A perturbing read that allows us to ponder guilt and innocence from new perspectives."

—*Kirkus Reviews* (starred)

"A true-crime narrative of extraordinary breadth and compassion. . . . *Facing the Wind* never disintegrates into a lurid tale of a sensational murder. Sensitive, moving, and disturbing, it is a masterful work of journalism."

—*Bookpage*

"Salamon—author of the previous best sellers *The Christmas Tree* and *The Devil's Candy*—has created a new genre. . . . But [she] goes far beyond the horror to include an in-depth look at the challenge of raising handicapped children and the use of the insanity defense. The result is a spellbinding narrative that's likely to simultaneously seduce and repulse readers."

—*Orlando Sentinel*

"Riveting. In documenting the stresses of raising a disabled child and Rowe's awful act and its aftermath, Salamon's book wrestles with a troubling and perhaps unanswerable question: Does a man who kills a family have the right to start over, once he has been acquitted of murder on the grounds he was insane?"

—*Pittsburgh Post-Gazette*

JULIE SALAMON is the author of *The Devil's Candy, The Christmas Tree, The Net of Dreams,* and *White Lies.* Formerly a reporter and film critic for *The Wall Street Journal,* she is now a television critic for *The New York Times.*

FACING THE WIND

A True Story of Tragedy and Reconciliation

JULIE SALAMON

RANDOM HOUSE
TRADE PAPERBACKS
NEW YORK

Grateful acknowledgment is made to the following for permission to reprint previously published
material: The New York Times: Excerpt from an "op-ed," by Anonymous, which appeared in the
March 28, 1978, issue of *The New York Times*. Copyright © 1978 by the New York Times Company. Reprinted by permission of *The New York Times*. Random House, Inc.: Four lines from
"Law Like Love," from *W. H. Auden: Collected Poems*, by W. H. Auden. Copyright © 1940 and
copyright renewed 1968 by W. H. Auden. Reprinted by permission of Random House, Inc.

Library of Congress Cataloging-in-Publication Data
Salamon, Julie.
Facing the wind : a true story of tragedy and reconciliation / Julie Salamon.—1st ed.
p.   cm.
ISBN 0-375-75940-9
1. Murder—New York (State)—New York.   2. Family violence—New York (State)—New York.
3. Uxoricide—New York (State)—New York.   4. Brooklyn (New York, N.Y.)—
Social conditions.   I. Title.
HV6534.N5 S35 2001   364.15'23'0974723—dc21
00-042532

Random House website address: www.atrandom.com
Printed in the United States of America on acid-free paper
2 4 6 8 9 7 5 3
First Trade Paperback Edition

Book design by J. K. Lambert

FOR BILL

CONTENTS

FOREWORD

I first heard of the Rowe family in the summer of 1995, when my second child was eight months old. It was a happy time for me. My children were healthy and well cared for—and I was incapable of making that assertion without knocking on wood. Why tempt fate? I knew terrible things could happen whether or not I lived up to my parental responsibilities.

I had been exploring various subjects to write about when a friend introduced me to Edith Patt, who for many years had been the chief social worker at the Industrial Home for the Blind in Brooklyn and had a story to tell. In the early 1970s, Edith had organized a support group for the mothers of blind children enrolled in the agency's nursery school. Some of the children had additional handicaps, including severe autism and inexplicable seizures, and there was one case of bilateral anophthalmia—a child who was born without eyes. The women had developed abiding friendships that helped them weather motherhood in its most difficult form. Now their children were grown and the women—the mothers, as they called themselves—were interested in having someone write about their experiences. Their higher purpose may have been to help others who found themselves in similar straits, but they also wanted recognition for the battles they'd fought on the domestic front. Their struggles may not have had the cinematic "glamour" of war, but they were as searing to the spirit. While most wars come to an end, caring for a handicapped child is a lifelong obligation.

I listened with fascination and sympathy and admiration—and terror. I wasn't sure I was prepared to immerse myself in the heartrending details that would force me to face my worst fears about being a mother. I was still hesitating when Edith's story took an unexpected turn.

The IHB mothers had become friends because of their children, but they were bound together when one of them was killed, along with her three children. The woman was Mary Rowe. The weapon was a baseball bat. The killer was her husband, and he had always been an exemplary father, a lawyer, a man the women knew and admired. Robert Rowe was declared not guilty by reason of insanity in 1978, spent two and a half years in mental hospitals before being released, and then tried to resume normal life.

It was a monstrous story, but Edith Patt assured me that this was not a monstrous man. I was drawn in. I spent the next four years learning as much as I could about these families, whose lives were yoked by contingency and fate. I interviewed the mothers and their husbands, children, doctors, and social workers. I studied Robert Rowe's court records and psychiatric files. I found out that the case had become a legal curiosity, provoking yet another debate about the limits and usefulness of the insanity defense. But I also discovered that for those who were involved, before and after the killings, this was a tragedy, not an intellectual exercise. From it arose a wellspring of questions about responsibility and guilt, retribution and forgiveness: We do what we can to hold chaos at bay, but what if we can't? Why can some people assume responsibilities in trying circumstances; why are others crushed by them?

The narrative that emerged was not "uplifting" in a conventional sense, though it included moving chronicles of survival and renewal. Nor was it condemnatory, though it contained an act of horrible violence. But in the stories of these mothers, fathers, and children I encountered uncommon strains of human resilience and was gratified, even as I prayed never to be tested—not like that.

PART I

In dreams begins responsibility.

—

from "Responsibilities"

W. B. YEATS

Prologue

In the summer of 1977, baseball was the only thing that mattered to Bobby Rowe and Jeffrey Mond. When they weren't hitting balls and playing catch, they were listening to games on the radio or rehashing old plays (both theirs and the Yankees') or speculating about whether the Yankees would actually win the World Series. They weren't being boyishly optimistic. For the first time in fifteen years—a lifetime for Bobby and Jeffrey, who were teenagers—there was general agreement that a championship seemed entirely possible.

Bobby and Jeffrey lived in Mill Basin. This was merely a fact of life for them but an accomplishment for their parents, who sounded like real estate brokers when they described this prosperous enclave in Brooklyn as the best of both worlds, with suburban amenities and urban convenience. The fathers of Mill Basin were lawyers, accountants, dentists, and shopkeepers. The mothers were homemakers, though some of them did work outside the house, often alongside their husbands in dry cleaning stores and other family-owned businesses. The population was mainly white and ethnic—Italian, Irish, Jewish—but the more liberal residents liked to mention the lovely black family who had moved into the neighborhood (noting with relief that both the husband and wife were doctors).

When Jeffrey heard a game on the radio, he'd call Bobby to report the score, and Bobby would do the same for him, even if they were both listening to the same game. When they played catch or shagged flies, they'd pretend to be Yankees stars—Catfish Hunter or Ron Guidry or Reggie Jackson. The boys played ball together a lot, even though Bobby, who was fourteen, was exactly four years and four days younger than Jeffrey. Jeffrey's mother nagged him about hanging around a younger kid so much, but he liked being with Bobby. Jeffrey was the youngest of three children and Bobby was the oldest of three. It was a novelty to play a different role. Jeffrey could be the big brother and Bobby could be the little one. Besides, they had the same interests. They liked to sail and to climb trees, and more than anything, they liked baseball.

Bobby was the gutsiest kid Jeffrey knew. When he had to use crutches for a couple of years because something was wrong with his hip, he'd leave them lying on the ground to climb the giant tree by his house, and then would expertly deal with his mother when she freaked out about it.

Jeffrey's affection for Bobby couldn't be disentangled from his warm feelings toward the entire Rowe family. That included Bobby's younger brother, Christopher, who could be a pain in the neck, and Jenna, his little sister, the youngest. One day, when Jeffrey's bicycle tire blew out far from home and he couldn't reach his own mother, he immediately called Mary Rowe to pick him up. She was the best lady on their street, as far as he was concerned. And Bob—Robert, Sr.—was the best, period. He had a way of making a summer night in Brooklyn feel like you were at sleepaway camp in the country. Bob taught the neighborhood kids how to build campfires in the backyard and which constellation was which, and sometimes he played the ukulele and sang. None of the other fathers jumped into the Sapolskys' swimming pool with the kids, splashing and yelling noisily when they played a game called Whale. Jeffrey certainly couldn't imagine Murray Sapolsky doing that. Mr. Sapolsky didn't play; he yelled. He was always afraid someone was going to drown in his pool. Jeffrey never saw Bob lose his temper.

Jeffrey always felt that when he had children, he'd want to raise them the way Bob raised his. He learned so much from Bob. Much as Jeffrey had a good time with Bobby, he also felt as though he were returning a favor to Bob when he taught Bobby things, like how to move quicker when he played ball. Bobby was fast, though not as fast as Jeffrey. The older boy spent hours drilling the kid, figuring out ways to help him put on speed. They worked on it all summer and into the fall. One day Bobby complained that his father's old bat was slowing him down. It was too heavy. Jeffrey was larger and his bat was lighter, so he told Bobby they should trade. He liked the idea of their having each other's bats. What better way to seal a friendship?

—

On February 22, 1978, four months after the thrilling Yankees World Series victory the previous fall, Jeffrey was looking out his bedroom window when he noticed lights flashing up the street and heard his mother come in from walking the dog. He knew something was wrong, because she slammed the door and shouted that something had happened at the Rowes'.

Jeffrey didn't hesitate. He pulled on his coat, ran out of the house, and raced past the half-dozen houses between his and Bobby's, where he found a bunch of neighbors standing in the icy night, watching policemen make tracks in the Rowes' front yard. The ground was still white from the blizzard a couple of weeks earlier that had dropped nearly seventeen inches of snow on Brooklyn in one day.

A grim-faced officer carrying a baseball bat in a plastic bag caught Jeffrey's attention. He did a double take when he noticed the distinctive dark wood and the dirty white tape around the handle. That was his bat. Why was the cop taking it away?

—

Assistant district attorney Michael Gary was on duty that night. He'd been hired by the Brooklyn D.A. four and a half years earlier, right after receiving his degree, magna cum laude, from New York University, but had only recently worked his way up to the premier bureau, the homicide division.

The twenty-eight-year-old assistant district attorney was a mild-looking man with a round face and small features and fair hair that was already sparse. More experienced lawyers had told him that eventually he'd get used to the brutality, the way most cops do, but he was still raw. The brutality got to him every time.

In the 1970s, the Brooklyn D.A.'s office worked under the theory of "vertical prosecution." The assistant district attorney who would eventually present evidence to the jury was supposed to be part of the case from the beginning, dispatched to crime scenes to help the police take statements, obtain search warrants, run lineups. That way, when the office was putting a prosecution together later, there wouldn't be any gaps. Plus, the ADAs wouldn't have to rely on photographs or secondhand descriptions of the crime scene, because they'd have checked it out for themselves.

Assistant district attorney Gary wasn't worried about arriving on time, because he was being taken by Rocky, one of the drivers assigned to the D.A.'s office. None of the ADAs seemed to know Rocky's last name, but they knew this: When Rocky was around, you didn't need a cop to lead the way. He could find any address in any police precinct in Brooklyn.

Gary didn't pay much attention to where they were going. He was tired. The call had come after nine o'clock, and he had a long night in front of him. He knew that killers didn't keep regular business hours, but why did the calls always seem to come at night? Still, despite the discomfort, he didn't mind riding cases. Early on in law school, he'd decided that he would do public-service work of some kind, either as a legal aid lawyer or as a prosecutor. He wanted the bad guys put away, but not at any cost, and the truth got smudged every time it passed through another pair of hands. It was worth a sleepless night to see a crime scene for yourself.

He shook himself out of a semi-snooze and looked out the window. Where were they? This didn't look like Brooklyn. The houses had space around them and the yards were real, not the patio extensions New Yorkers tried to pass off as yards. Just as it occurred to him that they'd been driving a long time, he realized that Rocky was lost.

"People don't get killed in Mill Basin," explained Rocky in embarrassment, as they drove in circles, up one quiet street and down the next, the monotony punctuated by the driver's apologies and his assurances of their imminent arrival.

Finally, a blast of light cut through the still, cold darkness. They'd reached their destination, 2443 East Sixty-fourth Street. The frigid air was smoky with exhaust fumes from police cruisers and ambulances. The neighbors gathered outside the house were silhouettes in the night, accented with little puffs of breath.

A detective met Gary at the door and escorted him up the short flight of steps that led to the living room of the split-level house so he could take a look at the first victim. A woman with brown hair was lying on the brown wall-to-wall carpeting, not far from the piano, close to a conversation nook created by two chairs that were set at angles near a side table. She was wearing red slacks and a colorful sweater and looked comfortable, as though she might have stretched out for a few winks before calling the kids down to supper. Gary had to get close to see the blood on the side of her head, the stain on the carpet.

A sicker than usual feeling came over him as he glanced around the room and took in the walls covered with paintings and family pictures, an antique clock. He followed the detective up another half-flight of stairs to the bedrooms. The smell of gas had penetrated the house, but that wasn't why the ADA felt woozy. This scene was too middle-class, too "tasteful," too familiar. Someone mentioned that the husband was a lawyer.

Michael Gary had seen horrible crime scenes, where the violence lingered in the air, like smoke after a fusillade of bullets, but he was far more unnerved by the deceptive tranquillity he found in the Rowes' home. How would he be able to excise the image of the three dead children lying in bed, wearing pajamas, peaceful, as if they'd happily succumbed to exhaustion after a busy day?

To dispel the harmonious illusion, it was necessary to turn the children's heads, to seek out the gashes and the dried blood. Before he did that, he might have thought nothing was wrong at all, except for the color of their skin, white as alabaster, eerily angelic.

This was the benefit of riding cases, wasn't it? No one had to tell you later where the bodies were discovered. You didn't have to look at a photograph to get the lay of the land. Lucky him. He had the opportunity to walk close to the children, to examine the head wounds that weren't apparent from the doorway, to see their blood on the sheets. Much better than a photograph. Lucky him.

CHAPTER I

The Beginning

When Bob Rowe first laid eyes on Mary Savage, he immediately began thinking of ways to improve her. It was 1950, and he was sitting in the cafeteria at St. John's University, in downtown Brooklyn. He watched her bounce across the room, nineteen years old, meeting and greeting like a ward heeler. She wasn't tall, but she moved with a big stride.

Good figure, he thought—maybe a little heavy in the hips. He decided the quilted skirt she was wearing was the problem. "That's got to go," he said to himself, and later recorded his thoughts in a journal.

A girl at Bob's table waved Mary over and Bob asked to be introduced. Her blue eyes, so tiny that they almost disappeared when she smiled, held the promise of mischief. As she stood there laughing and talking, he studied her for signs of ambivalence or anxiety but saw only a straightforward appreciation of life.

He had decided when he was eleven years old that he was going to move out of the social class to which he'd been born; his father had been an electrician for the Tastee Bread Company. Now he saw a girl who could help him with his plan. It didn't matter when he found out that Mary's family was even poorer than his. She didn't need money to be a good partner for him.

"Drive—that's what Mary was," he wrote. "Pure drive." He wasn't surprised to learn she'd been class president at St. Joseph's Commercial High School.

Mary Savage's mother, Laura, didn't want her daughter, her only child, to have anything to do with Bob Rowe. The Savages were so poor that they couldn't afford to fix the ceiling when it started falling in on them, piece by piece. Not many people were below them on the social scale, so Laura Savage used religion as her measuring stick. She looked down her nose at anyone who wasn't Catholic, and Bob was Lutheran. She addressed him, with neither irony nor affection, as "you Protestant bastard."

Bob and Mary maneuvered around the religion problem by having Jack O'Shaughnessy pick Mary up when she and Bob had a date. It was easy enough. Jack lived near Mary in Bay Ridge, and he would do almost anything for his fraternity brother—and closest friend—at St. John's. Jack would bring Mary to the DeKalb Avenue subway station and hand her off to Bob.

Mrs. Savage approved of Jack's Irish Catholicism, which made her approve of him. When Jack and Mary were about to leave, he'd tell a joke. "If we're not home by Tuesday, Mrs. Savage, call the police." She would laugh appreciatively and tell them to have a nice time. Or she'd shout out a ditty in her thick Irish brogue.

> Work while it's work time
> Play while it's play
> 'Tis the only way to be happy
> The only way to be gay.

Jack thought Mary was an attractive girl—no Miss America, but attractive. That was amazing considering her mother's face. There was no nice way to put it. Mrs. Savage was homely. "Born in a cave in County Cork,"

Bob said, and Jack didn't disagree. He described Mary as "bubbly, a girl you could have fun with," when he fondly remembered the night the three of them had spent wandering along the beach at Coney Island. They'd done nothing more than laugh and talk and run on the beach, but staying out all night seemed daring in those days just after World War II. People were trying to settle down, and Irish Catholic girls from "nice" families didn't venture far from home after dark. No matter that home was barely one step up from a shanty—a crucifix on every wall, a roach for every crack in the floor. At dawn it was up to Jack to take Mary back and make peace with Mrs. Savage.

Jack suspected that eventually Bob would have to make peace with Mary's mother. He'd watched a series of girls try to get their hooks into Bob—the nautical metaphor was Jack's—but he figured that Mary was going to be the one to anchor him.

Jack would meet *his* future wife, Nellie, a nursing student at St. John's, through Mary, who worked as a secretary at the nursing school. Bob was best man at Jack and Nellie's wedding; Jack was best man at Bob and Mary's. The connection between the women would make it easier for Bob and Jack to keep their friendship going after they both married. Things would become harder when the children arrived.

—

Jack knew it wouldn't be accurate to say that he and Bob had grown up together, because both of them had already served in the army by the time they met. Without the GI Bill, neither of them could have afforded the tuition at St. John's. But Jack felt that in a crucial way they *had* grown up together. They'd shared an intellectual awakening, and that was a kind of coming-of-age for inquisitive young men from working-class families.

Bob constantly interrogated Jack about Catholicism. He was drawn to the religion's melodramatic flourishes and theological gamesmanship and would have liked to please Mary by converting, but he was skeptical. His mother was scornful of Catholics, maybe because his father had been born one. One night Bob and Jack were wandering around the streets of Brooklyn talking about the Catholic doctrine of transubstantiation. Jack explained that the priest, by saying words of consecration, converts the

Eucharist wafer and wine into the body and blood of Christ. They stopped in front of a bakery window and Bob pointed to some buns. "You're going to tell me the priest says the words *Hoc est enim corpus meum* and then that bun is the body of Christ?"

"Yeah," said Jack. "He has the power, but it would be a horrendous sin, because he's not supposed to do it outside the mass."

He saw Bob file the information away. The guy never seemed to forget anything. Ask him about a potato, he'd give you a dissertation on the history of Ireland.

At the end of their first year at St. John's, they took summer jobs as orderlies on the midnight shift at Beth Israel Hospital in Manhattan. After classes, on their way to work, they'd go for some drinks in downtown Brooklyn and then walk across the Brooklyn Bridge into the city. Those were magical evenings, with the towers of the financial district looming like castles against the pink sky. They passed by the courthouses in Foley Square, quietly majestic in the after-hours calm. If it was early enough, they'd stop in Union Square, which in those days was New York's equivalent of Hyde Park Corner. The cold war was under way, so someone was always ranting about communism, pro or con. Bob would jump right in. He had an opinion about everything.

The nurses at Beth Israel called Bob "Red" and Jack "the Irish kid" and fed them Hungarian goulash in the middle of the night. In the morning, after their shift was over, Bob and Jack would steal a couple of scrub suits and stethoscopes and walk around the wards pretending to be doctors. Before going back to Brooklyn, they'd stop at a coffee shop and annoy the waitresses by ordering ice cream sodas while everyone else was having eggs and bagels and coffee.

Bob could do many things that Jack felt were out of his reach. The two of them were about the same height, five-foot-ten or so, but Bob was strapping while Jack was slight. Bob served in the army not once but twice—called up from the reserves and shipped to Korea for his second go-round. When he came out, he went back to school to become a lawyer, while Jack dropped out. Jack was hesitant; Bob was unafraid.

Jack saw Bob as an alchemist who could spin the dull gray of ordinary life into gold. Bob's father also had that gift. He was part Hawaiian, and the two of them, father and son, used to play the ukulele together. His father was as dark as Bob was fair. Bob took his looks from his mother, Mildred, whose family was Scandinavian. One night Jack and Bob were prowling around downtown Brooklyn and Jack found an old, cracked ukulele without strings. He bought it for three dollars. They took it to Bob's house. His father patched it up, put on new strings, and then managed to pull some pretty good music out of it.

—

In 1960, six years into their marriage, Bob and Mary moved to the Mill Basin peninsula and built their house on an empty sandlot on East Sixty-fourth Street. There was nothing between them and the water but other empty sandlots.

In the southeastern corner of Brooklyn, the smell of salt hung heavily in the air. This part of the Jamaica Bay tidal basin had been called Equandito—"broken lands"—by the local Canarsee Indians, who sold it in 1664 to white men, who kept its rural character intact for a couple of centuries. In all that time, the only industry worth mentioning was the sale of crabs, oysters, and clams. Then, in the early twentieth century, there were various attempts at commercial development of the neighborhood, but these were stalled when long-promised railroads weren't built. Finally, after World War II, people began moving in. The first homes, built in the late 1940s and early 1950s, were brick bungalows, but by the time the Rowes arrived, sizable houses on lots measuring fifty by one hundred feet were replacing them. Mill Basin would become even more upscale, but it was already regarded as a very good place to live.

Bob was a lawyer—a claims investigator for Allstate Insurance—and a company man. But the dullness of his professional life and his pursuit of bourgeois comfort didn't limit his imagination or cramp his style. Bob Rowe was also a visionary, who saw himself as part of a noble lineage, risen out of the sea: a descendant of Vikings on his mother's side and Hawaiian warriors on his father's. After he and Mary moved to Mill Basin they bought a sailboat, which they kept by the side of the house. Bob named it *King Kamehameha,* to honor his father's ancestors.

Bob liked feeling connected to the benevolent dictator-king who ruled

Hawaii from 1796 until 1819. Kamehameha was noted for his intelligence and character as well as his ferocity. During one of many battles he fought to become the first undisputed ruler of all the Hawaiian Islands, he led an attack against a small village. One of the village's defenders defiantly broke a paddle over Kamehameha's head. Years later, remembering the man's bravery, Kamehameha enacted the Mamalahoe, "Law of the Splintered Paddle," whose purpose was to protect the weak from the strong. The law is included in Hawaii's constitution, Article IX, Section 10:

> The law of the splintered paddle, mamalahoe kanawai, decreed by Kamehameha I—Let every elderly person, woman and child lie by the roadside in safety—shall be a unique and living symbol of the State's concern for safety.
>
> The State shall have the power to provide for the safety of the people from crimes against persons and property.

Within a few years, construction would overtake all the sandlots on Mill Basin, and Bob and Mary would no longer be able to see the water from their home.

Barbara and Murray Sapolsky moved to East Sixty-fourth Street one week after the Rowes, and soon there was a block full of young couples who had wanted bigger houses so that they could begin families. Until the children came along, however, they would think nothing of staying up until four in the morning at one house or the other. Saturday nights, they'd break out some beer and potato chips and just sit in someone's driveway and talk. Inevitably, a process of evaluation and comparison began. If their street had had a yearbook, Bob and Mary Rowe would have been designated the couple most likely to succeed.

"Everybody sort of envied them, their relationship—it was beautiful," Barbara Sapolsky said. "They both had strong personalities, and they were friendly. Bob could tell stories for hours, and you could howl when you heard the things he would tell you from his job. He was a very well-read person. He knew facts and things the average person would never think of."

His job at Allstate was to turn human mishap and tragedy into an actuarial calculation. His pleasure was to transform the calculations into stories. Bob told these gruesome tales as absurdist entertainments, horrifying and titillating yet reassuringly distant from placid Mill Basin.

There was the one about the fireman who battered his way through the wooden barrier in the "bedroom" window and then fell four floors to his death. The "bedroom" had in fact been an airshaft.

A metal-tipped pole fell out of a twelfth-story window in a Manhattan skyscraper and pierced the head of a nun walking below. A neurosurgeon had to trim the pole close to her skull so she could fit into the ambulance.

A musician driving off the Whitestone Bridge skidded onto a divider median. When he got out to survey the damage, he was hit by a car. He flew over a wall into high weeds eighteen feet away. A few hours later a policeman ticketed his car. A tow truck took it away. A construction worker discovered his body days later.

Mary didn't have Bob's education, but she had a sharp wit. She could hold her own with her husband, although Barbara Sapolsky thought Mary catered to him a little too much. Barbara, for example, would never have allowed Murray to go out and spend eighty dollars on a single book, the way Bob did—she didn't care how rare it was. Mary also catered to Bob's mother, who moved into the apartment downstairs. The houses had been built so they could be easily divided in two for rental income. Barbara's mother-in-law lived in her house, too.

Mildred Rowe had a wicked sense of humor, but she wasn't an easy woman. Mary confided to Barbara that Millie was the only person who criticized Bob, the older of her two sons, though he was her favorite. Millie seemed unimpressed even with Bob's diplomas. "So you're a lawyer," she said to him, the only one in the family who'd gone to college. "Why aren't you a judge?"

Chief among Bob's offenses, according to Millie, was his unwillingness to put his mother in front of his wife. Millie said she didn't like Mary because she was Catholic, but if religion hadn't been available, she would have found another reason. (Bob and Mary were married in a Catholic church, and Mildred attended the wedding.) Mary didn't like Millie, either, but she wouldn't think of confronting her, any more than she would have openly defied her own mother. She conformed to her description in *The Parmentier,* her high school yearbook: "capable, considerate, gracious." One year, when she and Bob were still living in a little apartment off Fort Hamilton Parkway, Mary invited her parents and Millie for Christmas dinner. Bob's father had died a few months before Bob and Mary got married, and Mary's father would be satisfied so long as there was plenty of whiskey on hand. The mothers would set the evening's stakes.

Mary's mother insisted on potato stuffing and Ocean Spray cranberry sauce, while Bob's mother wanted sausage-and-bread stuffing with lingonberries. Mary cleverly solved the problem. With a wink at Bob, she put a dish of lingonberries in front of her Scandinavian mother-in-law and a bowl of Ocean Spray cranberries in front of her Irish mother. She had punched holes in both ends of the turkey. Potatoes emerged from one end, sausage from the other.

—

At their first Christmas in Mill Basin, the Rowes had a joke of a tree, barely a foot high. But soon Bob felt the urge to put on a Santa Claus suit and to have children who would appreciate it. He planted hedges, a plum tree, and a white birch. As the yard thickened, the house acquired a look of permanence. Everything seemed ready.

But Mary didn't seem in a rush to become a mother. She wasn't the type to go peeking enviously into other people's baby carriages—maybe because she was an only child, speculated the women on the block, or maybe because she was having fun. She was working as a sales rep for the telephone company and liked her job. She and Bob lived well. They sailed in the summer, skied in the winter. Bob painted seascapes, which Mary displayed on the walls.

Barbara didn't think Mary was doing anything to prevent having kids besides being careful and being Catholic. Early on, Mary told Barbara about a group of friends they had from Bob's office. One of them was divorced. "I'm not really supposed to talk to him," Mary said. "He's divorced." But she wasn't closed-minded. She confessed to her friend that she had doubts about religion. "If I die and find out that all of this is garbage, I'm going to be so mad!"

Barbara became pregnant first. After her son Alan was born, she and the baby would hang out with Mary and her dog. She was a wonderful little mutt, but it still drove Barbara crazy when Mary couldn't get over the fact that Barbara's one-year-old son was smarter than her dog. "Mary," said Barbara. "If you ever compare my kid to a dog again, I'll kill you."

She wasn't really angry with Mary. They were more like sisters than neighbors. Only a row of bushes separated the Rowes' driveway from the Sapolskys'. Their houses were mirror images. Though Mary was an inch or two taller than Barbara, who was short and sturdy, they wore each other's clothes, size 12.

Barbara was thrilled when Bobby was born, on May 10, 1963 — Robert, Jr., after his father. Her nickname was Bobbie, too, so now there were a Bob, a Bobby, and a Bobbie. The connection between the neighbors seemed complete.

Poor Mary didn't know what to do with a baby, and her mother was no help. Mr. Savage had died the year before Bob and Mary moved to Mill Basin, and Mrs. Savage seemed lost in Mary's fine new house. There were cousins in Rockaway, but they rarely visited, and there was another cousin—a nun—in Boston. So Barbara and another neighbor, Natalie Mond, came over and helped Mary give the baby his first bath.

Bob wanted his firstborn to love everything he loved. He had the chess set ready; he bought a piano. Most of all, he couldn't wait to show Bobby the night. The stars would frequently appear in his paintings, especially Orion the Hunter, the tragic giant sadly traipsing across the sky carrying his club. Before Bobby could walk, his father would take him outside and tell him stories about the constellations. "Whenever you see Orion," he said to the boy, "you'll know that I am thinking of you and loving you."

CHAPTER 2

The Second Son

Christopher was born on August 20, 1965, two years after Bobby. He, too, was a beautiful blue-eyed baby boy, likely to be a redhead like his brother and his father, judging from the peach fuzz on his head. Bob and Mary noticed that one of his eyes was tiny, much smaller than the other, and asked the doctor about it. "Microphthalmic," said the pediatrician unhelpfully, simply translating what was clearly observable into clinical language. He assured the Rowes that the condition probably wouldn't affect Christopher's vision, though he might be a little cross-eyed.

Bob and Mary, optimists by nature and conditioning, didn't dwell on the "probably." Christopher was adorable and he seemed all right, except for some phlegm in his chest that made him rumble when he breathed. Maybe he would be asthmatic like Bobby, who'd scared them more than once by turning blue. But the asthma hadn't stopped Bobby from being an active boy. Before he'd turned two, Bob and Mary had him out on the ski slopes. Christopher would be fine, too.

They believed that for four days. Then, after a follow-up visit, the doctor put his hands on Bob's shoulders and said ominously, "We will have to watch the baby very closely. Where nature makes a mistake in one place, it often makes a mistake in other places."

Over the next few months, the pediatrician's general concerns became alarmingly specific. There were "mistakes" in many places: Christopher could barely see, he was almost deaf, he drooled almost constantly, he couldn't digest his formula, and he could hardly breathe. His chest had become so full of mucus that it rattled.

The Rowes went from one doctor to another, but none could help. Christopher would starve or suffocate if something wasn't done. They asked everyone for advice, including a chiropractor Bob had gone to for some back problems. The chiropractor turned Christopher upside down, cupped his hand, and pounded the baby's back. At the end of the session, Christopher rattled less. He kept some formula down that evening.

The treatment required daily visits, the chiropractor's office was almost a mile away, and Mary didn't have a car at home. Barbara told her to leave Bobby at the Sapolskys', but Mary never did. "He's no problem," she would say brightly. Or, "The fresh air is good for them." She and Bob must have been feeling alarm, but they suppressed their dread. They were not the type to cater to themselves—they liked to offer help, not ask for it. Mary called this her Irish pride, Bob called it his Hawaiian pride. She bundled up the two boys, put Christopher in his carriage, and they walked to the chiropractor's and back. Christopher's breathing and digestion improved markedly.

But none of the specialists, not even the helpful chiropractor, knew exactly what was wrong with Christopher except that he wasn't likely to be another Helen Keller, whose intelligence and creativity were imprisoned by sensory deprivation. All of them were fairly certain that Christopher was brain-damaged, that even if they could penetrate his deafness and blindness, they weren't likely to find much on the other side.

Finally, when Christopher was a few months old, Mary met a pediatrician with an explanation: She might have been exposed to the rubella virus when she was pregnant. A recent outbreak of rubella had brought on a new generation of blind children, he told her, many of whom were brain-damaged. Unfortunately, Christopher fit the profile.

The pediatrician's assessment broke Mary's optimism. After that, Bob would find her sitting with Christopher in her arms, staring at her silent son. Sometimes Bob found her alone, crying. Before that, he had seen her cry only one time, when her father, Jimmy Savage, died. He had been a drunk, had barely supported his family, but he was also an appealing man with a gift—he could refinish furniture like no one else. No matter how battered a piece might be, he found a way to coax out its beauty. But Jimmy Savage was dead and Christopher wasn't a piece of furniture, though when the drool was freshly wiped from his face, he looked like a porcelain doll, lovely but inscrutable. It would be so much easier to love him if he would smile—just once—if he could look at them adoringly, as Bobby did.

Bob had grown accustomed to being adored by his family and admired by everyone else. He had risen steadily through middle management at Allstate. Before he was forty, he was promoted to manager of a large branch in Brooklyn, in charge of 125 people, and he was a likely candidate for vice-president. His colleagues teased him for being precocious. "To be pope or vice-president of an insurance company you are supposed to be sixty" was the kind of joke they told at Allstate.

He was athletically ambitious as well. On the way home from work, he'd stop at a dojo in downtown Brooklyn and practice judo. His friend Silvio Caso, also a lawyer at Allstate, used to watch Bob compete against Japanese masters and became interested in martial arts. But he didn't like falling on the ground, so he went into karate instead. Bob began going to watch Silvio at his dojo in Manhattan, and then he joined him.

Bob's expertise in karate would reinforce the envy of the wives on East Sixty-fourth Street. A group of couples, including Bob and Mary and Stan and Natalie Mond, went to see the comedian Buddy Hackett perform at a nightclub on Flatbush Avenue. The place was mobbed. It was almost impossible to sit at one table without bumping into someone at the next. A man sitting near Mary kept putting his hand on the back of her chair and it bothered her. She asked him many times to stop it, but he persisted.

Bob turned around. "I have a black belt in karate," he told the man, "and I don't want to use it."

The man ignored him. No one could remember exactly who started the hitting, but within minutes it seemed that everyone was punching someone.

Natalie Mond considered herself a pacifist, but she was impressed and a little excited by this hands-on show of chivalry, unusual in their middle-class crowd. It seemed terribly romantic, especially because she thought of Bob as an intellectual, not a macho man. She didn't think he was showing off. She didn't stop to think what else this might mean about Bob. He was just watching out for Mary.

—

The "firsts" were the most difficult: the first time they took Christopher into a store, the first day at the playground, the first close look at another baby Christopher's age, all reminding them of the myriad ways this child was not going to fulfill the parental fantasy of replication-with-improvements. It was painful to be around other new mothers, with their cheerful, nervous chatter about formulas and sleeping patterns. They imagined everyone wondering about why Christopher dribbled, why he was so passive, why his eyes were crossed, why he didn't smile.

As they had with Bobby, they studied what had passed from them to their child. With Bobby the genealogical survey was a matter of pride. They traced his complexion to Mary, his musical talent to Bob; each jokingly attributed his big ears to the other. With Christopher they were looking for blame, even though their doctor assured them it wasn't anyone's fault. Bob understood the logic of the rubella explanation, but he wondered if Christopher's problems hadn't been inherited. His family always spoke of his creepy uncle Al as "retarded," though Bob had always thought of him simply as a slob and a degenerate who leered at young girls. Maybe there was a connection, maybe not.

Mildred Rowe, Bob's mother, treated her grandson as though he were a leper. She had willingly baby-sat for Bobby, but she refused to be alone with Christopher—or even to look at him. This infuriated Bob, who interpreted his mother's reaction to Christopher as an extension of her disdain for him.

As the first year passed, Christopher missed every milestone. Bob and Mary stopped wondering when their younger son would start to crawl and began hoping he would learn to sit—this when he should have been standing and taking his first steps. He was still small and cuddly, but what would happen to him when he was grown? Would he still be wearing diapers and sucking on a bottle? It had seemed so wise to wait to have children until they were settled. Now Bob, still in his thirties, was worried about growing old and foisting Christopher on Bobby.

In the early winter of 1966, a few months after Christopher's first birthday, Bob talked Mary into visiting the Willowbrook State School, on Staten Island, an institution of last resort for the severely retarded. Willowbrook sat on a huge campus that had been farmland until 1938, when the state bought the property for the Department of Mental Hygiene. The land was appropriated by the Veterans Administration during World War II, and became the site of the country's largest hospital for wounded soldiers. After the war, the hospital went back to the state and began admitting mentally disabled civilians, including infants.

Mary went along because she wouldn't argue with Bob, but she made it clear that she didn't want to put Christopher away. Bob assured her that they were just looking.

The weather was portentous as menacing clouds gathered on the horizon. A sorry-looking Christmas wreath hung dispiritedly on the ornate grillwork of the Willowbrook administration building's heavy oak door. Just before a housekeeper invited them in, an icy drizzle began to fall. She escorted them to a quiet sitting room, lit by a single Tiffany lamp that threw yellow and red sparkles onto the ceiling. An ancient grandfather clock ticked loudly in the corner. Feeling like characters in a horror movie, Bob and Mary sat in the dim room listening to the clock, waiting for the assistant director.

He was no Basil Rathbone character but rather a nice enough fellow, who tried to brighten things up with friendly chatter. After introducing himself, he took them on a tour—a driving tour, because the place was huge: 375 acres. They passed by the gym, the cafeteria, and the dormitories for young adults before they stopped in front of another building. He led them to the basement, where he proudly pointed out racks and racks of new tricycles waiting for action, not a scratch anywhere.

Bob nodded optimistically toward the tricycles, though Christopher hadn't yet begun to crawl.

Then back into the car and on to the next stop, two large red structures known as the "baby complex." The assistant director, whose name they would quickly forget, said he wanted them to take as much time as they wanted, so he'd leave them there. They could call him from the telephone inside when they were ready to be picked up.

As Bob and Mary stepped inside the cavernous ward, they understood instantly why the man didn't want to join them for this part of the tour. The air stank of sour milk and shit. In the faint light, they could make out rows and rows of cribs filled with children, some parked in wooden boxes that looked eerily like caskets.

Almost all the children seemed to be sleeping, though it was the middle of the day. Two black women moved slowly among the cribs and boxes, pushing a cart filled with bowls of hot cereal. At each child's bed, they stopped and tried to deposit some mush into an unreceptive mouth. The cereal dribbled out in almost every case, but the women kept moving. There were a lot of children to feed.

Bob realized why the tricycles so proudly presented by the assistant director were so pristine. They had probably never been used, and never would be.

Certainly not by their son. Christopher was staying home.

In 1972, a few years after Bob and Mary's visit, a television correspondent named Geraldo Rivera would become instantly famous for an exposé that made Willowbrook synonymous with Bedlam. "The conditions here are deplorable, but they are no worse than those in any other facility for the mentally retarded in this state," Jack Hammond, Willowbrook's director, told Rivera. The ratio of workers to patients was one to thirty or forty, depending on the day. The shortage of attendants was said to contribute to the horrifying death rate: three to four a month.

Rivera reported that toilets were broken, that there was excrement everywhere, and that children—some naked, some wearing only straitjackets—were found drinking from toilet bowls. In interviews, the parents of these young Willowbrook patients expressed horror at the way their children—most of them severely retarded—were being treated, but they felt they had to keep them there because they didn't know what else to do.

—

W hen parents are first informed about their children's disabilities they are likely to feel shock, disappointment, grief, sorrow, and re- morse," Rosalyn Benjamin Darling, director of a program for handi- capped children, wrote in a 1983 text for health-care professionals.

Strongly negative reactions are usually short-lived, however. Most par- ents receive encouragement and support from close friends and family members, but the strongest shaper of parental feelings is usually the handicapped infant itself. As parents live with their children, they learn to love them.

Most parents leave the postpartum period with the desire to do all they can for their children, because, like parents of typical children, their self-esteem as parents is based in some measure on their chil- dren's accomplishments. Although parents' goals may have to be ad- justed (the physically handicapped child may not become a star athlete, and the mentally handicapped child will not become a great scientist), most parents are able to find meaning and pleasure in the goals their children *can* accomplish, no matter how small. In our society, "good" parents do all they can for their children.

Mary had been temporarily immobilized by shock, disappointment, grief, sorrow, and remorse. But after the Willowbrook visit, she went into action. She was still the woman who had appeased two stubborn mothers at Christmas dinner and who had attracted her husband-to-be with her drive. She was going to find a way to communicate with her child, and Bob was going to help her. They determined to teach Christopher to move, to eat, and to use the toilet—whatever he could learn. They would learn how to be "good parents" for him. If doctors, therapists, and social workers couldn't show them the way, they would figure it out for them- selves.

With little solace forthcoming from traditional medicine, Bob and Mary were willing to experiment. He would be in charge of research. After all, he was the personal-injury expert, a specialty that required him to spend more hours with medical texts than with law books. She would do the fieldwork.

They put themselves in the hands of the Institutes for the Achievement of Human Potential, a center for alternative medicine based in Philadelphia, which had developed radical new therapies for brain-damaged and mentally retarded children. Normally, Bob, whose values were middle-of-the-mainstream, would have been skeptical of the institute's cultish name and unorthodox methods. But he had stopped living in the "normal" world when Christopher was born.

The Institutes had been established by Glenn Doman and Carl Delacato, who combined theories of evolution and biological development in a complex formulation that begins with the adages "You must crawl before you can creep, you must creep before you can walk, you must walk before you can run" and then argues that if the brain fails to set these stages in motion automatically, a manual override is possible: The body would teach the brain. If a child failed to crawl, for example, he could be trained. With one adult at each arm and each leg and another at the child's head, five people working in tandem could flex a child's arm and leg on one side while turning his head in that same direction and extending his other arm and leg. In theory, repeating this simulated crawling for at least five minutes four times a day would leave an imprint on the child's central nervous system, and, after a while, he would crawl by himself. They called this technique patterning.

Doman and Delacato also claimed their methods would make superior children out of normal ones: TRAIN YOUR BABY TO BE A GENIUS was the tantalizing headline on an article they wrote for *McCall's* magazine, in March 1965, five months before Christopher Rowe was born. The medical establishment was already dubious about Doman-Delacato and would become openly hostile after a series of clinical trials failed to substantiate their theories.

Bob was aware of the controversy, but he and Mary agreed that their choices were limited. They enrolled in a local branch of the Institutes, where they learned ways to try to jump-start Christopher's system. They put ice cubes on his back and pinched his toes to get him to move. They slid him down talcum-powdered Masonite slide boards and forced him through roped crawl boxes. They thrust blinking lights in front of his eyes and placed headsets on his ears, the volume turned up all the way.

They began patterning, which required an elaborate system of solicitation and scheduling, because they needed five adults at the ready—at the right times and every day. One of the criticisms of patterning would be the emotional and physical burden it placed on families: They became supplicants, constantly facing the fear of failure if someone didn't show up. Since Bob had to go to the office, Mary was in charge of recruiting, scheduling, and reminding. Resolutely good-natured, she was impossible to refuse. Almost every woman in the neighborhood enlisted, as did a few of the men. Barbara Sapolsky was on call as permanent understudy—until she was too far along in her pregnancy with her third child to help.

Day after day, for several months in 1967 and 1968, when Christopher was two years old, people trooped in and out of the Rowes' house and took turns moving the boy's feet and arms and head. At first the sessions were awkward and sober, but then they became social occasions. No one could be afraid of Christopher after they'd held on to his warm little feet and arms or spent time looking at his sweet face, which was off-kilter but still charming. He calmly allowed the adults to manipulate his limbs and head.

They didn't know whether the experiment would work. But even if Christopher wasn't being repatterned, Bob and Mary were—especially Bob, because once Mary got over the initial shock of Christopher's handicaps, she never seemed to doubt his place in the family. By forcing the neighbors to accept their son, Bob seemed to have accepted him, too. In the winter the neighbors would watch Bob standing with Christopher on the street corner facing the wind—as though defying nature to beat them back—so that Christopher could feel the breeze on his face. In the spring, there was Bob, lifting Christopher up to touch the buds on the trees, then kneeling with him to smell the flowers, to examine petals and leaves with his fingers. In the summer, Bob strapped Christopher into a life jacket and taught him to float in the Sapolskys' pool, just as he'd taught Bobby.

CHAPTER 3

Skills of Daily Living

I n the summer of 1968, when Christopher turned three, Bob and Mary decided he was ready for nursery school. He had learned how to smile and had begun taking his first, shaky steps and he recognized familiar people, though he couldn't yet feed himself and was still in diapers. They heard about a program for rubella babies at the Industrial Home for the Blind, on Willoughby Street in downtown Brooklyn, and made a call.

The IHB had been established in 1893 with a mandate "to furnish a home for deserving blind men and to provide them with suitable employment such as chair caning, mattress making and repairing." This was a progressive notion; a decade later, special commissions in both New York and Massachusetts endorsed the IHB's approach and recommended a large-scale effort to train blind adults for work in industry. The agency kept expanding its services in the first half of the twentieth century, and in 1945 it opened a children's program—though by then medical advances had greatly reduced the number of blind babies. In the beginning there were few clients, but one day the telephone started ringing and didn't stop. Betty Maloney, who ran the IHB's social-services department, remembered how awful it was.

"You would pick up the phone five times a day and hear a frightened mother saying, 'I've just come from the hospital, my baby is going to be released to me tomorrow, and I've just been told she's blind.' The baby had at that point been in the hospital for three months, so that early bonding with an infant didn't take place. They were in incubators; the mothers stood outside the glass panel. As soon as they reached five pounds, the doctors said, 'Here's your child. Unfortunately, he's blind.' You can't imagine what this did to the mothers. It was a tremendous shock, and they had not the least idea of what to do."

This mysterious epidemic was first identified in 1940 by a Boston ophthalmologist, Theodore Terry, who was startled when six blind babies were brought in for examination within a matter of months. Dr. Terry found two common characteristics among these infant patients: All of them had formed a curtain of fibrous scar tissue behind the lens of their eyes, and all of them had been born prematurely.

A terrible irony lay behind the disease. As incubators came into wide use in hospitals in the forties, allowing premature babies to survive earlier and earlier births, researchers discovered that doctors were inadvertently blinding the babies they were saving. The blasts of oxygen were overwhelming the still-developing blood vessels feeding the fragile retinas of the premature infants. The blood vessels hemorrhaged and scar tissue formed, which caused the retina to detach from its normal position.

Incidence of the disease, named retrolental fibroplasia (RLF) by Dr. Terry—referring to the curtain of fibrous scar tissue—rose dramatically over the next few years. In New York the number of cases would increase steadily from twelve in 1941 to more than three hundred in 1952.

By the late 1950s, as doctors learned to administer oxygen more judiciously, incidence of RLF declined dramatically. But then in 1964, an epidemic of German measles, or rubella, swept through the Northeast, and then across the country. The disease was relatively harmless, except to women in their first three months of pregnancy. Health officials estimated that half the babies born to those women would develop abnormalities, including mental retardation, cataracts, deafness, and defects of the heart. Ten thousand mothers miscarried because of the rubella virus in 1964 and 1965; twenty thousand bore children who were damaged.

Once again the IHB was inundated with calls. Betty Maloney (who wished she'd had six or seven children but never had any, and never married) pitied these parents, who had stepped into a universe for which they'd had no conditioning, even if they had other children—no, *especially* if they'd had other children. There was little guidance. They were a generation shy of the era of self-help books for almost every situation.

The parents found out quickly that many "natural" behaviors weren't innate, as they had believed, but learned. "How do you get a blind child to chew?" Betty Maloney would say. "Chewing is a learned skill. The child watches the parent. He doesn't chew automatically. Not at all. We tried all kinds of things at the nursery school. Ultimately, the thing that worked best for most children was applesauce with a little bit of solid food in it that had to be chewed. Eventually they got the idea. But some resisted completely. It was little things like chewing that could drive a parent straight up the wall."

Little things could drive the parents straight up the wall, but so could big ones—such as guilt. "No matter what you do," said Betty Maloney, "the mothers feel responsible for the blindness. Even though they know it was a medical thing, they know they didn't cause it, they feel responsible. I think the fathers felt it, too. Very deeply."

It was the custom of the Industrial Home for the Blind to send a social worker to visit parents soon after they first got in touch with the agency, to find out what they needed. If the child was too young to be enrolled in the nursery program, the IHB could arrange for help with the "skills of daily living"—sitting, crawling, walking, and chewing.

Edith Patt took the call from the Rowes. The agency's chief social worker, she liked to make the first visit to new families, and often the second and third as well. She was a careful woman who preferred to let a little silence gather while she composed her response to even the most casual question. This reserve made her seem aloof at times, remarkably cool for someone from the so-called helping professions. Yet her clients were comforted rather than intimidated by this woman, who always looked them directly in the eye while she was considering what to say. Most of the parents who called the IHB had had a surfeit of glib answers and uneasy sympathy from doctors, neighbors, and relatives—as well as from strangers. Edith never condescended with false hope or pity.

Her empathy was not born of direct experience, but she did know what it was to want one thing out of life and to get something else. Her friend and former neighbor Theodore Rubin, a psychiatrist and the author of *Lisa and David,* about the romance between two young mental patients, said of her: "My feeling is that there's an Edith who might have lived in Paris and had a hell of a time with Henry Miller. There's an artistic streak there somewhere, and she got pushed into an upper-middle-class bourgeois kind of life. I think there's a lot of frustration and a lot of pressure to keep down the wild girl, the artistic, the creative, the Village character." Ted Rubin liked Edith because she showed signs of eccentricity, which interested him, and because he liked to look at her. She was slim but full-breasted, and her face was complex: beautiful and alive when she smiled, otherwise a mask.

When they were neighbors in the 1950s, the Rubins and the Patts were living on Bedford Avenue, a leafy street in Brooklyn, and Edith was trying to convince herself that she wanted to be a perfect housewife—an unexpected ambition for a woman who had been the only one of her friends to complete college and then acquire a graduate degree. It was also surprising for a woman who, as a teenager, had happily gone to a progressive camp, where boys and girls were encouraged to swim nude and to share sleeping bags so that they could learn about sex.

Her lovely house became her nemesis. Everything associated with it seemed destined to cause her misery by reminding her that she didn't have the proper temperament to be a happy homemaker. She had promised her son, David, that she would buy him a dog when they moved into a house, and Edith always kept her promises. They went to the ASPCA and found Blackie, a gorgeous black cocker spaniel with big brown eyes. The dog and David became attached to each other immediately. Edith loved to watch them together, but the minute Blackie came into the house, his long hair matted with dirt and leaves, Edith couldn't breathe. It was almost an allergic reaction, though she wasn't allergic to dogs. She couldn't stand the chaos.

What had she been thinking? Dogs run around; they shed, they sit on your lap, jump on chairs. They are the antithesis of orderliness, and Edith ran an orderly household. One day each month she did nothing but cook a month's worth of meals, then packaged each one, labeled it, and put it in the freezer. Sometimes she baked—complicated pastries such as cream puffs, dozens at a time, and she would toss all of them in the garbage if they weren't perfect.

One day in the fall of 1957, Edith knocked on the Rubins' door and asked Ted to recommend a psychiatrist. David and Blackie had been playing in the house, and Edith couldn't stand it any longer. "We have to give the dog away!" she shouted.

She saw the hurt in her five-year-old son's eyes. "How can you give the dog away?" he demanded. "You promised me. It's my dog."

She thought her husband, Ray, would be on her side, because the dog hated Ray. But he looked at her and said, "How can you give the dog away? Look how the dog looks at you! Look how the dog loves you!"

She looked at the dog and saw that he did indeed love her. In fact, his brown eyes looked exactly like her father's eyes. Her father who had never yelled at her but had had merely to look at her and say, "Tootsie dear, how could you?"

The dog was looking at her as if to say, "But, Tootsie dear, how could you give me away?"

At the first session with her psychiatrist, she cried about the dog. She explained that if she had one more thing that loved her, she wouldn't be able to stand it. She didn't want it, didn't need it, but how could she give it away? It loved her.

When her time was up, the doctor had a question: "How are you going to finance this therapy?" he asked.

By the next session she had an answer. She'd found a job through an ad in *The New York Times*. The Industrial Home for the Blind needed a social worker part-time. Never mind that the only blind child Edith had ever seen was at her son's nursery school. She wasn't looking for a career. Working the two and a half hours a day that David was at nursery school, Edith could earn just enough to cover the cost of therapy.

She wouldn't have predicted that she'd find her life's work among the damaged bodies and souls at the IHB. "I didn't see myself as a Florence Nightingale," she would say. She agreed with her therapist, who believed she had deliberately gravitated to clients who were so traumatized that she couldn't do them any more harm. "My feeling about working with these people was that it would have been worse had I not been there. Not that I could do such great things, but that things were so lousy I couldn't make them any worse."

When Edith left her clients, she often felt in desperate need of air, to clear her head of the suffocating sadness she had just been dealing with, but with the Rowes it was different: She was revitalized after her first visit with them. Bob and Mary were optimistic yet realistic—enthusiasts, not zealots.

Edith admitted that she was first attracted by their looks. Bob was physically imposing, a powerfully built man who looked like he could fix things. (This was a sore spot for Edith, whose husband, also a lawyer, was baffled by repair work and happy to leave it all to her.) Mary had let her hair grow into a thick black mane, and, together with her hearty laugh, it gave the impression of coltish enthusiasm. Mary's laugh startled Edith at first. She was more accustomed to tears from new clients.

Edith was also fascinated by the experiments they were conducting with Christopher. She'd read about patterning but had never met anyone who'd actually tried it. Bob confessed that he wasn't convinced it was patterning that was helping Christopher, but he was beginning to take steps, contrary to the predictions of many doctors. Even if the patterning hadn't rerouted the signals from Christopher's brain, Bob told her, it had introduced their son to their neighbors. "Christopher became known to all of the mothers and all of their children as they were helping us," he told her in an interview she taped. "Therefore, he was not an oddity. He was simply a child being helped by their mothers. As a result, when we go out in the street and Christopher does something as simple as cough, they all say how wonderful it is that he can cough.

"We never had a ridicule problem in the neighborhood, simply because we had about sixty people a week coming into the house. The entire neighborhood has gotten to know Christopher, and when he walks down the street, people take pride in what he is doing and greet him by name. This also makes it easier on his brother, who has assumed that all babies are patterned. I think it is a big thing that he doesn't see anything wrong with having Christopher in the family or at home, or that there is anything to be ashamed of."

Most impressive to Edith was Bob's forthrightness about his own deficiencies. She'd learned to expect self-reproach from the mothers but hardly ever from the fathers. "I remember something, and I'm very ashamed of it now," Bob told her. "Before Christopher was born to this family, there was a retarded child that lived on the block. He was a very large boy and very gross-looking. He had all the features I am now familiar with—crossed eyes, shambling gait, drooling. The first time I came upon him, I was really shocked. I have tried to analyze my feelings, which were, What the hell is he doing walking around on the street—why isn't he locked up somewhere? I feel that I must have been in a very primitive stage at that point. And a good deal of the public is still at that point."

During her third or fourth visit, the Rowes told Edith they wanted another child, for many reasons, including the ones that anyone might have: They loved children; they'd like a daughter after two sons. But the most important reason was particular to families like theirs: They didn't want Bobby to inherit the burden of Christopher alone. They had decided to adopt, they told her, because while they were fairly certain Mary had been exposed to rubella during pregnancy, they weren't 100 percent certain about what had caused Christopher's problems, and they didn't want to take a chance. However, the adoption agency had made it clear that Bob and Mary weren't desirable candidates because of their age (both of them were pushing forty) and because of Christopher. They asked Edith to write a letter of recommendation.

She didn't tell them that her only child, David, was adopted. Nor did she tell them that he was away at a military boarding school because it had become clear that he and her husband, Ray, couldn't live in the same house anymore. David was bright and blond—and blue-eyed and athletic. He had figured out soon enough that being the only child of two only children was a rotten position to be in. He got tired of being the last chance for them—especially his father—to correct every mistake they'd made when they were young.

David didn't want to go anywhere Ray pushed him. The pattern was always the same as he transferred from school to school: great test scores, lousy performance. He'd make any team he tried out for and then he would quit. Success didn't elude him—he ran away from it. Finally, they sent him to military school—a desperate move for a couple of liberal urban Jews like Ray and Edith.

But there were happy memories, too—summers in the little boarding-house in North Truro, on Cape Cod, where you could walk to the bay side and tell instantly when the stripers would be running because all the guys who usually hung around the hardware store would have headed for the water. They'd eat big steaming bowls of clam chowder together and travel through old whaling towns, where David, a talented artist, learned the painstaking craft of scrimshaw. Edith remembered waking up with Ray and David in motel rooms in fog-covered valleys on visits to Civil War battlegrounds and roaming together through all the great museums of New York. Because Ray liked only the plainest foods—egg salad was an exotic departure for him—David was Edith's gastronomic companion. He was eating Japanese food long before it became fashionable; he tasted snails before he tried a fish stick.

Once, when David was a little boy and having lunch with a friend, Edith overheard the boys discussing her work. The friend was perplexed, because this was at a time when mothers usually didn't work. "What does she do?" the friend asked. "Oh," said David. "She tells other people how to bring up their children." Edith had had to stop herself from a vigorous self-defense. *I would never presume to tell someone else how to bring up their children.* Then she understood. "Of course that's how he would see it. What else was he supposed to think?"

She was always grateful to have had David's perceptions, and was glad that she and Ray had adopted him, even with all the attendant heartache. So when the Rowes asked Edith if she would recommend them as adoptive parents, she didn't hesitate. In her letter to the adoption agency, she described them as "lucid and capable—an ideal family."

It took a couple of years for the adoption to go through, but on October 19, 1970, the Rowes brought home a three-week-old baby girl, five pounds, ten ounces, whom they named Jennifer Laura, after Laura Savage, Mary's mother.

By then, Christopher had been at the IHB nursery school for two years. He had begun to acquire skills of daily living. He could feed himself, he could signal that he had to go to the toilet, and he had learned to walk—not gracefully or efficiently, but all the same, it seemed miraculous. Critics of the Doman-Delacato method would argue that Christopher's progress wasn't a miracle, that even the most severely damaged children will grow and develop, especially if they are prodded.

Mary and Bob didn't know if Christopher had been rewired by the Doman-Delacato method or if his muscles had simply responded to all the stimulus or if he had simply developed in his own sweet time—and they didn't care. Christopher was progressing, in his way.

CHAPTER 4

The Mothers

Helen Keller was still alive—still young and healthy—when she was transformed into an object lesson, her life into a parable. Inspiration abounded in the story of the blind and deaf girl who grew up to be an accomplished woman who was courted by the world's luminaries but who also championed the underdog. She would become one of the twentieth century's most enduring celebrities, memorialized on stage and screen, the subject of numerous books, and an author herself. She represented the noblest attributes of humankind: perseverance and compassion and good-humored selflessness.

But for most of the parents at the Industrial Home for the Blind (whose name would one day be changed to Helen Keller Services), this exemplary story was irrelevant, even reproachful. Few children—with or without disabilities—could hope to match Keller's brilliance. Before entering Radcliffe College (class of 1904) Keller was an honors student who had mastered ancient history and advanced German, French, and Latin—in Braille. As a sought-after speaker, she would travel the world.

For the mothers who brought their children to the IHB, the likely point of identification would be Kate Keller, Helen's mother—loving and protective (she dismissed the suggestion that Helen should be institutionalized), but ineffectual when dealing with her damaged child. "Mrs. Keller was an aloof person, very private, fastidious, whom an error of taste offended more than a real fault," wrote biographer Joseph Lash. "She did not like to acknowledge, scarcely to publish, the difficulties she had in her household, or the dreadful troubles they had with little Helen after she was stricken and before Annie Sullivan took her in hand." Annie Sullivan, of course, was Helen Keller's teacher—the Miracle Worker, as she was referred to in the Broadway and Hollywood versions of Keller's life. Annie Sullivan would become almost as famous as her student, certainly among schoolchildren who were assigned to read about Sullivan by *their* teachers. Kate Keller would always be a supporting character, and not a very sympathetic one.

Not until the 1960s, just about the time Christopher Rowe was born, did social workers, teachers, therapists, and doctors even begin to consider parents as potential partners rather than obstacles to their children's progress. For many years before that, proponents of education for the blind urged parents to send their children off to special schools as soon as possible—before the parents could inflict too much damage.

Edith Patt had always hated the way the mothers were treated. The fathers, too—but it was the mothers who bore the brunt of the disapproval, because they took care of the children. Edith had been introduced to officialdom's low regard for mothers when she was a young social worker taking foster children to medical clinics, where they would sit knee to knee with the poor women who had brought their own children. There were no appointments, so they'd have to wait for hours. Naturally, the children would start squirming and running around and making noise. The clerks would bark out: "*Mother! Mother!* Can't you keep that child quiet?" It amazed Edith to see how an ordinary word, a potentially lovely word, could be twisted by those bureaucratic mouths into an epithet for an inferior species that couldn't even control its children.

When Betty Maloney hired her at the IHB, she told Edith that her job was to help the parents navigate the world of the handicapped, with its alien customs, bureaucracies, fantasies, and fears. They would ask her: Where would their children go to school? How would they get there? What kind of work could they do? What would happen to them when their parents were dead? Edith would help them understand that there were more immediate questions, which had no obvious answers: How would the children learn to feed themselves, to dress themselves, to walk, to use the toilet?

"Sometimes a shortcut turns out to be the long way around," she would say, "and a parent may need help in learning to wait, and waiting with someone is better than waiting alone."

The early 1970s was a heady time for the social services. The federal government and many states began, for the first time, to devote significant amounts of money to the education of handicapped people. Edith was invigorated by the proliferation of theories and programs, and she participated enthusiastically in many symposia. In 1972 she asked Betty if she could try an experiment. She had the notion that the mothers of blind children might help one another more than a professional could. She wanted to organize a group from the IHB to meet every week and talk about anything they wanted. Besides, she needed an assignment for Marti Kopp, a graduate student who was on loan to the IHB. Marti had agreed to act as the group's moderator. Neither Edith nor Marti had ever organized a group before, but Marti had one crucial qualification: She was available.

Edith's method of choosing the women for the group was similarly unscientific. She simply picked the mothers who seemed to need the most help. Some had children who were brain-damaged as well as blind, others "simply" couldn't see. They were a fully integrated group, racially and economically—not because Edith planned it that way, but because blindness was an equal-opportunity affliction. The mothers agreed to meet once a week in the conference room while their children were at the nursery school.

The room was nondescript—Marti Kopp dubbed it the brown room—and the plan was nonexistent. Marti had read that people in groups were supposed to form some "identification" with one another, but she wasn't able to convert this abstract notion into a plan. What if identification occurred and she missed it? She didn't confide her concerns to Edith.

When Marti walked into the brown room the first day, she nervously asked people to say who they were and why they were there. She didn't have to do anything else. The women responded to these bare-bones introductions with the appetite of the starved. Though strangers, they formed an immediate intimacy with the kind of thunderclap recognition Marti associated with the meeting of lovers. "Identification" was no longer an abstraction.

For eight months, the duration of her graduate school course, Marti Kopp listened to the women talk, always fascinated but always feeling somewhat apart, daunted by the experiences she hoped she would never share. Marti was almost twenty-nine years old and in the process of divorcing her first husband, with whom she hadn't had children. "I don't think I could have tolerated it if I had kids," she said later, when she did have children of her own and more fully appreciated the sorrow to which she had been privy week after week. "It would have been too painful."

At the time, she was swept up in the drama of witnessing the remarkable conversion of grief into action. "I felt envious that each woman in that group was able to have a positive sense of her life, to keep families going, to wake up in the morning and do whatever they had to do and not let the situation stop them from functioning. I don't know if I could do that. Over the years I've thought about that, whether I would have the strength each of them had to keep their situations in perspective and go on with life with an optimistic sense about the future."

Marti would move on. She would write a paper about her experience at the IHB and finish graduate school before migrating to California, where she would marry a pediatrician, raise two children, and become a therapist in private practice. The mothers at the IHB stayed behind and kept on talking.

The country would eventually overdose on support-group intimacy as special interests multiplied in number and kind and as revelation, no matter how gross or outrageous or insipid, became a staple of television talk shows. But for the mothers who first met on Willoughby Street in 1972, it was astonishing to be able to talk openly about the grief and guilt that terrorized them. No matter what the diagnosis, they felt responsible for what had happened to their children: If only they hadn't taken that pill, walked that extra block, exposed themselves to disease, been born with the wrong genetic code. In that room they could recall the moment their children were born the way other mothers did, but with a dreadful difference, and without worrying about being treated like freaks.

They began to think of the brown room as their DMZ. There, it was safe to crack jokes about their predicament, and no apologies were necessary for feeling insecure or miserable—or happy, for that matter. Outside, they spent so much of their time getting on with it, trying to appear normal, to protect their other children, if they had them, to keep themselves from going mad. But in the brown room they were the norm. Each of them had a child who bumped into walls or drooled or jabbered or couldn't quite put two and two together. All of them had children who someone had looked at and thought: *monster.* Some of them had—secretly—the same thought themselves.

Rose Mauro felt unaccountably happy to be among women who felt the way she did and who could talk of their weakness without shame. Before she met these mothers, Rose had stopped trying to explain her feelings for her daughter Anne, her fourth child, born three years earlier, very prematurely, at twenty-eight weeks. All of Rose's babies had been small, but when she first peeked at this one in the preemie nursery, she was shocked. Twelve inches long and the color of an eggplant, Anne looked like a doll that had been dropped in ink. But Rose didn't care. She wanted to clutch her purple baby close, but she could only stare at her through glass like a specimen.

Anne was so little that the doctors wouldn't give odds on her survival, and it didn't help that Rose's husband, John, kept saying, "We don't have another baby yet."

For weeks it seemed like Anne was always bad or worse, never better. Her weight dropped below one pound, and her skin went from blue to yellow when she became jaundiced. As if God had prepared her for this—Rose had kept the faith of her devout Italian-Catholic family—Rose's blood was transfusion-friendly, AB positive, containing antibodies needed by premature babies. She couldn't feed her baby or hold her, but she could give her blood, and that was much better than nothing.

Rose was oblivious of Vietnam and racial problems and everything else that was going on in the world. None of it meant anything to her. She was caught up in life—three kids at home to feed, dress, keep from killing one another—and death, that place where Anne kept one scrawny foot. But she would never forget the day the astronauts landed on the moon. It was about to happen, she heard on the radio, when she was summoned to the hospital, the afternoon of July 20, 1969.

When she reached the nursery, the curtains were shut. Usually they were open so that you could look in and see the babies, so Rose sensed something was wrong even before the doctor told her Anne was in trouble. There wasn't anywhere left in her body to put a needle. Her veins had collapsed. Rose thought about the baby's legs, no bigger than an adult's finger, poked with needles so often that Rose half expected her to start spraying like a water sprinkler when they put anything into her, like a cartoon character.

"Can I go in to her?" Rose asked. Until that day she'd never touched her child, only looked at her through the glass, though Anne was more than two months old. The doctor and nurses thought about it for a minute and then told Rose to scrub up and put on a surgical gown. Clearly, they figured it was miracle time. "Go in and talk to her," one of the nurses said. "Sometimes, they say, a child can hear the mother's voice even in the womb."

Rose's hands were shaking. Three children at home, and she felt as though she'd never touched a baby before. Carefully, she laid her hand on Anne's stomach, the only surface big enough for her to rest it. "Hi, Anne," she said. "Please get better. We're all praying for you. We love you."

Then there was nothing left to do but wait.

That night, at 11:01, five minutes after Neil Armstrong stepped onto the surface of the moon, the telephone rang at the Mauros' house. "She's rallying," Rose heard the doctor say.

From then on, the miracles would be linked in Rose's mind: the man on the moon and her baby daughter, both contesting the laws of nature with scientific know-how. After that, Anne started to put on weight and her skin lost its blue cast and turned pink, like a real baby's, though she remained attached to the many machines that were womb substitutes, since many of her basic reflexes—including breathing—hadn't kicked in yet.

The hospital treated Anne as a prized possession. A public-relations person showed up at the house to interview Rose and her husband for a promotional booklet on the hospital's facilities for premature babies, with Anne featured as proof positive that medical science could produce miracles. The booklet was never published. Anne lost a great deal of credibility in the miracle-baby department when it was discovered that she was blind.

She had retrolental fibroplasia. Though doctors thought they had RLF under control by the time Anne was born, they had learned that it wasn't easy to trick fate. Too much oxygen caused blindness; an insufficient amount could result in brain damage or death. Anne's doctor had decided to take the risk of blindness.

Rose's husband handled the situation by avoiding it. John had just bought his own gas station, and he used the business as an excuse for coming home late and drinking too much. But Rose felt she could handle Anne and the other three children—if only there weren't so many jerks in the world conspiring to make her feel lousy, like one of her "best friends," who called her up one day shortly after Anne came home and mused, "Maybe the baby should have just died."

—

The conversations in the brown room were a release, the mere articulation of fear and frustration an exercise that built a muscularity of spirit. That's how it was for Ellen Alboher. For six months after October 22, 1971, when her second daughter, Elyse, was born without eyes, Ellen had begun the day ritually, with a shower followed by a debate: Should she kill herself or kill the baby? But after she got out of the shower, she went and turned on the television in one room and the radio in another, because the social worker had said it was important to stimulate the baby. Sometimes she picked up the booklet someone had given her that described the kinds of toys that would be helpful for very young blind children. As she read the introduction, with its calm, wise prescriptions, she began to laugh. This obviously wasn't written with someone like her in mind, a hysterical woman in Brooklyn who had the shakes because she was nervous all the time.

On good days, when her weight was down, Ellen was a statuesque beauty with a hint of eastern Europe in her almond-shaped eyes. Her distinctively Brooklyn voice often erupted into a wild cackle, especially after she'd had a few drinks. She called herself a yo-yo person, losing fifty pounds, gaining sixty. If Weight Watchers had given frequent-flier miles, she would joke, she could have traveled around the world on the weight she'd gained and lost.

She noticed that the booklet was distributed by the office of public education in Illinois, and began to laugh again. That explained it, she thought. Midwesterners!

The way you accept your blind child is the way he will be accepted by the people around you. Do not talk about the things he cannot do, but about the things he can do now and will be able to do in the future.

Your blind child is a challenge. He will depend on you for many things which will help him grow up to be a respected, independent citizen in our sighted world.

Remember that your blind child is first your baby, needing your tenderness and love, and then that he is a baby who is blind, needing a little more than a child who can see. He cannot see the smile on your face nor the love in your eyes as you pass his crib; therefore, you must show it in your voice by singing to him, talking to him and handling him perhaps more than you might if he could see. Do not be afraid to cuddle him and encourage your friends, relatives and neighbors to do so, too.

But when Ellen hugged Elyse, the baby resisted. Her little hand would find Ellen's chest and push her away. Ellen shrugged it off, telling herself, I don't like to be touched either, especially by a stranger. Of course, she wasn't a stranger; she was Elyse's mother. She kept trying, in those early months, to find the smallest connection to Elyse, to find a hint of the familiar.

Perhaps when Elyse would finally smile, Ellen thought, it would make a difference. And one day she heard a gurgling noise from the direction of Elyse's crib. Ellen ran into the room and found her baby daughter laughing. At nothing! Ellen hadn't been able to coax a smile out of her, and now Elyse was chuckling away, at a joke she would never be able to explain to her mother, not even when she had the language to do it. They would become commonplace, the bursts of laughter from Elyse's crib. "She's an alien," Ellen's mother told her, in one of the rare moments when she bothered to acknowledge her younger granddaughter. "She's from another planet."

Elyse the alien became part of the family shtick, the black humor that crops up in cancer wards and on battlefields and among the handicapped as a protective cover. It would be easier if she *were* from another planet, Ellen would tell herself in those early months.

She was terrified that she would lose everything she'd been given by her older daughter, Lori. For five years Ellen had felt the current of pleasure that can run between a mother and child, a vitality that made her feel as though she were situated at the center of the universe, the strange sensation that her existence actually mattered. Her mother had made her feel superfluous from the time she was very young, and Ellen had accepted her expendability as a matter of fact. So she had been apathetic about school, apathetic about religion, and apathetic about the political upheavals of the sixties—and was apathetic about her husband, Al (after the brief thrill of courtship), except when she was angry with him.

Lori had changed everything: She *needed* Ellen. Suddenly, Ellen felt connected to her emotions; she became wired into the meaning of tenderness, of exhilaration, and of fear. But when Elyse was born, Ellen realized that there were still vast unexplored territories in her heart and that her base camp was terror. She began to realize that if Lori had made her a new person, Elyse would make her quite another.

When the hospital pediatrician examined Elyse, he gave Ellen the telephone number of one of his patients. She was the mother of two blind children, and she happened to live in the large, impersonal apartment complex right next to the impersonal apartment complex where the Albohers lived. Ellen thanked the doctor, and when she got home, she put the phone number in a drawer. She had no desire to meet Phyllis Roth or her sightless children, to commiserate, to compare notes. The doctor had told her that the Roth children were brain-damaged as well as blind. Bitterly, Ellen tried to imagine their conversation. Let's see, she thought. I could tell her about my mornings: I get up, then remember and decide I don't want to get up. But I have to get up because of Lori. I get up and have my coffee and get into the shower, and in the shower I decide whether I'm going to kill Elyse or kill myself or kill everyone. This runs through my mind. How am I going to get through this, and how am I going to live with this, and what about Lori? How is Lori going to live with this?

She could imagine how her complaints would fly with Phyllis Roth, who had no normal children, just the two girls "with problems"—Ellen had begun to use the euphemism even when talking to herself. At least she had Lori.

But when Elyse was a few months old, Ellen found herself sitting in a brown room with drab leather furniture, together with Phyllis Roth, whom she had finally called, and a handful of other women. They were telling one another how they truly felt about their children and their husbands and their doctors. They made no effort to appear wise or calm or polite. And for the first time since Elyse was born, Ellen didn't feel incompetent, crazy, or alone.

—

The Industrial Home for the Blind had in fact been involved with the Albohers almost immediately after Elyse was born, when the maternity nurse on duty called for help.

"We have a kid here born without eyes, and we don't know what to do," the nurse told Edith Patt.

Though Edith usually went to the parents' homes herself, she sent someone else to see Ellen Alboher. At first she tried to rationalize her decision by telling herself that the caseworker she was sending had far more experience with blind children than she. But that was ridiculous—Edith had been at the IHB for almost fifteen years by then. She had seen all kinds of children and had heard all kinds of heart-wrenching stories. Could anything be more horrifying than the little boy who had been able to see perfectly well until his face was eaten by acid, thrown at him by an insane neighbor, who had meant to maim somebody else?

For reasons Edith couldn't explain, a damaged part was easier for her to deal with than a missing part. She couldn't stop herself from thinking that this situation was especially awful because the Alboher baby was a girl, and for a girl, beauty is what matters. A girl without eyes! She wasn't proud of these thoughts, but they persisted, and she felt they would interfere with her personal credo, suggested by the Hippocratic Oath: First, do no harm. So the social worker who arrived at Ellen's house a day after she got home from the hospital wasn't Edith but Nan Siegal, a sensitive woman who didn't flinch when she met Elyse.

"What do I do with her?" Ellen asked.

"You treat her like a baby," said Nan Siegal. "She's a baby. And you're her mother."

___

CHAPTER 5

The Happy Family

An excursion through the Rowe family albums reveals a portrait of blossoming domesticity. The shrubbery Bob planted grows denser and taller; the Christmas trees become larger and more elaborate; toys, birthday cakes, and bicycles appear. Everyone is smiling, especially after Jennifer joins the picture (pictures, plural—hundreds of them). Jennifer, who likes to dress up like a princess, is blond and adorable and flirts coyly with the camera, or whoever is holding it, usually Bob.

The albums are Bob's domain. He hasn't placed the photos haphazardly. He has installed them, along with family artifacts such as the printed announcement of Jennifer's arrival. Sometimes he takes three pictures of the same scene, crops them, and pastes them together to create a panoramic view—of the pink house where they stayed in Bermuda, of an Indian fort in upstate New York, of the sand dunes at the Jersey shore. Mary has taken to wearing dramatic scarves, which Bob bought her to draw attention away from her hips.

Bobby's hair grows shaggy and seems to be cut specially to cover his ears, which have embarrassed him because they seem too big for such a thin face. In one picture, he is playing the piano his father bought for him before he was born; in another, he seems to be beating Bob at chess while both of them laugh about his victory.

The Rowes are almost always laughing, often while they are gathered near a body of water. Sometimes they are at the Sapolskys' big backyard pool, paid for by Murray's mother so that she could keep an eye on her grandchildren. Sometimes the body of water is very small, in a bathtub, where the children appear alone or together. Most often, the family is seen sailing on the *King Kamehameha.* They look exceptionally healthy, burnished by the sun and wind and salt, a perfect family proudly displaying its less-than-perfect parts. Christopher is always easiest to spot—not so much because he is very small for his age or because of the way he never looks at the camera, but because his eyes are a startling blue, his hair the color of a freshly peeled carrot.

Yet life must not have been as easy as they made it seem, because when Edith Patt asked Mary Rowe in 1973 if she would like to join the IHB's mothers' group, which was then several months old, Mary eagerly accepted the invitation.

Thus began a relationship that would continue for years, long after the children who brought them together were grown and long after Mary Rowe was dead. The mothers' stories would forever be linked to Mary's, at first because of the pressures they had endured and helped one another survive and then because of what happened to Mary when those pressures overwhelmed Bob.

Edith introduced Mary to the mothers by playing them a tape of a conversation she'd had with Mary and Bob about raising Christopher. Edith had made the recording after the Rowes had told her they would like to help other parents who found themselves wandering unassisted in the universe of the handicapped. She used the tape at seminars in the way she sometimes used Ellen Alboher at such gatherings: to make student teachers feel empathetic rather than adversarial toward the parents.

The tape riveted the group. Mary's hearty laugh and sly Brooklyn humor made her seem instantly familiar, but it was Bob who gave them a jolt. How many hours had the mothers passed in extended analysis of their husbands, most of whom indulged their wives' passion for the group even if they didn't see the point of all the talk? When cornered into a discussion about their handicapped infants and toddlers, the husbands would do little but ask the familiar questions about the future: What kind of job can he get? Will she be able to live alone? What will happen when I die? The mothers were consumed with *now*—with school, with doctors, with mobility training. And here was Bob Rowe, a man who talked the way they did. He was argumentative and conciliatory, whining and wise. He even made fun of himself for talking too much.

He was a big talker, but Mary didn't let him overwhelm her. A high spirit connected them; you could hear the way they pumped energy back and forth. They were discussing the kinds of toys that would be good for blind children, and she said to Bob, "I remember when your mother gave Christopher a brown teddy bear as a present and I thought, What a stupid thing to give a child. A brown teddy bear—it wasn't even a bright color, and it did nothing. Then, being the heroes, we got him the light that flashed on and off. Buy toys not based on what salespeople or TV ads say is acceptable for children but which are practical and adaptable to the handicapped child."

Bob picked up where she left off. "Mary is talking about a big light that you would put in your car for protection if you broke down. It had a big bright white light on one side, and when you push a button on the other side, a red light flashes on and off. This really wasn't a toy for a child, but when we gave it to him, he loved it. So you have to buy for the handicapped child and not what is being sold for his normal age group. I guess it's like saying that sometimes you buy a toy and the child throws it away and plays with the box it came in."

After Elyse's birth, Ellen Alboher thought nothing could surprise her again, but in the mothers' group she encountered startling permutations of human grief and resourcefulness. Then, when Elyse was barely a toddler, Nan Siegal, the social worker who had encouraged Ellen to treat Elyse like any other baby, died of breast cancer. Ellen was in her twenties, but she felt prematurely old, mired in disappointment and death.

Hearing Bob Rowe reinvigorated her. From her perspective, he seemed a man of the world—simply because he was a lawyer—yet he also seemed to share the frustrations that preoccupied the mothers: getting help for their handicapped children without ignoring their other children; battling the professionals who behaved as though the parents were also handicapped, congenitally stupid; trying to not let their children's condition destroy them and their families. Ellen had come to think of these as women's problems and therefore insignificant to anyone but other mothers. Their husbands might weep with them, but then they distracted themselves with work, drink, the track, or the nightly news.

The literature supported Ellen's evaluation. Psychoanalyst Dorothy Burlingham, who with Anna Freud operated the Hampstead War Nurseries during World War II, in 1972 published *Psychoanalytic Studies of the Sighted and the Blind*. No coincidence that she called her opening chapter "Child Analysis and the Mother." Burlingham explained, "In this paper I shall talk chiefly of mothers, because it is almost exclusively with them that the analyst must deal." Accordingly, the book's index lists twenty-seven references under "mother," ranging from "aggression toward unborn infant" to "warding off child's seduction." An additional ten references fall under the heading of "mother-child relationship" and two more under "mother guidance." The heading of "father," however, contains two references: "of twins" and "death of."

Similarly, in psychoanalyst Selma Fraiberg's groundbreaking studies of blind children, the mother's burden is assumed. "While the developing ego of the sighted infant is insured when the mother is unexceptional or even less than adequate," wrote Fraiberg, "the blind infant's ego development is imperiled when his mother does not have adaptive capacities which are exceptional."

But here was Bob Rowe, a robust man, a professional man, turning the full force of male authority toward his child's problems. "I had a terrible time getting information about my own son," Bob said. "They would give me the same routine: 'We will send the report to your doctor.' I would wind up with editorialized reports. Why, why is everything a great big secret if they have some information—and they had some good information about the capacity of this child's eyes early in the game. I asked for a report; I didn't get one. They said they sent it to my doctor, and later—I won't tell you how it happened, but I did read the report. I found out a tremendous amount about the boy's eyes I would never have known. My doctor for one reason or another editorialized; he didn't tell me or he didn't think it was important or the guy was too busy. Probably it was the last, because most pediatricians are very busy, but if a parent can handle the information, why not give it to him? Why do doctors hold back everything?"

Ellen nodded, amazed at Bob's frankness and comprehension, and inevitably made comparisons to her husband. Al was sweet to Elyse and helpful with feedings and diapers. But ask him about Elyse's condition, about her present and her future, and he would instantly defer to Ellen. "I'm good at playing with my babies. I love them," said Al. "They can jump on me, roll on me, that's no problem. I'm a good daddy that way. But of course everything boils down to Mom. Mom is in the house; Dad goes out to work." Yeah, Ellen said to herself, thinking of Al, *and then he goes to the track, has a few glasses of booze, and sinks into the moment, him and his trotters.* It seemed sinful to feel jealous of people with so much trouble—and Edith had told them that the Rowes' boy was severely handicapped—but she did. She envied Mary Rowe for having a husband who seemed so in sync with her.

The Rowes spoke freely about things most of them couldn't bear to whisper to themselves—institutionalization, for example: the subject that was most loaded with guilt and yearning. How could you give your child away? But what would it be like to be free of the crushing minute-to-minute responsibility? The Rowes had considered institutionalization and had even gone to visit Willowbrook, but were disgusted by what they saw. "Kids were like blocks of cement—you put them in a place and they stayed there all day," Bob said, his voice low and angry. His voice lifted when he described taking Christopher sailing and to the beach, how they had gone to the Jersey shore recently and gone together into the heavy waves. "Wherever we go, he goes," said Bob. "He has a good time."

Geri Smith almost cried at that, but then she'd been susceptible to tears since her son, Eric, was born. She was a small woman with dark eyes who strongly resembled the young Judy Garland. Geri came to the mothers' group as often as she could, but rarely said a word. Every time she started to speak, she stopped herself. How could she talk about her problems, which seemed so minor, when Ellen's daughter had no eyes and Phyllis Roth had two children who were severely disabled?

People blithely speak about being "in denial," whereas a true practitioner, like Geri, denies the denying. Putting a bright face on a lousy situation was a lifelong habit. Geri had learned how to fake a big smile when she was a kid and went to the butcher's and pretended she didn't see him shaking his head and raising his eyebrows as if to say, "No fooling, you want a pound of beef livers sliced thin like you do every other day." Hers was yet another sad story of a poor Irish girl, part of a brood brought up by a drunken father and a stoic mother, whom they loved when she was alive and loved even more when she died young.

So when Geri noticed that Eric wasn't progressing in step with his peers, she constructed a rationale for his lagging development. While Geri had been recovering from labor, her doctor had come into her hospital room and shoved a sketch of a very underdeveloped penis and testicles under her nose. "Your son was born with a genital abnormality," he told her coldly. Eric had been born with hypospadias, a birth defect in which the urinary tract opening isn't at the tip of the penis. Because he was "genitally ambiguous," Eric's case was complex.

"How did this happen to my baby?" Geri asked the doctor.

"How can we question what God has done?" replied the doctor, instinctively knowing the right answer to give Geri, who hadn't yet discarded her mother's Catholicism. "To me, it is a miracle to see so many perfect babies being born."

He told Geri that Eric could be repaired with surgery.

Eric also suffered from aniridia, the absence of an iris, which made him sensitive to light, so he liked to keep his eyes closed. When they were open, they fluttered uncontrollably. But an ophthalmologist had assured her that Eric would be able to see normally with tinted glasses.

Geri told herself that Eric's problems would eventually be fixed, and neither friends nor family questioned her sanguinity, because no one wanted to pry and because Eric was so "easy." He slept well at night, napped frequently, and occupied himself when he was awake. He especially liked shiny objects, particularly tiny race cars that he lined up in rows, often for hours. "What a good boy," people would say. "He looks like a little angel." But when Geri tried to distract the little angel from his task, the obsessive organization and reorganization of his miniature cars, he had a fit.

When a carpenter doing work in Geri's kitchen told her he thought Eric was abnormally sensitive to the sound of a banging hammer, Geri responded by taking Eric for a walk when the carpenter came to work. When a neighbor's three-year-old son, more than a year younger than Eric, asked his father for a sweater because he was cold and Geri's husband said to her, "Do you realize Eric never does things like that?" she got angry at her husband.

"Why can't you ever see the positive?" she asked him furiously, and began rattling off all the things Eric could do. He could recite the alphabet, sing all the lyrics to "Puff the Magic Dragon" and "It's Raining, It's Pouring," and had memorized lines from several of his favorite Dr. Seuss books. He could repeat all the Bert and Ernie routines from *Sesame Street* and, courtesy of *Mr. Rogers' Neighborhood,* he could identify his body parts when singing along to "Everything Grows Together." She would often have him perform for friends. She was determined to believe that he was in the realm of normal.

Geri enlarged and framed a photograph she had taken of Eric in Prospect Park when he was three years old, an idyllic portrait of a child running across a field, sunlight bouncing off his curly blond hair, red overalls bright against the green field, dandelions at his feet. He could have been any happy little boy engaged with the world around him. She loved looking at the boy in the picture, even though she knew the image was false.

She snapped the picture the day she took Eric to the zoo with a neighbor's son, John-John, who was six months younger than Eric. John-John did everything a boy is supposed to do on such an outing: laughed at the monkeys, prattled on about the tigers, screamed with delight at the seals. Eric walked along brushing his hand along the fence; the animals were of no interest to him. Geri pointed his head toward the tigers and the seals and the monkeys, but he would have none of it. Finally, when an elephant lifted his trunk toward them and sent a powerful gush of water their way, Eric looked startled.

"Elephant!" exulted Geri.

"Elephant," said Eric.

Geri was euphoric. As they left the zoo, she told herself that all Eric had needed to command his attention was a little drama.

Her desire to have Eric be what he wasn't made her life take on the surreal shape and coloring of a child's drawing, in which fantasy and reality merged. She and her husband bought a dilapidated brownstone in Park Slope and became absorbed in restoring it to its original elegance. She planted a vegetable garden and got involved in community politics. She was happy to be among her peers—young industrious parents of small children, amateur contractors eager to dig out marble fireplaces whose beauty was submerged beneath layers of paint. In this vision of herself, there was nothing out of the ordinary except for Eric, the little boy sitting apart from it all, lining up cars one after the other ad infinitum, and Geri, his mother, cracking her kitchen sink with a pot thrown in a rage because she secretly knew the truth about her son. His limitations weren't only physical, they were mental, and he might never get better.

As she listened to the Rowes talk, Geri couldn't wait to meet these people, to introduce Bob Rowe to her husband. They'd had many fights about his refusal to take Eric out of the house. He didn't ignore Eric. He'd patiently sing and strum on the guitar with the boy. He just didn't want to be seen with him.

Most difficult for Geri was hearing about Jennifer, the baby girl the Rowes had adopted. "Christopher walks around with her holding her hand, and they have their own special relationship," Bob said. "I don't know to what extent they communicate, but they do have a thing going between them, whatever it is. They pat each other on the head, talk in baby language over in a corner, and I'm thinking to myself that if he were in an institution, he would have missed all that experience with Jenna. He must be learning something from it."

Geri's husband had made it clear that he was not interested in having any more children: Eric was more than enough. As she listened to Bob Rowe, she imagined what it would be like to have an ordinary child who could give her ordinary pleasure—and who might even teach her new ways to get through to Eric.

—

When the mothers later described the meet-the-Rowes session, they could have been talking about a revival meeting, recalling their responses to Bob and Mary with head nodding and responsive murmurs.

"One attitude I run into lately and that I hate," the women heard Bob say, "is when people find out that you have a problem. They say something along these lines: 'Well, God only sends you a problem you can bear.' "

Geri nodded vigorously at that. "Yeah, God gave you this to make you a stronger person. I hate that."

Rose Mauro muttered, "Next time someone says something like that to me, I'll tell them, 'Suppose I give my *special* person to you so you can be a *special* person.' " The cynicism was unusually pronounced for Rose, whose voice generally conveyed the sense that she was slightly surprised. It made her sound puzzled rather than bitter when things didn't work out as she thought they were supposed to.

The Rowes were appealing not only because of their bracing bluntness. They sounded like a team, enviably in sync. Mary said she had taken a course in the care of handicapped children which was so impressive that she reenrolled with Bob. They merged their experience into a single narrative, each filling in details for the other. Though he was the dominant speaker, Bob seemed in no way to be domineering. Both his inflection and his words indicated respect and love.

Bob Rowe's final words on the tape gave his listeners a small thrill. He put into words the secret desire in all of them, a desire that felt shameful and selfish. He understood that they all wanted the best for their children but that none of them wanted to be martyrs. Only later would they see the horrifying implications of what he had said, the terrible irony in his insistence on including Mary, even in this: "Mary and I got the attitude right from the beginning that we are not going to engage in a life of self-sacrifice to the extent that we were going to be suffering. God sent this to us, or somebody sent this, or this is a cross we must bear. Our major theme has been that we are going to be happy, and if we can be happy with Christopher, great. If we can't be happy with Christopher, if he is going to be a tragedy, if he is going to make a tragedy of our life and our family, then he has to go. This may sound a little cold-blooded, but the fact of the matter is that this is how it's worked out. We are a very happy family."

CHAPTER 6

Neither Here nor There

The Rowes became a touchstone for many of the mothers. If they could carry on with Christopher, who was far more damaged than many other children at the IHB, then carrying on was possible. Bob and Mary showed them that a family with a handicapped child had to set its own standards for success. This was the only hope for happiness. But the Rowes' example was also perplexing. The mothers found themselves wondering why their husbands didn't live up to their responsibilities the way Bob did, why they themselves couldn't be optimistic and cheerful like Mary.

Mary Gaskin—Mady, her family called her—remembered sitting in the Rowes' living room sometime in the early seventies and feeling ashamed for her envious thoughts. She was ashamed because she had just been in the Sapolskys' swimming pool with Mary and Christopher and other rubella children from the IHB and she had been a nervous wreck, worrying that the kids were getting chlorine in their eyes, that they hated being in the water, that one of them would drown, while Mary—who had arranged the outing for the kids—had seemed so cool, bouncing up and down with Christopher as though neither one of them had a care.

Though Mady's own child had attended the IHB nursery school, she then began working at the IHB with the rubella group as a teacher, and she knew how stingy the rewards were. Maybe when the children were six or seven they'd learn how to make the sign for the toilet, so you wouldn't have to keep changing their diapers (which seemed gigantic, even though these children tended to be small for their age). Maybe after you'd put a spoon to their mouths a thousand times they'd do it themselves, or maybe not. She knew how hard life with Christopher must be.

But Mady couldn't stop herself. She still envied Bob and Mary—their home, their neighborhood, his professional accomplishment. Mainly she envied the way they seemed to fit in wherever they were. She'd watched them at IHB fund-raisers and parties, where Bob would speak eloquently about all kinds of things, including the rights of handicapped children, and Mary would crack up the women with her deliberately tasteless repertoire of Helen Keller jokes.

Their self-assurance underscored Mady's insecurity, her feeling that she was neither here nor there. She had been Edith Patt's first client at the IHB and had become one of the social worker's closest friends, yet Edith had discouraged her from joining the mothers' group when her friend Silvia White had asked her to join. (Only later would Mady learn that Edith didn't want to share her friendship.) Mady's son wasn't blind, but he couldn't see very well, and he wasn't retarded, but he wasn't normal, either. She had a handsome, engaging, and glamorous husband, who claimed he worshiped her, but he routinely cheated on her. And then for Mady Gaskin there was another, even more essential discrepancy: She was a black woman who looked white.

Mady had always been on the outside, starting with her upbringing in Mobile, Alabama, on Carolina Avenue, an isolated black enclave in the richest white section, rented out to the maids and yard men who tended the mansions on either side. She went to school at Most Pure Heart of Mary, Mobile's black Catholic school, where the kids mocked her. *Yellow nigger,* they called her. The white Josephite nuns didn't step in and protect the black child who looked alarmingly like them.

Mady's parents had headed for New York when she was a baby, leaving their five children behind in Mobile to be raised by Mady's grandmother. Mady didn't see her parents again until she was thirteen and was called to join them in New York. Her mother didn't bother to come to the station to greet her.

Mady grew up tall and skinny, a striking girl with long black hair and olive skin. She drifted through Girls' Commercial High School in Brooklyn, emerging with a 77 average and a skill: She could type. And she could party. Her older sisters, light-skinned and good-looking like her, were the kind of women that rich black men liked to have with them on the cocktail circuit in Harlem and Brooklyn, at the clubs where black celebrities mingled with black money.

After high school, the partying became an escape from Mady's double life.

In the 1940s, there were jobs for white girls who could type, and when Mady discovered this, she began to pass—never lying, exactly, just not offering more information than she was asked to give. Her attitude toward life became *Que sera, sera,* because she never let herself feel part of anything. She'd drink with her sisters up to a point and then stop, or date a man and then be done with it.

Then she met Leonard Gaskin. Later she'd tell herself she should have listened when he told her that music was the love of his life. He'd bought his first bass when he was seventeen, named it Dolores, and kept the receipt forever in a special drawer, like a marriage certificate. By the late forties, he was playing with the most famous musicians—Billie Holliday, Louis Armstrong, Dizzy Gillespie. He didn't waste his passion on women, which wasn't to say he didn't appreciate them. Even as he grew old, when Leonard would talk about a woman being *attractive,* his voice would drop into a happy purr. This was a man who couldn't resist sex, the way some people can't resist rich food. He'd indulge no matter how much heartburn he'd have to suffer.

He said he wanted to marry Mady and have a family, but he was in no rush. His performing life was richly diverse and exciting. He moved easily between white and black musicians, playing conventional music on the radio and experimenting in the clubs. There wasn't a great player around that he hadn't worked with: Charlie Parker, Miles Davis, Thelonious Monk. He was drawn to the possibilities in the different kinds of music, and the instrument he played gave him a wide range of choices. There were plenty of jobs for a talented bass player willing to explore, and Leonard was willing. He went to Chicago for a while to learn Gypsy music, hooked up with a classical group at the YMHA to learn what Schumann and Bach were all about, and played country and gospel, too.

He had been seeing Mady for eight years when their son, Leonard, Jr., was born—and he still wasn't ready to get married. He had his career to tend to. But he didn't abandon them. He gave Mady money and kept on seeing her, but he didn't give up his other women. He saw nothing wrong with his behavior—at least he wasn't like some of the fellows he worked with, who bragged about meeting a grown child for the first time. "That to me is a tragedy," he would say. "I may not have been the most moral person, but that goes too far. I could not have impregnated a woman and then walked away from her. I can brag about that because I seem to be the only one in the whole world who hasn't done it."

He was sorry for all Mady was going through, but he also felt there was only so much he could do. He couldn't imagine settling down and being a dedicated family man—even if Leonard, Jr., had been perfect, which he certainly was not.

LEONARD O. GASKIN, JR.

Medical Record, compiled by his mother

1952. Born 3 months premature

Weight 3 lbs. 9 oz. Brooklyn Hosp. Remained in hospital 3 mos in incubator.

August 20, 1953. Operated for congenital cataracts both eyes at Brooklyn Eye & Ear Hosp.

Cataracts grew back and several successive operations were performed.

Glasses prescribed at the age of 11 months

May 12, 1954 Enrolled in New York Hospital pediatric & eye clinics

May 28, 1954—Right eye removed—glaucoma

June 7, 1954 Operated right eyelid to shorten elevator nerve. Operation not successful.

February 1954—Confined to Brooklyn Hospital for dehydration. FIRST CONVULSION

September 30, 1954 SECOND CONVULSION while under anesthesia in NY Hospital

Diagnosed as having abnormal forming of cerebellum

Operated on both eyelids—unsuccessful

January 1, 1955 THIRD CONVULSION. Prescribed ¼ grain phenobarbital 2 × per day.

March 18, 1955—Leonard has undergone 10 operations for the eyes\April 27, 1955 Operated on both eyelids to attempt to open eyes.

June 13, 1955—Weight 23 lbs height 2 ft. prescribed seconal by pediatric clinic to enable Leonard to sleep.

July 14, 1955—Had seizure during night. Admitted to NY Hospital because of postseizure coma. Released July 21. Prescribed 3 tsp phenobarb 3 × day

August 8, 1955—two severe seizures.

August 16, 1955 Height 3'2" [sic]—Phenobarb increased to 4 tsp per day

November 1955 Seizure

December 1955—Seizure

January 21, 1956—Seizure

January 24, 1956 Weight 27 lbs 3' 1½" [sic]—Phenobarb increased to 6 tsp per day

March 15, 1956—Seizure

May 14, 1956—Very lethargic staggered all day and fell down several times temp 106

Aug 15, 1956—Slight seizure—threw up green bile and complained of being cold

Nov 16, 1956—Seizure

January 19, 1957—Seizure—apparently petit mal

February 16, 1957—Same type petit mal seizure

March Medication—Mysoline ½ tsp 2 × per day

July 7, 1957—Seizure

July 27, 1957—Seizure

August 12, 1957 Two seizures ½ hour apart

Sept. 17, Medication—Dilantin 1 tsp—4tsp phenobarb & ½ tsp mysolin

Reduced Dilantin to ½ tsp on September 20, 1957

November 12, Medication: 2 tsp Pheno 3 × day; ½ tsp mysolin 2 × day;
½ tsp dilantin 1 × day

January 12, 1958 Seizure

May 11, 1958—Seizure

July 31, 1958—Left eyelid operation—Nider procedure—tied muscle
to inside of lid

August 5, 1958 Right eyelid operated on—opened permanently

August 8, 1958—Hernia on right side and hydrocele left side operation—
NY Hospital

October 15, 1958—Seizure

Nov. 26, 1958 Operated on NY Hospital left eyelid—Post–Nider procedure

Feb 1959—Dr took Leonard off benadryl

April 5, 1960—Seizure free for 2 years. Dr. says unlikely he will have
another

Feb. 14, 1961—Leonard jerks arms so took to Pediatric Neuro clinic.
Dilantin increased.

March 14, 1961—Leonard has not been doing well—jerking of arms
increased and he has not been alert. Dr. decided medication too
intense reduced it took him off reserpine and substituted amphetamine

April 21, reduced mysoline—Leonard continues to jerk

May 20, 1961—Reduced dilantin for 2 weeks then stop. reduce phenobarb to 3 pills per day ¼ grain amphetamine 1 per day—Dr.
thinks Leonard can be pulled out of withdrawal

June 15, 1961—reduced amphetamine to ½ tsp per day

With reduction in medication—Leonard remained seizure free—He
decided to discontinue the medication when he was about 16
years old.

During her second pregnancy Mady had vowed that she wouldn't do
anything wrong the way she must have with Leonard, Jr., and then she
would get so worried thinking about it that she'd need a cigarette to calm
herself down. When Poppy was born and the nurses brought her to her

mother's bed, Mady immediately took everything off—the covers, the baby's clothes, everything. She counted Poppy's toes one by one, then her fingers, and then she counted them all again. She was so transfixed by the baby's perfection that she wouldn't let the nurses wrap the poor child back up. Poppy had to lie there naked on her blankets until her mother fell asleep and couldn't look at her any longer.

Still, while Mady knew people thought of Leonard, Jr., as a mistake, she never had, even when he was born three months premature, his eyes clamped shut. The doctor's first words to her had been "Well, you have a boy, but don't send out any birth notices."

Even with all her son's sickness, she was determined not to turn him into an invalid. She always believed he could do more than it appeared he could do, and she encouraged him to try. Leonard hopped on the tricycle she bought him and rode the hell out of it, and she let him, knowing he would run into the fence and run home bleeding. She'd patch him up and send him out again. Then he'd try to climb the fence and she'd let him do that, too, and she'd patch him up again when he fell. The neighbors criticized her for all the blood Leonard, Jr., spilled on the street, but Mady didn't care.

She wasn't a saint. When Leonard, Jr., ran wild, she found herself smacking him, even knowing that the more she hit him, the wilder he'd run. Spanking reason into Leonard was as useless as trying to dig her way to China, though she would often feel at the end of the day that she had run there and back, running after the little boy who was chasing demons she would never understand. When he turned five, she decided it was time for him to go to kindergarten, just like all the other kids. Off they went to the neighborhood school, a tall, striking white-looking woman with long black hair and a tiny African-American boy with glasses so thick you could barely see his eyes. *No way, lady,* they told her. He was legally blind and intellectually dubious. How could they handle him?

She called the Industrial Home for the Blind. She was told that a social worker would have to come for a visit. That terrified her, because she knew what Leonard, Sr., would have to say about that. Even though she seldom defied him, she knew she was going to defy him now.

He responded according to script: "I don't need any social workers coming in here asking about my business, my income, wanting to know this and that about my life," he told Mady. "I don't want to talk to her, and I don't want her in the house."

They were living with Leonard's father in the Bedford-Stuyvesant section of Brooklyn. The house was a brownstone laid out in a grand style, with nineteen-foot ceilings and huge rooms, which Mady couldn't begin to fill with furniture, because they had no money. It could have been a gracious living space if Mady had had the slightest idea what to do with it. She'd covered the floor with wall-to-wall carpeting in a shade that might as well have been called Discount Blue. The walls were painted a different blue, and there was yet another blue for the slipcover on the chair. The couch was red.

Mady hated that ugly room, but that's where she received the social worker, because she thought she was supposed to. The kitchen and dining room were on the ground floor, and even though the kitchen was big enough for her children to use as a racetrack for their tricycles and roller skates when they grew older, it always felt cozy to her. But she was so intimidated by the thought of a social worker coming to her house that she wouldn't have dreamed of trying to have a casual tête-à-tête over coffee, especially when Edith Patt showed up looking as though she'd just stepped out of a fashion magazine. Mady could tell that the scarf had been chosen to bring out something in the sweater and that the sweater was coordinated with the skirt.

After a half-dozen visits that were stiffly polite, Edith asked Mady if she could have a cup of coffee. Mady was startled. Had she been rude all this time, not even offering the woman a glass of water? As soon as they went downstairs and seated themselves at the kitchen table, things were different. Though it would take a long time before Mady would stop calling Edith Mrs. Patt, she always felt their friendship took root that day. From then on, Edith came in through the downstairs door and Mady already had the cups laid out.

Mady felt no hesitation about telling this woman, whom she didn't know, everything about her life with Leonard, Jr. These were matters she never discussed with anybody, because she could see that most people felt no qualms about judging her. She had grown accustomed to assuming an air of quiet competence, because she had learned that weakness attracted bad advice and idiotic commentary.

Edith's visits had the aura of an illicit affair. Mady found herself wondering if Mrs. Patt took special care with the way she dressed just because she was coming to see her. She found herself speaking so low that she was almost whispering, for fear of waking Leonard, Sr., who generally slept during the day. She was always afraid he would come in and say something rude—though on the occasions when he did meet Mrs. Patt, he was unfailingly courteous and charming.

Mady had never known a woman like Edith, who had the confidence and competence of a man. After years of stumbling along alone, trying to find out what to do, she had finally found someone who could say, *This is what you do. This is where you go. This is who you call.*

Leonard, Jr., loved the IHB nursery school, which he started attending in 1958. For the first time in his life he held an advantage, because most of the kids were blind and he could see a little. When he was ready to leave, Edith not only found a school for him; on his first day, she accompanied him there.

A few years later, Edith also encouraged Mady to go back to school. Still, Mady knew that she wouldn't have gotten her college degree if it hadn't been for her husband. She had to give Leonard, Sr., credit for that. When she sat in those classes with students almost young enough to be her children, she was ashamed to open her mouth, because every one of them seemed smarter than she was. The first time one of her professors referred to Aeschylus as if his name were commonly known, like Louis Armstrong's, Mary was ready to bolt.

Leonard sent her back in, like the manager of an inexperienced fighter who gets the jitters when he tastes his own blood. He bragged about her to everyone, and he stayed with the kids so that she could study. When she got her master's degree in education from Columbia University, Leonard—who had been known to miss a family Thanksgiving dinner when he had a gig—took the day off to come to the ceremony.

Mady could see why people might think they were the perfect couple, and she wouldn't want them to think anything else. Yet knowing all that about herself didn't stop her from envying Bob and Mary Rowe.

One Sees, the Other Doesn't

In 1973, as the mothers' group sat in the brown room at the IHB grappling with the day-to-day problems of raising their children, Bryan Magee, a British philosopher, was a visiting fellow at All Souls College, Oxford, where he met a lawyer who had lost his vision as a baby. Their discussions sparked a desire in Magee to determine how deeply our understanding of the world depends on sight. He wanted to collaborate with the blind lawyer, but the lawyer died, so Magee began to look for another collaborator, someone with specific characteristics: He must be a scholar whose intellect complemented Magee's, and he must be blind—from birth or, failing that, from earliest childhood, since the memory of sight would completely alter the inquiry.

Magee found his man in Martin Milligan, chairman of the philosophy department at the University of Leeds, who had become blind as an infant and who was eager to join Magee on his philosophical journey. Milligan had been raised in one of the poorest slums in Britain—the Gorbals of Glasgow, Scotland. Despite the double handicap of poverty and blindness, he won a scholarship to Balliol College, Oxford, where he became an honors student. A combative thinker, Milligan had spent much of his life fighting what he believed were unfounded postulations about the capabilities and feelings of those who couldn't see. His own academic and professional advancement notwithstanding, he became a fierce advocate for the sightless, most of whom, he understood, didn't possess his intellectual advantages.

The correspondence between Magee and Milligan, recorded in a book called *On Blindness,* quickly moves from a philosophical debate into a personal discussion of blindness. In one of his letters, Magee tried to understand the blind person's point of view by thinking about bats. Bats are born with a kind of radar that all humans lack, he observed, but most of us don't feel deprived because we register sound waves within a much more narrow range of frequencies than bats do. Carrying on this line of reasoning, he mused, "We are almost certainly all in the same boat with regard to total reality: it is nearly all passing us by without our having any means of knowing what we are missing. It seems to me that the difference between what the blind miss and what the sighted miss must be as almost nothing compared with what we all miss."

But even as he articulates this "transcendental perspective," Magee doesn't seem to believe it. In a departure from the cool intellectual tone of his inquiry, with its learned digressions on Kant and Schopenhauer and Hegel and bats, he describes a heart-stopping moment of visual pleasure with great emotion. "What conception can you have of natural beauty?" he asks Milligan. "Recently I was in Kenya and visited a lake called Lake Nakuru. It has a high alkaline content, in which thrive certain algae, on which thrive flamingoes, a bird so beautiful that even my impersonal encyclopedia describes it as beautiful. The lake is of a size that can be embraced in a single act of vision from a distance of a few hundred yards. So I found myself standing looking at a whole African lake whose shore was lined by over a million flamingoes. The sight was so breathtakingly beautiful it gave me gooseflesh all over my body, and I shall remember it for the rest of my life. What, I wonder, can you make of that experience?"

Professor Milligan, who would die before he and Magee had completed their debate, couldn't fully grasp the fear and pity he aroused in people who could see because they thought he was missing so much. He was much more concerned with the practical problems, the inconvenience of being blind in a world designed for the sighted.

"One thing that is true is that neither I nor, I think, most blind people who don't remember seeing miss the *pleasures* of sight very much," he wrote to Magee. "It is not that we don't believe that these pleasures are many and intense: I for my part wholly accept that for many sighted people the loss of the pleasures of sight are a major part of the total loss that blindness brings, and for some by far the most important part. But although, as I argued in my last letter, one can long for pleasures one has not experienced, I don't think that people born blind or without memory of seeing do pine for the pleasures of seeing flowers, sunsets, works of art, or even the faces of loved ones."

—

Silvia White wasn't a philosopher like Magee or Milligan, nor was she of a philosophical bent, but perhaps more than any other mother in the group she understood the conundrum of seeing and not seeing. One of her twins was blind and the other wasn't.

Like Rose Mauro's daughter Anne, Silvia's twins were RLF babies, born in 1963, so tiny at birth that no one really expected them to live. Silvia hoped to protect them by naming them after holy women—Elizabeth Seton, the founder of the Sisters of Charity, and Madeleine Sophie, founder of the order of nuns who taught at Silvia's college. Her prayers were answered.

The twins remained in the hospital for almost three months after they were born. Elizabeth came home two weeks before Madeleine, who was kept behind because her chest was congested. When Madeleine arrived, Silvia noticed that her eyes didn't match—one was blue; the other was brown. But she was more concerned about Elizabeth, whose eyes matched but seemed indistinct when compared with Madeleine's.

Silvia didn't pay much attention at first. She had four older children, and her two skinny babies needed to be fattened up. Unsentimental and practical, Silvia was a natural at organization and management; it was her favorite part of motherhood. She was especially proud of a device she'd concocted for her older children called the Plunger, a cake decorator with a nipple on top, which made feedings more efficient. She brought it out for the twins, who'd suck down a plungerful of whole milk, fruit, and cereal for breakfast and another plungerful of beans and vegetables for lunch. No problem with those two—they were good babies.

Silvia liked to talk about her brood insouciantly, as if they were the Brady bunch, a happy-go-lucky sitcom clan. They lived in a roomy home in Forest Hills Gardens, the prosperous enclave of Queens designed in the early 1900s by Frederick Law Olmsted, Jr., whose father was the architect of Central Park. Forest Hills Gardens was a planned community, conceived by its organizers as "a humanist reaction to the industrial revolution." Silvia had spent almost her entire life within six blocks of her home.

But all that familiarity was no protection from fate's mischief. She married a man from the neighborhood, a doctor, and they had two children, who were still babies when drugs and depression caught up with her husband, who killed himself. It was horrible, of course, but as Silvia would say, she wasn't one to dwell on things. Two years later, while her girls were still toddlers, she married Tom White, a man with Kennedy-esque looks, who sold advertising for one of the television networks. In her version of the family lore, she cast herself as the bad cop, the mean disciplinarian, and Tom as the good cop, slightly distracted and often away on business trips but with a firm grip on the kids' hearts. The truth? Silvia was in way over her head. She'd been the only child of upwardly mobile immigrants. Her Cuban father was a manager at Westinghouse, where he edited a company publication. Her Puerto Rican mother had been a schoolteacher. Her childhood home was quiet and orderly, a poor training ground for someone who would be the mother of six children, one with poor vision and one with none.

Silvia frequently lost her temper, but she didn't complain. She didn't have patience for people who moaned about their lot and didn't do anything about it. That's what she liked about the mothers at the IHB. They didn't ignore their problems, but they didn't whine.

Silvia sent the twins to the IHB nursery school, and then she took a job there as a liaison between the parents and the administration. She first joined the mothers' group as an adviser but then, in 1974, became part of it. After the group began organizing fund-raisers for the IHB, they started socializing at one another's homes. Silvia could be hilarious, sexy, and provocative, and she, like Mary Rowe, had a sardonic wit. Like the other mothers, after she'd had a few glasses of wine, she was able to cut loose at these parties, where no one had to fear the dread "Tell me about your children."

—

Later, when the girls were grown, they would have a different take on things.

From the minute she realized that she was being lumped together with her twin, Madeleine White did everything to make sure it was absolutely clear that she was Madeleine, not Elizabeth. She instructed her family not to refer to them as "the twins." No matter how much she protested, however, it was always "the twins" this and "the twins" that. She couldn't say whether that was what made her rebel or whether rebellion was intrinsic to her nature, but she detested being categorized by anyone—especially her mother. It was anathema to Madeleine to be referred to as "visually impaired"—not because she objected to the jargon, but because she didn't consider herself visually impaired, even though one of her eyes needed a strong corrective lens. If people felt compelled to make a distinction between her eyes, they could point out that one was blue and the other was brown. If they insisted on comparing, she could live with them saying that she had a dominant eye and a not-so-dominant one, and they could even specify that the dominant one was blue.

She was fairly certain that she wouldn't be so sensitive if it weren't for Elizabeth, but Elizabeth was always there, the monkey on her back. As Madeleine grew older, she would tell herself that Elizabeth wasn't the monkey, the monkey was the circumstance—and the circumstance wasn't their twinness but Elizabeth's blindness. That's what made Madeleine her sister's keeper, whether she wanted to be or not. For that she blamed her mother, who would fob Liz off on Madeleine or their older sister Judy whenever she could.

Yet Madeleine also admired her mother, who fought like the devil to "mainstream" her and her sister rather than isolate them in an academic tributary for handicapped children. When Madeleine and Elizabeth were ready for first grade, Silvia insisted that they be allowed to attend Our Lady Queen of Martyrs, the parochial school Silvia had attended and had sent her older children to. Because the school didn't have a special program for the blind, Silvia arranged through the diocese to have a traveling teacher teach Braille to Liz at school, and then Silvia learned it, too, so she could make sure her daughter kept up with her schoolwork.

But usually Madeleine fought with Silvia, who could lose her temper just because the table wasn't set properly. Her mother became Madeleine's compass. If Silvia pointed north, Madeleine headed south.

When she was young, Elizabeth didn't feel that she was treated differently because she was blind. She never felt like the odd one out. She learned to ride a bike at the same age as everyone else, frightening the neighbors when she whizzed down the street, crashed into trees, got back on the bike, and then crashed again. She went to the same school as the rest of her family, and she was expected to do her share of the chores.

She felt more normal, in fact, around her friends who could see than she did around her blind friends from nursery school and summer camp in Vermont. Of course, the blind kids understood certain things better than her sighted friends did—most of them practical, like how to approach one another (sighted people had a tendency to just pop up next to you without warning and start talking). And when she was with blind people, she wasn't likely to barge into a conversation at an inappropriate moment, as she sometimes did with sighted people, lacking the visual clues they use. But most of the camp kids went to schools for the blind, so they were from a different world.

She really didn't feel different at all from the sighted kids until seventh grade: Boys were afraid of her, because they didn't know how to approach her. Even if they were friends, they didn't know how to treat her as a girlfriend, what the etiquette was. But that was on the outside. At home, the etiquette seemed straightforward: Liz was treated like everyone else. She was coddled by her father and organized and terrorized by her mother.

"She was absent," Liz would later say, "and I don't mean physically.

She wasn't the one I'd come to when I needed an ear. She was the one I'd come to when I expected to get disciplined for something."

It would have been easier if Silvia had been consistent, but she was erratic. Liz's older sister Mimi used to make her friends wait outside to see what kind of mood Silvia was in before bringing them into the house. With her father, you always knew what to expect. Liz never had to ask him if he loved her—she just knew it. He always showed her; he always told her. But Liz was also certain that without her mother around, she would never have been mainstreamed. Her father wouldn't have had the guts or the resourcefulness to figure out how to manage the system. Her father wouldn't have pushed her into Our Lady Queen of Martyrs.

When she'd lived away from home long enough to be able to think coolly about her mother's explosions, Liz concluded that there were too many kids—one of them blind, one with poor eyesight—and not enough money for the life Silvia had wanted for her family. She was so busy getting things done that she didn't realize her children needed her to stop and do nothing, nothing but grab them and let them love her. None of the White children missed that hugging and kissing more than Liz, who could hear her mother yell but couldn't see her smile.

CHAPTER 8

Acceptance

Ligia Monzon, a social worker at the IHB, needed to occupy her two younger sons over school vacation during the summer of 1972, so she brought them to work with her. To make the boys feel useful and keep them happy, she paid them to help out with the children in the rubella program—the agency's hardest cases. Her friend Claudelina Irala, who was, like her, from Paraguay, was the teacher in charge of the rubella kids and could use the extra hands.

Almost all the teaching was physical. Claudelina—who had been a physical-education instructor back home—spent her days manipulating small arms and legs, wrapping fingers around spoons, then repeatedly bringing the spoons from plates to mouths, hoping that one day the movements would register and the kids would start feeding themselves. She sat on the floor with the "advanced" children in this low-functioning group and helped them learn to play with toys designed to stimulate the senses—large blocks, trucks and wagons with big wheels, musical instruments, and wind chimes. Children who responded to no one else came to life with Claudelina, who looked at them as if they could see her when she talked to them, and never hesitated to cradle a child in her sturdy arms. She was solid and sure, even when she was dealing with the parents, who often had to struggle to understand her heavily accented English. With Claudelina, Ligia knew her sons would be in good hands.

Ligia's youngest son, Santiago, was eleven years old when he began his summer job at the IHB. It seemed like a fine deal to him. His mother was going to give him money to play with a bunch of kids. She'd explained that he would have to be patient, because even though some of the children weren't much younger than he was, they had been born with many problems. He quickly got over his nervousness when he saw all the great toys and when Claudelina explained that she needed him and his brother to hold the children's hands when they went to a nearby park and to help teach them how to play ball. It sounded like fun.

On their first outing, Santiago was put in charge of Christopher Rowe, by then a tiny seven-year-old—tiny except for his head, which was large. Claudelina told Santiago that Christopher didn't speak and could barely see or hear, which explained the big glasses and the hearing aid.

Santiago placed his hand in Christopher's. The boy seemed oblivious to him. They were walking along when Christopher started making a funny sound: *"Oy-oy-oy-oy-oy-oy."*

Santiago thought perhaps Christopher was trying to talk to him, so he leaned over and tried to mimic the sound—loudly, so Christopher could hear him: *"Oy-oy-oy-oy-oy."*

Christopher replied with a huge smile.

Santiago couldn't believe it. His mother had warned him not to be disappointed if the kids didn't respond to him. It wasn't personal, she'd told him—most of them couldn't connect. But Christopher had connected with him.

As the summer wore on, Santiago knew the connection wasn't in his imagination, because Christopher became his special charge—or, rather, he became Christopher's. They developed a ritual. Santiago would greet Christopher with an *"Oy-oy-oy"* and Christopher would smile and reach with his thin, freckled arm to grab the older boy. When they walked to the park, Christopher would lean against Santiago, clutching his elbow. At the park Santiago would roll balls to Christopher and fetch them when Christopher failed to roll them back, which was almost every time.

Santiago was young, but he understood the rareness of Christopher's recognizing him. He would never forget that summer—though the reasons would change over time.

—

It seems that Christopher, with all his imperfections, had inherited his parents' magnetism. When Irene Wagner visited the IHB nursery school the year after Santiago's summer there, in 1973, she couldn't take her eyes off this adorable child with the bright red hair and freckles. Looking at him more closely, she noticed how thick his glasses were, that he was wearing a hearing aid, and that he walked awkwardly. But, for her, his disabilities only added to his appeal.

Claudelina saw Irene staring at Christopher.

"He's very fortunate," she said. "His parents are very involved and dedicated. You should meet his father. It's very unusual to find fathers who are as involved as this father is."

Claudelina offered this observation because Irene had explained why she was visiting the nursery school. As the parent of a handicapped child—her son had been diagnosed first as retarded, then as learning-disabled—she was acutely aware of the misunderstandings, even hostilities, that often developed between the parents of such children and their teachers. When Irene's son finished high school, she decided to put to good use her years of battling teachers and the Board of Education. She went back to school to earn advanced degrees in the study of mental retardation and learning disabilities and became an instructor at Brooklyn College, where she now taught in the graduate program for special-education teachers. Her goal was to produce teachers who would be sensitive to parents: the kind of teachers her son had never had. To that end, she regularly brought the parents of handicapped children into the class she taught to explain what their life was like at home—the same kind of thing Edith Patt was doing, but more systematically. Irene believed that if teachers understood what it was like at home for a family like hers, they would behave differently. Her "parents' panels" became part of her curriculum. She found participants by going where the handicapped children were, including the Industrial Home for the Blind.

Irene herself was regularly amazed by the things her students heard from the parents on her panels. People were still generally private about such matters in those days—repressed, Irene would say—but her students received intimate insight from primary sources. They heard from a mother who said she wasn't a great brain but she knew she could be a good mother if only her disabled child wouldn't make her feel like a total failure. They heard about a doctor who had asked the parents of a handicapped child if they had other children and, when they said yes, told them, "Thank God you have someone else." They heard about grandparents who blamed their own children for the handicaps of their grandchildren, and mothers and fathers who blamed each other.

These were the lessons Irene Wagner taught in her classroom.

An unusual father. That's all Irene Wagner needed to hear. Mothers were readily available for her panels, but it was almost impossible to find fathers. The men often found it difficult to assign words to the terrible things they felt. On one of her recent panels, only two of the dozen panelists were fathers, and one of them was frozen in sad silence, unable to speak. Christopher Rowe's unusually involved father was an alluring prospect.

When she heard that Christopher lived only a couple of blocks away from her in Mill Basin and that he was going home on one of the IHB's little schoolbuses, Irene made sure she was on the bus with him. Irene, a lively woman with dark, seductive features and enormous enthusiasm, got off the bus and headed straight for Bob Rowe, who was waiting for Christopher. In a burst of volubility, she introduced herself, told him what a darling child Christopher was, informed him that they were practically neighbors, and began telling him what she wanted from him. Then she stopped. The bewildered expression on his face told her she'd gone too fast.

She started over and took it more slowly this time. As she explained that she, too, had a handicapped child, she noticed that Bob Rowe's blue eyes were no longer glacial but rather warm and sympathetic. By the time she waved good-bye, she'd recruited him to come talk to her class, and asked him to talk to Mary and Bobby about volunteering as well.

Bob interested her more than Mary, because she already had a large pool of mothers; Bobby interested her most of all. She had wanted to start a "siblings' panel" for some time, and, if Bobby was anything like his father, he would be a perfect candidate.

Hearing from the brothers and sisters was extremely important, Wagner felt. It was her second child who had been born with a heart condition that required him to be carried frequently, to keep him from turning blue. His sister, two years older, was very jealous of this sickly creature, who had displaced her as center of the universe. One day she said to her mother, "I wish I was born with a heart condition. Then you would carry me."

Though most of Wagner's time would be devoted to her son, who also suffered from neurological problems, she was acutely aware of her daughter's trauma—she understood anger and feelings of inadequacy and unfairness and frustration, because she felt them all herself as she fought to help her son make his way in the world.

Bobby Rowe couldn't have been a more persuasive spokesman. When he appeared on her first siblings' panel, he was as appealing as a ten-year-old boy can be. While his affection for his brother was obvious, Bobby didn't pretend that their life together was carefree. He spoke about the anger that would build up inside him when he would find someone taunting his brother or saying mean things about him, how hurt he felt when he heard that some children weren't allowed to play with him because of his brother.

Bobby's comments were recorded only in the notebooks of diligent students and in Irene Wagner's memory, so details are missing, but Irene was touched and impressed. "He was a charming boy, the mirror image of his parents," she would later say. "Genuinely caring people."

Though Irene and her husband would begin to socialize with the Rowes, the couple were elevated in Irene's mind to a higher plane than mere friends. She thought of them as collaborators in her quest to integrate handicapped children and their families into the world.

Like many of the women who would later talk about the Rowes, Irene spoke in superlatives. "He adored Mary and she adored him—it was so obvious to anyone who got to know them," she recalled. "The way they treated each other, things they would say about each other. One time we had gone there for dinner and Bob said, 'Isn't she a great cook? Isn't she wonderful, the way she takes care of so many things?' That impressed me, because not many men acknowledge what their wives do. The way they talked to each other, looked at each other, sometimes holding hands. And they had so many obstacles to overcome."

Mary was a good cook—at least a better one than Irene, which, Irene acknowledged, wasn't saying much. Mary's house was spotless, her children were always well groomed, and she was both high-spirited and down-to-earth, the kind of woman who would copy down a recipe for you after you'd complimented her on a dish she'd prepared. If Christopher hadn't been in the picture, Mary would have seemed like a lovely, competent housewife. But Christopher *was* in the picture. So, in addition to the normal tumult of dressing, feeding, transporting, and loving three children, there were all the special arrangements for Christopher, who continued to need a diaper at night, even though he was eight when Irene met him and had learned to use the toilet. All the usual chores became unusually difficult because of Christopher. Indeed, under those circumstances, being a lovely, competent housewife could be seen as a form of heroism. But mothers were expected to adapt, and they usually did.

Irene Wagner had taught her students that there were several stages through which almost every parent of a handicapped child would pass. These were similar to the five stages of death explored by the psychiatrist Elisabeth Kübler-Ross in her classic study *On Death and Dying*—but different because death limits the process of dying, while caring for a handicapped child can be a lifelong occupation.

Shock comes first, accompanied by thoughts of suicide and infanticide. Some parents also go through a theological crisis: *If there is a God, how can this happen?* Or, *I've sinned and God is punishing me.*

Denial is next as parents try to do whatever they can to make their child whole—megavitamin therapy, patterning, crash tutoring, even witch doctors. Yes, Irene Wagner would tell her students, she had a friend (a highly intelligent friend, she specified) whose wife, frustrated by conflicting diagnoses and consistent lack of progress, took their son to a witch doctor, whose treatment—passing a feather over the boy—proved to be no more (but also no less) successful than any other.

Then guilt. Irene, for example, had decided that her son's problems resulted from her decision to move a couch when she was pregnant because she thought she saw a cockroach.

Next is withdrawal. During this stage, the parent (usually the mother) becomes obsessed with care of the child to the exclusion of everything else, or the parent (usually the father) withdraws from the situation either by leaving altogether or by staying but finding any excuse for not being at home.

The final stage, she would explain to them, was acceptance. At this point, the parents accept the child as he is, not for what he could be if only he were someone else. They accept themselves as well, what they can and cannot do. For some, this means placing their child in an institution. Others manage to adapt household rhythms and expectations so that their "special" child feels like part of the family rather than an intruder.

Wagner warned her students not to expect these stages to follow one after the other in an orderly fashion. Parents could spend years in denial, for example, and they might never reach acceptance. When parents came to speak to the class, she often spent the next session classifying them with her students, who would then try to determine what stage the parents were in.

Quite often, opinions varied about a particular parent, and some parents seemed to be in many stages simultaneously. But in the discussion of Bob Rowe there was unanimity. He had not only reached the stage of acceptance, he had gone beyond acceptance to an even higher level—to helping other families become as well adjusted as his.

CHAPTER 9

The Ocularist

Elyse Alboher was five years old, and her mother, Ellen, still had never looked behind her eyelids to see what was there. She had been told that she would find not a hole but a pinkish membrane, tissue given its healthy color by a network of capillaries. But no matter how hard she tried to take a clinical perspective, her curiosity was always overruled by revulsion. Even as she regularly cleaned the outside of Elyse's lids with water, she never once peeked inside, never once risked sliding back into the despair that had immobilized her after Elyse's birth.

When the time came for Elyse to begin kindergarten, Ellen told her husband, Al, and her older daughter, Lori, who was then ten years old, that she wanted to have Elyse fitted for prostheses. Their reaction was immediate: We're not doing this.

Lori thought the whole idea was scary and disgusting. Al didn't tell Ellen, but she suspected—correctly, he would affirm—that he had vivid memories of a high school friend, a boy named Frankie, who liked to remove his fake eye and wave it around. But Al had another fear, especially strong, because it was bound up with his most fervent secret hope. What if they made these *things* for Elyse, put them in her sockets, and then someone discovered a way to make her see and the fake eyes interfered? He could never forgive himself. He also knew he was being foolish, just as Ellen said he was, so he didn't offer an explanation for his position— he simply said no.

"I don't care what you say," Ellen shrieked at them. Ellen had always been a screamer, but she had tried to lower the decibel level after Elyse was born, because the baby could not tolerate loud noise. The choice was clear: speak softly, or Elyse would cry, uncontrollably. So Ellen lowered the volume for Elyse, but inevitably the urge to shriek would build and she would explode, usually at Al or Lori, when Elyse was in another room. It simply wasn't natural for Ellen to be a mother cooing, *What do you want, honey?*

Still, Ellen's voice automatically softened when she talked about Elyse, from years of consciously forcing herself to tone herself down around her sensitive daughter, and from tenderness. "Her demands were really very little—she never really wanted anything," she would later say. "She didn't know there was anything to want."

Ellen had learned to appreciate Elyse as she was, which wasn't diffi cult. She was a funny little girl, with a shrewd sense of humor. When Ellen's friend Irving called the house, he would say to Elyse, "Listen, I want you to come over today. Leave them home."

"How am I going to get there?" Elyse would reply on cue.

"Get in the car and drive."

"I can't drive."

"Why not?"

Elyse would wait a beat and then reply, "I'm too young!"

Yet despite her precocious banter, Elyse seemed to Ellen to be discon nected in a way that wasn't obvious to most people. Like a smooth guest at a cocktail party, Elyse knew how to give the appropriate response, al ways with a warm smile, whose charm gave her an aura of brightness. Few people noticed that while she could define the words she was utter ing, she often missed the point of the conversation she was carrying on so well. Over the years Elyse would be tested frequently, and while it was agreed on that she was "neurologically impaired," the exact nature of the impairment would never be clearly defined.

While Ellen would do anything in the world for Lori, Elyse made her a warrior. She knew she would have to fight for this child, for whom the operating manual hadn't been written. Ellen became obsessed with artificial eyes, reasoning that Elyse lived in a sighted world and that people were cruel. Even if Elyse couldn't see, she would be able to feel people staring at her. Prostheses might shield her.

But protecting Elyse was only part of it. Ellen was forthright about her desire to look at her daughter without flinching, even knowing that the eyes looking back at her would be no more useful than a pair of marbles. Appearances mattered—and they always had.

In the sixteenth century, the Parisian author of a book on surgery described the "Eclepharon," an artificial eye made by the process of enameling gold and silver, with lids and brow painted on an oval leather shield attached to a metal spring band that circled the patient's head. Not exactly what Shakespeare had in mind when he wrote *Love's Labour's Lost,* just around the time the Eclepharon was created. "From women's eyes this doctrine I derive: They sparkle still the right Promethean fire; They are the books, the arts, the academes, That show, contain and nourish all the world."

The eye makers turned from metal to glass, which fit much more comfortably onto the tissue behind the eyelids and looked more natural than metal prostheses. Still, the glass models were far from perfect. Because they weren't implants, they didn't fill the empty sockets, so the eyes of the people wearing them usually seemed sunken in. In addition, the glass shells had to be removed at night, for the comfort of the wearer and protection of the prostheses, which were fragile.

Not surprisingly, Ludwig Mueller-Uri, the man credited with revolutionizing the glass eye in the nineteenth century, was a father whose seven-year-old-son lost his eye in an accident. At the time, Mueller-Uri was a glassblower living in a remote German mountain village who had acquired a measure of fame for making dolls' eyes with a human glint. Why not do the same for his son?

His contemporaries simply painted iris colors on glass globes, producing prostheses that had the look and shape of an eye but no depth or character. Through a complicated process of melting and twisting thin strips of "bone glass," which approximated the shining white sclera color, and dispersing them throughout a glass eyeball, Mueller-Uri approximated the twinkle of an eye with startling authenticity. Later, the Mueller family would develop a new kind of acrylic/glass combination that was hard and light and less irritating, and Germany, as the provider of this rare material, would dominate the world of artificial eyes—until World War II. Unable to import the rare German glass, U.S. dental technicians developed the first plastic eye, a major advance in the field of ocular prosthetics. The new plastic eyes were versatile—they could be molded into any shape and allowed a greater variety of color—and they were unbreakable.

Helen Keller owned a pair of the prewar German acrylic eyes. "For years she had always been carefully photographed in right profile to hide her left eye, which was protruding and obviously blind," writes Dorothy Herrmann in *Helen Keller, A Life.* "Aware that she would now be exposed to the merciless gaze of the public, she had both eyes surgically removed and replaced with glass ones. Aside from the medical benefits of replacing unseeing eyes with prosthetics, the operation drastically improved her appearance. No longer did Helen Keller have to be photographed in profile, and from then on, most photographs would show her gazing straight ahead. She was often described in newspaper interviews as having 'big, wide, open, blue eyes,' few reporters realizing that such a luminous countenance came out of a box."

—

When Elyse was an infant, her ophthalmologist told Ellen that he couldn't say whether the child was a good candidate for artificial eyes, but he suspected that prostheses would require complicated surgery. Then he admitted he wasn't knowledgeable enough to give an expert opinion. Ellen stopped listening when she heard "surgery." She agreed with Al that they shouldn't impose another trauma on Elyse.

But with kindergarten looming, Ellen decided to revisit the question. Because she was more convinced than ever that the world abounded with medical opinions that were in general misinformed, she turned, as she usually did, to Edith Patt, who made a few phone calls and came up with a name: the LeGrand Company, a manufacturer of ocular prosthetics, with an office at Columbia Presbyterian Hospital. When Edith heard that Al wanted no part of this experiment, she offered to go with Ellen.

The youth and jauntiness of the man who greeted them when they arrived at the LeGrand Company's New York office surprised both women. Sandy-haired, he looked like a jock (and carried a great baseball pitcher's name), not a specialist in an arcane field that required an understanding of ocular anatomy, an artistic sensibility, and a gentle touch. He was an immature jock at that. Walter Johnson was twenty-two years old and seemed even younger.

None of this quelled Ellen's shakes. But when Johnson began speaking to them in his friendly, authoritative voice, making sure to include five-year-old Elyse in the conversation, Ellen calmed down: Walter Johnson knew what he was doing—there wasn't a doubt in her mind about it. She admired him for his expertise, but she fell in love with him for the way he looked at her daughter and lit up with a sense of possibility, something no one else had done—including Ellen.

It is highly unlikely that Walter Johnson would have become an ocularist if his left eye hadn't been sliced open during an ice-hockey game when he was sixteen years old. Determined not to let that twist of fate alter his ambition to be a professional hockey player, he kept playing. But after a year on his college team, he realized he didn't have it in him to be the athlete he wanted to be—and not because of his eye. So he followed his mother's advice and asked the man who had made his artificial eye if he needed an apprentice.

That's how he joined a group of rarefied specialists—there are 114 licensed ocularists in the United States—whose work technically resembles dental sculpture but is really sui generis. Most practitioners come to the profession from the dental field or through inheritance. It's a skill passed down from generation to generation, like baking or palm reading. But some, like Walter Johnson, actually wear the eyes they have made.

Though he was only twenty-two when Ellen met him, Johnson had acquired unusual maturity from constant exposure to loss. He saw all kinds of patients: people like him, who had lost eyes in accidents, and people who had lost eyes to disease and people who had been born without eyes. There was no such thing as a casual visit to an ocularist. Johnson's patients always came swaddled in trauma.

Nothing touched him more than babies and their mothers. Typically, ocularists and ophthalmic surgeons like to insert prostheses into the eye sockets of babies born without eyes—or without one eye—within a few days of birth if possible. That way, as the child grows, the socket will enlarge gradually as larger and larger prostheses are inserted and they keep stimulating the tissue to grow. The procedure takes place in a climate of grief and hysteria. Walter had seen mothers still worn-out from delivery explaining the procedure to frantic relatives. He had heard mothers screaming that they wanted to give their babies away even as they pressed him for information about the artificial eyes he could make for them. The technical part of his job, painstaking though it might be, was a lark compared with the psychological. Nevertheless, he began to feel the passion he'd had for ice hockey filtering into his new professional life, and the bravura that had sent him hurtling down the ice was transformed into emotional daring. There was almost nothing he wouldn't try to make the process easier for one of his patients. When he realized that the best way to get through to some of them was to talk about himself, he told them exactly what had happened to him. He described the procedure as thoroughly and clearly as possible, because he knew from experience that the fear was the hardest part.

Ellen was exhausted after spending hours in the ocularist's office watching this young man *mutche*—annoy—her daughter. Though she was devoutly irreligious—Will a crutch help me? she'd ask—she fell back on the Yiddish of her parents and grandparents in times of stress. She tried to pay attention as Walter told her what he had concluded from all the probing and measuring. Elyse wouldn't need an operation, he said—she was a lucky exception to the rule among children with congenital anophthalmia.

Ellen snapped to full attention. This was the first time she could remember anyone describing Elyse as lucky.

Walter continued his brief introduction to the prosthetic management of congenital anophthalmia. Quite often, children whose eyes stopped developing during gestation also suffered from noticeable facial deformity. Their eyelids may not have fully grown; they could have cleft mouths or noses. These were problems Elyse didn't have.

His major concern was her age. He was worried that her sockets, which hadn't been growing along with the rest of her face, wouldn't be able to catch up. Usually, he began the process with newborns because the major development of a child's head takes place during the earliest years. Elyse had come to him very late.

The first step would be to insert small orbs of plastic, called conformers, into Elyse's sockets to stimulate tissue growth. The conformers were not works of art, just little orbs of plastic painted solid colors, and were much cheaper and easier to make than artificial eyes, which would be crafted when Elyse was ready for them. If things went according to plan, Walter would replace the first conformers with larger ones, then larger ones, until there was enough room for the final prostheses.

As Walter inserted the first set of conformers in Elyse's eyes, Ellen looked doubtfully at her daughter, who now had a blue wedge poking out from beneath her eyelid.

"What do I do if it falls out?" she asked Walter, shuddering.

"You put it back in," he told her.

Walter saw from the terrified look on Ellen's face that he had to act quickly. "I've bothered her enough," he said, glancing at Elyse, who was sitting there calmly. Without missing a beat, he reached into his left eye socket and pulled out his own prosthesis and gently showed Ellen how to put it back in.

This was the method Walter used as a last resort to convince parents. As it had many times before, the trick worked.

"It was so private, to do this in front of a stranger," Ellen said. "Like baring your soul. So intimate. It endeared him to me. I looked at him with awe that he was able to do that for me. We bonded. From that time on, we were friends."

As it turned out, Elyse's progress would amaze Johnson; in fact, she turned out to be an ideal patient. Though she liked to put things into her mouth, she never once tried to see what the conformers tasted like. They came in many colors, but the blue ones, which were the color of a robin's egg, had an unforeseen advantage. When one popped out one night while Lori was taking care of her sister, the bright blue made it easy to find on the brown shag carpet. The conformers made Elyse look odder than ever, and the family silently began to think of her as the alien once again. Walter kept increasing the size of the conformers until they were so large that he began to wonder if something was wrong. So he had a doctor take a CAT scan of Elyse's head and discovered that she simply had a lot of space in there. Everything he saw indicated that her eyes, had they developed, would have been large, like her father's and sister's.

Although Ellen was rarely at a loss for words, she was never able to adequately explain how she felt the first day Elyse wore the eyeballs Walter had crafted. Their hazel irises and shape were so authentic that Ellen barely noticed the slight droop that would remain in Elyse's eyes until it was corrected with a later set of prostheses. On the rare occasion that Elyse took the prostheses out, Ellen put them back as casually as she might a contact lens.

The prosthetic eye, of course, offers a psychological benefit, not a physical one; it makes not a whit of difference in how one sees—or, rather, doesn't see—only in how one is *seen*. For Ellen it was exhilarating to see something actually work out for Elyse the way it was supposed to. Elyse's feelings were, understandably, different.

"It was kind of scary for me, because I didn't know what my condition was until then," Elyse would remember when she was a grown woman, living on her own with a roommate. "I didn't know I was born without eyes. I didn't know what that meant, if you want to know the truth. I knew that I couldn't see and the rest of my family could. When I was a kid, people would ask my mom, 'Is she blind?' But what did that mean?"

Though she would always be a cheerful and fluid conversationalist, Elyse didn't probe deeply into the philosophical aspects of her condition. She had been bewildered rather than upset by the revelation that she had no eyes and had felt sad only when her father finally told her the story of her birth. She felt sorry for her mother and father, not for herself.

On her first visit to the ocularist she was nervous, because she didn't understand what was going on—even though her mother had explained it to her. When she met Walter, she felt more at ease because he seemed so nice, though she was still a little scared of him. Actually, the whole process was frightening. She could tell from her mother's voice that she wanted this very much, and Elyse wanted her mom to feel better, even if she didn't understand why it was all such a big deal. She loved her mother, even though she talked much too loudly and often sounded harsh—especially when their relatives came over and they all started talking at once. Elyse would feel sick then, because they made her so nervous. But her mother was also funny, and Elyse liked that. She had been praised so often for her own sense of humor that she particularly liked people who knew a good joke when they heard it, even if they couldn't tell one themselves. She could tell that Walter had a good sense of humor, and that made it easier for her to let him keep touching her face in unfamiliar ways.

She had also been unnerved when she heard Edith Patt's voice that morning. Edith's voice was nice and low, a soothing voice, but what was it doing in that unfamiliar setting? Edith belonged at the nursery school— it felt unnatural to have her here, even if Edith kept her mother calm.

Walter was very good about explaining what he was doing, but it still hurt when he put the conformers in. She didn't like the way they felt at all, pressing against skin in a strange new place inside her head somewhere. It had never bothered her not to have eyes until then—this seemed like an imposition. But she could tell from the way her mother sounded that this was very important, so Elyse forced herself to sit still while Walter did what he had to do.

Although she understood that she wasn't supposed to take out the prostheses, when the artificial eyes were finished and she heard how excited everyone was, she wanted to know what the fuss was about. She took them out and slid her fingers all over them. She liked the way they felt—really interesting, like a peanut, but smooth. She couldn't explain why, but she got a kick out of their shape.

Eventually, she became so accustomed to the artificial eyes she didn't think about them any more than she thought about her fingernails or her hair. They were part of being presentable, and this too, she knew from her mother, was important. When she was young, she'd stopped rocking and putting her hands in her mouth, because her mother let her know these "blindisms" were not acceptable. When she grew older, she dieted, because she knew that being thin was part of being presentable, and she would put makeup on her eyelids and her lips, also part of being presentable. Yet she didn't really associate being presentable with how she looked, because she never really imagined what she looked like. What she worried about was how she felt when she touched herself. Once, she had felt like her mother, thick and heavy. Now she was slim, and her skin was smooth and clean. That's what mattered. The artificial eyes didn't mean much to her at all.

CHAPTER 10

Unraveling

Barbara Sapolsky had a big pot of water boiling on the stove, for spaghetti, when she heard a knock at the door. It was early evening, a cool spring evening, April 9, 1975, two years after Mary had joined the mothers' group at the IHB. The Rowe kids were standing there—Bobby, Christopher, and Jennifer.

That wasn't unusual. The Sapolskys and the Rowes spent a lot of time together. The kids didn't think about where one yard began and the other one ended. The Rowe children knew they could use the Sapolskys' pool whenever they wanted, so long as an adult was around. When Bobby and her boys, Joel and Alan, used to make igloos out of the snow that piled up between the houses, it didn't matter where they started to dig—in one yard or the other. The families celebrated Christmas together at the Rowes', Chanukah at the Sapolskys', went ice-skating together at Abe Stark's Coney Island rink.

Now Barbara sensed that something was wrong when Bobby Rowe told her, "Mommy said to come over and stay here." That wasn't like

Mary. She wouldn't want her kids to be a bother at dinnertime. Still, they didn't seem especially alarmed, so Barbara decided to wait for her husband, Murray, to come home before doing anything. She made spaghetti and fed all six kids, hers and the Rowes'. When Murray arrived, she sent him next door to see what was going on.

Murray walked into Bob and Mary's house and found them on the landing between the front door and the living room. Bob looked at Murray as though he'd been expecting him, and handed him some rope.

"Tie me up, Murray," he said. "Before I do something terrible."

Murray Sapolsky wasn't a man given to asking questions. He walked up the steps, took the rope, and tied Bob's hands to the wrought-iron railing.

Later, when Barbara pressed him for details, Murray told her he didn't know much—just that Kenny, Bob's younger brother, was on his way over to the house, and so was a psychiatrist that Bob had apparently been seeing. They were taking him to a hospital in the city. Barbara was perplexed. How could she not have known that Bob was seeing a psychiatrist? If there were problems, Mary would have confided in her. She and Mary told each other everything—though lately, since Barbara had started to work again, there hadn't been much time for conversation. It was possible that a couple of weeks had gone by since she and Mary had talked. But what could happen in a couple of weeks?

—

A man could unravel. He could be forty-five years old and feel tired of believing in himself. He could stop pretending he wasn't angry at everything that had gone wrong. He could break down.

Three weeks before he asked Murray to tie him up, Bob Rowe had had a vision. He woke up in the middle of the night and saw the face of his mother, who had died two years earlier. He heard her whisper, "Kill your family."

He got out of bed and ran downstairs to the front door. He wanted to leave, because he was afraid he would obey his mother. Mary, never able to sleep without Bob beside her, instantly woke up and followed him. "Stay away from me," he said. "I want to harm you."

He told Mary he'd seen Millie. She was back from the dead to torment him as she had in life—as though she knew he'd never mourned her passing. She was the only critic of the picture he'd carefully painted of Bob Rowe—successful manager, dedicated family man. Millie judged him a lowly bureaucrat, head of a damaged household—a fake. She'd once told him she aborted two children before he was born and had considered making him number three. But he had tolerated Millie and tried to appease her by looking the other way when she shunned Christopher, answering her nasty comments with jokes.

When he was a child, he hadn't been able to shut out his mother's constant nagging at his father for more attention, more money. His father coped by coming home drunk, and that would set her off again. But she was also pretty, charming, and young—she was only sixteen when they had married. Bob's friends liked her, called her "little mother."

When Bob was seventeen, he dropped out of high school and joined the army. He was a bright boy bored by school and tired of loving and hating Millie. Rebellious but not a rebel, he sent home money every month, which he asked Millie to save for him. When he returned, he gave the money to his father for a trip home to Hawaii, hoping he'd be asked to go along. Instead, his father thanked him and took Kenny—the son who looked Hawaiian, though he showed no interest in his island ancestry—because it was understood in the family that Bob belonged to Millie.

No, he didn't mourn her passing. He was glad when she died, even before he found out that she had disinherited him—and he was the child who carried her imprint, her coloring, her ambition. She left everything to Kenny—Kenny, who had never gone to college and had then risen through the ranks at the Automobile Association of America to management, to earn more money than Bob. "Everything" was only five or six thousand dollars, and Kenny immediately offered to split the money with Bob. But neither Kenny's guilt nor his generosity could undo the hurt of Millie's final rejection.

Mary listened to Bob and talked to him, maybe took his hand—they still held hands after all their years together. She knew she had to take him away from Millie again, to let him know that she, Mary, would always see him the way he wanted to be seen. Mary had spent her adult life believing in Bob Rowe, and she wasn't going to stop now.

She managed to coax him back upstairs. "You won't hurt me," she told him. He listened to her, wanting to believe her. He never doubted her love—she was endlessly affectionate, though not sexual, always resisting what she regarded as carnal pleasure, the Catholic schoolgirl into middle age. If he resented Mary's reticence in bed, he never admitted it to any of the many psychiatrists he would encounter. "She loved me too much," he said.

A few nights later, he was again overcome by a frightening desire: He wanted to slam the children's heads together; he wanted to kill Mary. "I was right to tell you not to marry a Catholic woman," he heard his mother saying. "Go ahead and kill her." He went to the kitchen and began to pull a knife out of a drawer but ran out of the house instead.

Mary decided that this was the moment to stop being self-sufficient. She could no longer handle this alone. She called Pat, Kenny's wife. Mary didn't believe much in psychiatrists, but Pat convinced her that Bob needed help.

It was the end of March.

Bob went to see William Distelman, a psychiatrist in Mill Basin. Bob was calm, the doctor would remember. Bob told Dr. Distelman that he felt his problems were related to his work. He had left Allstate a few months earlier, after twenty years with the company, and had just started a new job, for which he didn't feel prepared. He was convinced he was about to be fired. Also, he told the psychiatrist, he'd forgotten to file some papers for a trust case he was handling privately and thought that his client would retaliate by having him disbarred. He was afraid to sleep— because of the visions—and he couldn't eat.

Dr. Distelman prescribed Mellaril, an antipsychotic, and Elavil, an antidepressant, and suggested that Bob consider treatment in a psychiatric hospital. The next week, however, Bob told the doctor that he and Mary had agreed they could take care of his problems at home.

He took his medication, which helped him get through the day. He put on a suit and went to the office and played with the children when he came home. But he had no control over what happened at night.

Millie reappeared more than once to taunt him. "Come to me," she told him one night. "Come to me."

Bob left a note for Mary, slipped out of the house, and drove his car to the Verrazano-Narrows, the long, lovely suspension bridge that links Staten Island to Brooklyn. He drove to the middle of the bridge and stopped the car, wanting to get out and throw himself over the side.

He didn't know how long he sat there. It could have been minutes or hours. He couldn't remember what he thought about or if he thought about anything. He just sat there and didn't budge until drivers behind him began honking their horns at him. Then he started the engine and went home to Mary.

———

Mary called Jack O'Shaughnessy at work. "Bob blew," their old friend heard Mary say. She told him Bob had been screaming that he had to get out of the house or he was going to hurt her. Some neighbors had helped calm him down, and now he was in the hospital. He wanted Jack to visit him.

Jack couldn't believe that Bob had come to this. Only a couple of years had passed since Allstate had suggested that Bob transfer to Skokie, Illinois, company headquarters. Jack worked in the insurance business and knew what that meant: Bob had been picked as a comer. Within two years he'd be a vice-president. He was moving fast.

But Bob and Mary had talked it over and decided to turn down the offer. It had taken years to arrange appropriate schooling and therapy for Christopher, and they couldn't imagine starting all of that over somewhere else. What if they uprooted themselves to Skokie, the logistics complicated a hundredfold because of Christopher, and then the company decided it was time to move again? They couldn't handle that.

Jack understood, but he was surprised that Bob had passed up the opportunity. It was unusual for him to restrict his plans because of Christopher. He and Mary took the boy everywhere they went. If they felt terrible pain about Christopher—and Jack knew they must—they never talked about it. Jack sometimes found it tiring to watch Bob and Mary hold it all together, but neither of *them* showed the strain.

Bob told Jack he was worried that turning down the promotion would relegate him to the sidelines. He'd seen that happen to a lot of men. When they didn't follow the company's plans for them, they were written off. Forty-three was young when you were on the way up but old if you weren't going anywhere. But, he said, he didn't want to stay in negligence claims. His specialty—assessing the damages in automobile accidents—had become obsolete after no-fault insurance was introduced. "It's like being a blacksmith and the horseless carriage comes in," he would say.

Bob didn't want to look like a has-been, so he asked for a transfer to the litigation department—a high-pressure job. He handled EBT work, examination before trial—dress rehearsals to see how witnesses would handle themselves on the stand. He had to anticipate every question the other side might pose. It wasn't unusual for him to be juggling sixty files a day, never knowing which one would be up for trial next.

After being the man in charge in the claims department, a vice-presidential contender, he was a rookie, trying to prove himself once again. He stayed up nights preparing for the interrogations, he told Jack. Though he never felt on top of things, he seemed to have the new job under control. By December 1974, not more than a year after moving into litigation, he was promoted to senior trial attorney.

That's when Jack started to notice a change in his old friend. The man who had always exuded confidence suddenly seemed unsure, sometimes even panicky. So Jack wasn't surprised when Bob called to tell him that the company wanted to take him out of litigation and put him back in management. It sounded like a good idea to Jack—a way to reduce the pressure—but Bob insisted that he wanted to stay in litigation. He decided to leave Allstate, the only place he'd ever worked, after twenty years.

Jack didn't think Bob would have any problem learning the ropes at Commercial Union, the insurance company that hired him. But it was a big step. Allstate's clients were primarily drivers and homeowners and small businesses, so the claims Bob was accustomed to handling were relatively small—less than $100,000 and often only $5,000 or $10,000. At Commercial Union, he would be handling complex claims—sometimes for millions of dollars—against the directors and officers of corporations. Bob didn't have that kind of experience. But Jack wasn't worried about his friend. Bob had a good mind. He was a capable man.

—

At ten o'clock on the night of April 9, 1975, a few hours after the Rowe children knocked on Barbara Sapolsky's door, Bob was admitted to Gracie Square Hospital, a private psychiatric facility on the Upper East Side of Manhattan. Diagnosis: psychotic depression. Treatment: drugs (a continuation of Mellaril and Elavil) and psychotherapy.

Bob was lucid from the outset, clearly explaining why he was there to Max Brandt, the psychiatrist assigned to his case. "Talks re his preoccupation with mother who died about two years ago," Dr. Brandt scribbled in Bob's daily progress notes. "He was glad she died as he felt her to be a burden. Now he hears her say, 'I was right' about not wanting him to marry his wife Mary. Pt. apparently never had a mourning reaction to mother's death."

Yet almost immediately after entering Gracie Square, Bob was putting a good face forward, smiling at the nurses, socializing with other patients. His chart notes that he hurt his right forefinger playing volleyball. The day after the volleyball injury he told Dr. Brandt, "I still feel the image of my mother telling me to hurt my wife, but the medicine puts a blanket on it, like on a fire."

The nurses liked him. "Quietly pleasant," observed one RN. "Shows interest in activities, maintains good behavior, well groomed and eating fairly well."

He read books, he made a belt for Bobby, he built a model Viking ship, and he received visitors. Jack O'Shaughnessy stopped by. Mary insisted on coming every day, and Bob's brother, Kenny, drove her. She brought twelve-year-old Bobby along one weekend. Sometimes they stayed in the hospital, but more often they went off the grounds. The nurses didn't know where Bob went, but they observed that he was almost always in good spirits when he returned.

However, on April 28, almost three weeks into his stay, Bob became so upset when Mary was there that he sent a nurse to find his psychiatrist.

"He was in unit punching at a mattress when I entered room," Dr. Brandt reported in Bob's daily progress notes. "Was with wife earlier, discussing financing his hospitalization. He became upset and was afraid he would hurt her and requested placement in Seclusion Unit. Spoke at length about the job he quit, his handicapped son, feelings toward his mother when she died. He had a desire to strike out at something, is extremely anxious and angry and asking for additional external controls at this time. Mellaril upped to 100 mg."

The next day Bob woke up in a panic. He was supposed to start a new job at Home Insurance on May 12, and he was worried that he wouldn't get out of the hospital in time. He told one of the nurses he needed more medication, because he felt he was "going to explode." By the next day, however, though his chart reported that he was "tense and somewhat depressed," he was able to divert himself with a game of chess.

Over the next few days, Bob pressed Dr. Brandt to discharge him because his insurance covered only 60 percent of the hospital bill. "You want my money," he told the psychiatrist, whose May 1, 1975, entry contained this observation: "Denies he's really ill and thought he shouldn't have told anyone about how he felt about his wish to kill his family."

By May 9, Bob was taking a regimen of drugs considered moderate for patients with psychotic depression: 100 milligrams of Mellaril four times a day; 5 milligrams of Stelazine, another antipsychotic drug, twice a day; and 50 milligrams of Elavil, the antidepressant, three times a day.

His mood had been steadily improving. On May 8, Dr. Brandt reported, "Wonders how he could have contemplated suicide. Wants to try possible overnite this weekend. I will allow it and would have brought it up myself if he hadn't."

On May 12, he came back from a weekend at home "relaxed, playful," reported one of the nurses. Dr. Brandt cut the daily dosage of Bob's antipsychotic medication in half but kept the antidepressant at 150 milligrams. The next day Bob admitted to Dr. Brandt that he "doesn't take criticism well. Feels he can control himself if he has physical activity—like punching bag, a wall, etc."

By May 16, six weeks after he arrived at Gracie Square suffering from homicidal and suicidal urges and diagnosed by Dr. Brandt as "grossly psychotic," Bob Rowe was declared ready to be discharged from the hospital—but in need of a diet. "Pt. is in good spirits this a.m.," observed Dr. Brandt. "Is eating very large quantities of food and he has gained about 20 pounds since here. Discussed his need to control appetite and possible relation to his medication."

On May 17, 1975, Mary came to the hospital and took him home.

—

Bob had gotten fat. That was the first thing Jack O'Shaughnessy noticed about his friend when he got out of Gracie Square. He'd always been stocky but athletic. Now he was eating yogurt for lunch, trying to lose weight.

That wasn't the only change. Bob, who had always been so quick, seemed sluggish and disoriented. Jack felt his words disappearing into a fog before they reached Bob's brain. It was the medication, Bob told him. He was still taking antidepressants, and they had a dulling effect on him.

Bob began—and lost—his job at Home Insurance not long after he was discharged from Gracie Square, and applied for a position at American Insurance, where Jack worked. Jack urged his boss to hire Bob, figuring he could tutor his old friend, who would be handling much bigger claims than he had before.

But that was the old Bob he was thinking about. Now, the most routine claims threw Bob into a panic. He'd call Jack four, five times a day to go over cases with him. Then the calls from Bob began to dwindle, and Jack figured he had snapped back and was handling things. But one day in the spring of 1976 he was on the street outside the office, waiting for a cab to take him to the airport, and there was Bob.

"I've been let go," he said to Jack, who told him not to do anything until he returned from his trip. By the time he got back, however, Bob was working somewhere else.

—

No matter how low Bob sank, Mary remained confident. She assured him that he was going to get better, that he'd work as a lawyer again. Until then, she would earn the family's living. She reminded him that she'd been a working girl before their marriage and for nine years after, until Bobby was born. Now the kids were in school for much of the day, and Bob could tend to them when they came home.

She didn't have to go far for employment. The Silverglates, who'd moved across the street in the summer of 1975, owned a company, Smiles Fuel Oil. In the fall of 1976, Risa Silverglate told Mary they could use help. Her job—secretary, gofer—carried no title, but it paid the bills.

Bob continued to see Dr. Distelman twice a month and to look for work. Dr. Distelman observed in a report, "He held several jobs for rather brief periods of time, often accepting a position that he felt unqualified for so that he might be able to earn a living, hoping that he would master the job requirements as time passed. Some jobs provided no challenge, while others required skills or knowledge that he did not possess; he left a job if he was severely criticized in order to avoid humiliation by the boss, or he was fired. Although somewhat apprehensive about his abilities, and fearful that his students might find him to be inadequate, Mr. Rowe taught an adult education course for a period of time.

"Early in 1977, Mr. Rowe began driving a taxi cab," wrote Dr. Distelman. "At first he felt embarrassed and somewhat anxious lest his close associates become aware that a man who is an attorney was now driving a cab. However, he was capable of dealing with these feelings and recognized that his need to support his family overcame his sense of wounded pride. Mr. Rowe then purchased his own cab, and was more optimistic about his opportunities to earn a living."

—

Irene Wagner, the teacher who ran the parents' panels, didn't suddenly stop seeing Bob and Mary Rowe—it just seemed that way when it occurred to Irene that they hadn't gotten together for a very long time. It occurred to her the day she bumped into Mary on the street, sometime in the late spring of 1977.

Mary was "not herself." By that, Irene meant that Mary was noticeably upset. In a rush of words, she told Irene that Bob was down in the dumps because he'd lost his job and couldn't find work as a lawyer. He didn't want to hear of her going to work at first, because it was too humiliating—and what could she earn, anyway? But she had gotten a job as combination clerk and errand girl for a small oil company. Bob had taken a big chunk of their savings—$25,000—to buy a cab medallion, but then he left his cab outside a Papaya King stand, the motor running, while he ran in for a glass of juice. When he came back out, the cab was gone. Twenty-five thousand dollars down the drain. Now Bob was home taking care of the kids.

Bobby's hip had been hurting him lately, she continued. He suffered from Legg-Calvé-Perthes disease, a degenerative condition of the skeletal system that most often occurs in young boys. He'd had to use crutches for a couple of years when he was little, and their pediatrician had assured them the disease wasn't necessarily crippling, or even likely to be. But a doctor had recently told them Bobby might end up in a wheelchair one day. That did it for Bob, Mary told Irene. He felt like the walls were crumbling. You won't recognize him, she told Irene.

They agreed to get together for dinner, and Irene was shocked at how accurate Mary's description was. This lumpy zombie wasn't the Bob she knew. Not that he had been vain—she wouldn't say that—but he had been a nice-looking man who took care of himself, someone who paid attention to what he saw in the mirror each morning. How could he bear to look at himself now?

Mary was nervous, chattering more than usual, as if trying to make up for Bob's silence—usually he was the one who set the pace, offering up a good story. After a while, the conversation began to register, and he joined in. Only then did Irene see a glimmer of the old Bob making its way through the fleshy exterior.

Not long after that dinner, Irene called to ask Bob to speak to her students that fall. He begged off.

"I'm really not up to it," he told her.

"Is there anything I can do?" she asked.

"No," he said. "There's nothing anyone can do."

She tried again. "We've had our problems, too, and in the past we've helped each other. Sometimes it helps to talk to someone."

"No," he said.

"Why don't you think about it," she said, but didn't press further.

CHAPTER 11

Afraid

In the summer of 1977, the heat was breaking records, and Bobby Rowe and Jeffrey Mond were spending their days playing baseball and listening to Yankees games, and sometimes they went sailing with Bob. That summer, Jeffrey gave Bobby his baseball bat, because it was lighter and would help Bobby move faster. In return Bobby gave Jeffrey the one he used, his father's old bat.

At nights the boys sat in the backyard studying the stars with Bob, and Bob told Bobby, as he had since he was small, to look for Orion. "Whenever you see Orion, you'll know I am thinking of you and loving you," he said, same as always.

Bob was still seeing Dr. Distelman twice a month and taking his pills. He was working now and again but was having trouble concentrating, because of the medicine. He wanted clarity—to be able to read a book and remember it, to challenge his mind without fear of another breakdown. He was certain he couldn't hold a job, because the drugs interfered with his concentration. He stopped taking his medication to see what would happen. He hadn't had any hallucinations since he'd left Gracie Square, more than two years earlier. Millie seemed to have settled into her grave and was leaving him alone. Besides making him groggy, the drugs were expensive. But without them to blunt his anxiety, he worried even more about money. He became terrified of losing his house, which had come to mean everything to him. Soon he was even terrified to leave it, as if he thought it might not be there when he got back.

On October 13, Bob called Dr. Distelman to cancel his session. He told the psychiatrist he had decided to end therapy. He felt treatment was no longer necessary, and, he said, his wife agreed. He didn't tell the doctor that he was more and more fearful that his family was headed for poverty and that he didn't want to spend fifty dollars an hour to talk about his troubles and that he wanted off the pills. Their savings were down to $14,000, and he was in constant dread of losing the money, even though Mary was working steadily.

On October 18, one of the happiest days of Bobby Rowe's life, Reggie Jackson hit the three consecutive home runs that helped the Yankees defeat the Los Angeles Dodgers and win the World Series.

—

The winter was as extreme as the summer had been. Nineteen seventy-eight blew in with a vengeance and froze New York solid, but that didn't stop the mothers' group from getting together. They were meeting at Rose Mauro's house in early January as planned, weather or no weather.

Ellen Alboher had picked up Mary Rowe to drive her to Rose's. When Mary got into the car, she told Ellen that Bob hadn't wanted her to go to the meeting. Ellen wanted to hear about *that*. Bob had always seemed to encourage the group. He always attended occasions to which husbands were invited, even after he came out of Gracie Square. All of them knew that he had been in the hospital and why. The Rowes hadn't kept his breakdown a secret, nor had they talked about it much. Everyone was busy. In those years—1975, 1976, 1977—the mothers had devoted much of their meeting time to raising money to support the Industrial Home for the Blind, which was privately funded. They'd pledged to raise $100,000 over a ten-year period and had embarked on a series of fund-raising events—dances and auctions—that gave them a sense of authority and power and community, but it also left little time for the intimate discussions that had brought them together in the first place.

True, the last time the men and women had all had dinner together, Ellen noticed that Bob seemed especially out of it. He'd grown heavy in the past few years, too—though, because Ellen's weight was up and down so much, she didn't think that was so strange. Now that she thought about it, however, she realized he had become more and more disengaged—not so different from the other men, unlike himself. His usual gregariousness was absent.

Mary said she was rattled because Bob had stopped taking his medication recently, and whenever she went out, she didn't know what shape he'd be in when she got home. He's been very depressed, she said.

Ellen was blunt. "Are you afraid?" she asked.

Mary dismissed the suggestion behind the question. She told Ellen she felt that Bob's willingness to express his fears—that he wanted to hurt her—meant he wouldn't do it. He'd never laid a hand on her—not before or after the hallucinations. She wasn't afraid for herself; she was afraid for Bob. He was very upset about her having to go to work, even though she told him she didn't mind at all. But he wanted her home with the family.

When the two women arrived at Rose's house, they began drinking wine and settled in for an evening of food and revelation. Mary began talking to Betty Burr, who had joined the group shortly after it began. Her son Cliffy was more damaged than Christopher, and Betty's husband, Kenny, was the most involved father besides Bob. Betty often felt annoyed with Kenny and always wished she could be more like Mary, who liked to indulge Bob—buying him a Japanese robe because he liked Asian culture, serving him tea in bed.

Mary confessed to Betty that Bob was losing touch. The last time it snowed, she said, Bob asked her what he should do about the snow outside the front door.

"I told him you pick up the shovel and throw the snow into the street!" Mary was laughing, making a joke out of it, but her eyes seemed sad.

Listening to Mary, Betty wanted to tell her that she didn't have to have a perfect house when she was working all day. You don't have to bathe a child every night, she wanted to say. You let it go. You don't wear yourself out. You work all day and come home to bathe the children and then make some time with your husband. It's too much. You cut out bathing them every night. You just sponge them off.

But Betty didn't say any of that, because she knew Mary would go on bathing her kids every night no matter what.

Mary seemed uncharacteristically nervous that evening. Every so often, she excused herself and went to call Bob, who was home with the kids. Finally, she told them that he had stopped taking his medication and that she was worried he would have another breakdown.

The mothers converged on her. "Why don't you get out—take the kids and go live someplace," they urged her. "You can't live like this."

"I can't do that to Bob," Mary said tersely.

Rose Mauro was struck by Mary's fierceness, which she understood well. She knew how it felt to be fed up with a husband, but she also knew that Mary couldn't just throw twenty years of marriage out the window—not after all she and Bob had been through together.

Before Mary left that night, she said to Rose, "I can't do anything to hurt Bob." There was no compromise in her voice. "He would never do that to me."

—

Mary left for work early every morning. She met Risa Silverglate across the street, and they went to work together.

Bob hadn't had a job since he'd stopped seeing Dr. Distelman, so he got the kids ready for school and he was waiting for them when they came home. He helped with the chores as much as he could. He prepared meals; he cleaned the house. He tried to read and to paint, but he often just sat and stared out the window. When he thought about Mary being the breadwinner, he sank into shame. The only image that held his attention during his hours alone was his bank account, which was shrinking steadily.

Christopher came home from school by two o'clock. For the first time, Bob was with him all day without Mary, day after day. He watched

Christopher amuse himself by banging himself on the head with a coat hanger. He noticed how much laundry there was, because Christopher, who was twelve, still wet the bed almost every night.

Since that long-ago visit to Willowbrook, Bob had never second-guessed their decision to keep Christopher at home. He'd collaborated in Mary's spirited construction of a happy family. He'd learned how to calibrate Christopher's achievements against Bobby's and Jennifer's, to find rough equivalencies for "special" and "normal." He'd helped their other two children understand that Christopher by necessity was the axis around which the household revolved, and he was touched by their acceptance. He loved watching Jennifer with Christopher. They could spend hours together, playing or curled up on a bed watching television, always teasing and gentle with each other. Bobby was old enough to evaluate his brother more dispassionately, and while the obligation to care for him and to occasionally defend him was sometimes a burden, he too was affectionate to Christopher and rarely complained about having to help. Surrounded by the goodwill he'd helped bring about, Bob had taught himself to love Christopher too, or to believe that he had.

But now he was finding it harder and harder to distinguish himself from his damaged son. Both of them were cripples. Christopher was his disgrace; Bob was the family's disgrace. Neither of them was worth the space he took up. Bob began to fantasize about fixing things for Mary and Bobby and Jennifer by killing himself and Christopher. With the broken parts out of the way, they could be happy and productive, as they were meant to be.

One day in January, without divulging his death fantasy, he told Mary that they should reconsider the question of putting Christopher in a home for the handicapped. What would happen to him when he could no longer go to school? What would happen to them? How would they provide for their children when he, Bob, couldn't figure out how to shovel the snow?

Like many people fueled by faith, Mary always found a way to be optimistic, no matter how tortured the path. She always believed Bob was on the verge of improvement, about to reemerge as the man she thought she knew. Even when he was in Gracie Square, pronounced "psychotically depressed," she had assumed that he could manage a rational discussion of the family's finances—and she had been shocked when he exploded at her then.

Now, when he told her that he wanted to send Christopher away, she responded truthfully. "That would break my heart," she said. She assured him that when he felt better, things would look brighter. He was exaggerating how difficult it was to have Christopher at home, because he didn't feel well.

—

In early February, the sky opened up and snow poured onto Brooklyn. Almost seventeen inches would fall before the storm was over, leaving Mill Basin looking even lovelier than usual, trees and hedges trimmed with white, postcard-pretty and even more peaceful than usual, because sound was muffled by the snow.

But for people trying to get somewhere, the snowstorm was an annoyance. Natalie Mond, Jeffrey's mother, was creeping toward Sixty-fourth Street, trying—unsuccessfully—to keep her car steady. She was sliding all over the place, and she could barely see where she was going. The windshield wipers couldn't keep up. Up ahead, she saw a man and child struggling to make their way through the thick heaps of snow along the road. She recognized Bob Rowe and his little girl, both of them light-haired, with bright red cheeks, both of them laughing as Jennifer kept falling in the drifts and excavating herself, happily brushing herself off and then plunging into the next pile, dragging Bob with her.

Natalie always got a kick out of Jenna, a frisky seven-year-old with a real mouth on her. Watching the two of them play made her feel better about the storm. She pulled over and popped open the door on the passenger side.

"Want a lift?" she asked them.

Bob started to put his foot in the car, but Jenna shook her head and pulled him back. "No!" she shouted, tilting her face so she could catch the snow, laughing. "I'm walking with my daddy!"

Bob smiled at Natalie, shrugged as if to say, "She's the boss," and closed the door. She watched them make their way through the snow, hand in hand.

The ground was still white when the Presidents' Day vacation began a couple of weeks later. The kids, ready for a weeklong break from school, had made plans. Bobby, Christopher, and Jennifer were going bowling with the Sapolsky kids. The lanes were nearby. They didn't need a grown-up to take them.

On Tuesday morning, February 21, around nine o'clock, thirteen-year-old Joel Sapolsky, the middle child, answered the telephone. He recognized Bob Rowe's voice immediately. Joel was disappointed when Mr. Rowe told him that their bowling date was canceled. He had a job interview and had decided to take the kids with him. Joel went bowling anyway.

Late that afternoon, Mary got a call from Bob at the office. When she got off the telephone she told Risa Silverglate that she had to leave earlier than usual. She seemed animated.

"Bob told me to come home as soon as possible," she said. "He said he has a big surprise for me."

Mary said that Bob had had an interview that day. "He must have gotten a job," she told Risa, who was aware of Bob's troubles. Then Mary joked lightly, "Or maybe Christopher started to talk."

She finished what she had to do and then went home.

Risa worked late that night. At around eight o'clock, she remembered that she'd forgotten to turn on her answering machine at home. She decided to call Mary and ask her to run across the street and do it for her. Bob answered the phone and told her that Mary had gone out to visit friends and wouldn't be home until "very, very late."

The Rowes had rented their downstairs apartment—the one Millie had lived in—to a young couple. They'd lived there for a little more than a year, for the past three months with their new baby daughter. That evening, before Mary came home, the tenant, John Farrell, on his way into the house, saw Bob standing in the living room, wearing slacks and a white shirt, looking out the window. Farrell saw that the curtains were blowing and realized the window was open. That seemed odd to him. It was freezing cold.

Bob was just staring at the street.

"How are you doing, Bob?" said Farrell. Bob looked at him for a few seconds and then waved. Farrell went inside.

—

The next morning, Phillip Silverglate saw Bob standing in front of his house. It was six-forty and still dark on that winter morning.

Phillip called to him from across the street: "What are you doing up this early?" Then he said to tell Mary to meet Risa later, because he was leaving now.

Bob replied, "Mary's taking the day off from work today. Don't interrupt her—she's going to sleep the whole day."

"Okay," said Phillip. "Whatever you want." He left for the office.

A few minutes later, the phone rang at the Silverglates'. Risa answered.

Bob Rowe told her that Mary wasn't feeling well and wouldn't be coming to work. He asked her to do him a favor and not call during the day because he was putting Mary to sleep. He had already taken care of the children, he said, and he wanted Mary to get her eight hours.

"Okay, fine," said Risa. "No hassle."

All day long Risa thought about calling Mary to see how she was doing, but held back. Finally, at seven that evening, the twenty-second of February, Risa called the Rowes' house.

No one answered. She assumed the family had gone out to dinner or something like that.

CHAPTER 12

Clarity

For months his depression had felt like a physical thing, as uncontrollable as a voracious weed, consuming his will, withering his logic. He could think of little else but the house, convinced that it would vanish unless he took action. The all-American dream house, he used to call it wryly—this icon of the life he and Mary had built so carefully. While he often appeared to be staring numbly into space, he was struggling to develop a plan that would restore him as provider and protector, and rescue his family from destitution.

Monday, February 20, was Presidents' Day, the beginning of winter vacation for public schools, though for Bob the day's significance lay elsewhere. It was the day he realized that his children didn't have to suffer the dire scenarios he'd envisioned for their future. That day, Bob Rowe decided he could keep his place as head of the family. He had found clarity, an honest way out.

He didn't feel afraid—nothing like the way he'd felt before Gracie Square, when his mother had come to him and ordered him to harm Mary and the children. The hatred in her command had frightened him and he'd run away. This is insanity, he'd told himself then. The hallucinations had come at him in uncontrolled bursts of hatred. He didn't feel that way now. Now he was calm, for the first time in months.

The children were still asleep when Mary left the house early Tuesday, before dawn. Though she and Bob usually ate breakfast together, they didn't that morning. She just slipped away.

Bob kept an eye on the clock. He would have to cancel the kids' bowling date with the Sapolskys, but he was a considerate man and didn't want to call too early. The Sapolsky boys were teenagers like Bobby, likely to be sleeping in on a holiday. He decided to wait awhile.

Bobby slept late, but Christopher and Jennifer woke up and crawled into the big bed in Bob and Mary's room so that they could snuggle together under the blankets and watch television.

At nine o'clock Bob went to the telephone and lied to Joel Sapolsky about his plans for the day. (There was no job interview; he wasn't taking the children with him.)

He went upstairs to Bobby's room, closed the door, and stood at the head of his son's bed, watching him sleep. More than anything, Bob had wanted Bobby to admire him, and nothing made him happier than Bobby's efforts to follow in his footsteps. Images of those efforts were etched in his memory: Bobby straining at the jib sheets on the *King Kamehameha,* Bobby skidding with terrifying speed down an icy ski trail, Bobby riding big waves at the Jersey shore. Bob always imagined that Bobby was thinking: I can do it, Dad—see me, I can do it. Someday I am going to be as fine as you.

When Bobby was twelve, Bob took him to Lincoln Center, to a performance of *Tosca,* hoping the scenery-shaking action sequences would seduce the boy as they'd seduced him. Bob wanted his son to share his passion for opera, especially the melodramatic tales of doomed love by Giacomo Puccini, whose music splendidly echoed Bob's grand yearnings.

Bobby succeeded in pleasing Bob in many ways, but none more than when the boy declared that he loved *Tosca*—until they went to see *Madame Butterfly* together and Bobby said, "It's even better than *Tosca,*" echoing his father's opinion. Bob had been happily amazed by Bobby's critical judgment. *Tosca* contained the kind of lurid action he expected a boy would like: a torture scene, a dramatic murder, and an execution by firing squad. Bob interpreted Bobby's preference for *Madame Butterfly*'s surging romantic score as a sign of sophistication and taste, assurance that he had taught his son well.

For twenty minutes on the morning of February 21, Bob stood at the head of Bobby's bed and watched him sleep. He loved him. Bobby could not be disillusioned by his father. Bob couldn't bear that.

As he struck Bobby's head with the baseball bat Jeffrey Mond had given him, Bob believed, as he was killing his son, that he was loving him. For twenty years Bob had studied medical texts to analyze insurance claims. He aimed the blow so his son would not feel pain, and then brought the bat down a second time to make sure that Bobby wouldn't survive with brain damage.

"What have I done?" he would remember saying when it was over, but then he reassured himself that he had done what he had to do. He'd decided there was nothing else that could have been done.

He left Bobby in bed and walked down the hall to Jennifer's room, to be alone. Jennifer was still watching television in the master bedroom with Christopher.

For two hours he stayed there by himself, waiting, though he didn't know for what. He might have kept sitting there, but Jennifer came to him.

"Daddy," she said. "Bobby's sleeping too late."

He saw her looking at him curiously and realized he was crying. It was time to continue.

"Get back into bed with Christopher," he told her.

The Rowe children were obedient. Jennifer returned to her parents' room and crawled into bed with her brother. When she was settled, Bob followed her into the room, carrying the bat.

"We're going to play a game," he said to his daughter. "Close your eyes."

There was no reason for her not to trust her father. Without hesitation, Jennifer closed her eyes. The blows were swift and sure, just like the ones that had killed Bobby.

Christopher was turned toward the television and couldn't hear well, but he sensed that something had happened behind him. He began to rise, but he was knocked down, again and again.

It was over.

Bob sat in a chair near Jennifer and Christopher, who were lying in bed in their pajamas. He stayed there for several hours, standing up every so often to stretch, but he felt nothing. He didn't turn off the television, but he didn't watch it.

Sometime that afternoon a thought occurred to him. If Mary came home and saw the children, she would suffer horribly. How could she live with the children gone?

At five o'clock it was already dark outside. He called Mary at work and told her to come home because he had a surprise for her. He went downstairs to the living room and stood at the window, waiting. He opened the window to let the cold night air blow into the house. John Farrell, the tenant, called to him from outside and asked him how he was doing. Bob stared at him a few seconds and then waved. Farrell went inside.

The living room was one landing up from the front entrance, so Bob was looking down at Mary when she walked in the door at six-fifteen.

"Come up and stand in the middle of the room with your eyes closed," he told her. "The children have a surprise for you."

Mary took off her jacket and climbed the stairs. She was wearing a bright sweater and red slacks, something cheerful against the winter gloom. She stood near the piano and closed her eyes.

After that, only one part of his plan, as he would describe it, remained unfinished. He was supposed to join his family.

That night, after Risa Silverglate called looking for Mary, he got into his car and began to drive. His destination was the Manhattan Bridge, which links Brooklyn to Canal Street in lower Manhattan. He would jump from there. But every time he came close to the bridge, he drove away. He stopped several times and lay down in the backseat, telling himself he had to jump. But he was afraid of pain, of a slow death by drowning.

The last time he approached the bridge, he didn't turn back. He shouted, "Get out and jump," but he couldn't. He kept driving, went into Manhattan, then turned around and went back to Brooklyn.

Then he was home again, standing by the driveway. It was early in the morning, and there was Phillip Silverglate across the street asking him what he was doing up so early.

"Mary's taking the day off from work today," Bob told him. "Don't interrupt her—she's going to sleep the whole day."

Bob was afraid Phillip would forget to tell Risa, so he called her to make sure she didn't pop in to get Mary for work. He spent the day in the house with his dead family, unable to leave them, unable to think or move. Eventually, he swallowed a handful of sleeping pills and pulled the kitchen table next to the stove. He turned on the gas, climbed onto the table, and lay down. As he pushed his head into the oven, he pulled a sheet of cellophane wrap over the stove and his head, thinking this would help the fumes do their work more effectively.

He fell unconscious.

—

When John Farrell stepped inside the foyer of his apartment on the ground floor of the split-level house at around eight-thirty that evening, he smelled gas. His wife said she didn't smell anything, but Farrell opened a window anyway, and called the gas company. He wanted to see if the gas had leaked into the Rowes' place, but the door connecting his apartment with their lower floor was jammed. His wife dialed the Rowes' number, but no one answered the telephone.

A man from the gas company arrived at around nine o'clock. Farrell took him to check the gas meters, then they went upstairs. The door leading into the Rowes' kitchen was unlocked, but the lights were off. When John Farrell turned on the light, he saw Bob lying on the floor beneath the wall oven, next to a table that was pushed up against the stove. He was wheezing, his eyes were shut, and his skin was pale.

The tenant ran downstairs to his apartment and dialed 911 to report a possible heart attack. Then he returned to the Rowes' place. In the living room, he saw Mary lying on the floor. He called 911 again. There were more victims, he told the dispatcher, possibly overcome by gas.

Farrell asked the gas man to help him carry Mary outside for fresh air, but when he kneeled down next to her and shook her shoulders, he saw that there was blood on his hands and on the floor. He noticed a baseball bat leaning against a chair.

This was too much for him to handle alone. He barely knew the Rowes, and now he was privy to this ghastly intimacy. He ran across the driveway to the Sapolskys' and knocked on the door.

It was the second time someone had knocked on their door that evening. Three hours earlier, Barbara had been starting to prepare dinner when Bob stopped by, wearing an overcoat. He asked her if she had a flashlight, and she sent her older son, Alan, to the basement to get one. She didn't ask Bob why he needed it, and she would never find out.

When she heard the second knock, she assumed it was Bob again. Who besides a next-door neighbor would drop by on a night like this? The temperature was dropping into the teens, and she'd heard on the radio that the windchill would make it feel like twenty below zero. Through the window she could see the wind blowing the snow around. There was still almost a foot of it on the ground.

When she opened the door, it took her a while to identify the young man standing on her stoop. Then she realized he was the Rowes' tenant.

He was saying something about gas and Bob and Mary, and he asked her to come next door with him. She shivered as she followed him through the snow and wished that Murray, her husband, would come home already.

She followed the tenant into Bob and Mary's house and up the stairs, and then she saw Mary. They say awful things happen in a blur, but Barbara saw Mary very clearly that night: She was lying on the living room floor and she was wearing slacks.

Barbara ran up the stairs to look for the children. She found Bobby in his room, then Jennifer and Christopher in the master bedroom, still, as if in deep sleep, but Barbara knew they were dead, like their mother.

"Oh my God," she shouted, and ran outside as the instinct to protect her own children overwhelmed all other sensation. She just wanted to be gone, away from this horror. All she could think of were her children. What if they followed her and saw what she had seen?

So she ran. There was nothing she could do for poor Mary and the kids. Just as she reached her front door, a car pulled into her driveway.

She stood frozen, squinting at the headlights, their brightness intensified by the ground's icy reflection.

It was Murray.

Barbara would leave it to him to talk to the police when they came. She would not be a witness. She couldn't bear it.

—

Natalie Mond didn't want to step out into the wind that night, but Prince George DuMond had to go, cold or no cold.

She bundled up and said to her schnauzer, "Okay, darling, I'm ready."

The two of them had walked past a few houses on the block when Natalie saw the police cars. She tugged at Prince George's leash as she picked up the pace. Murray Sapolsky was standing in the driveway between his house and the Rowes'. "What's going on?" she asked, unable to see his face clearly in the dark, not yet realizing that he was distraught.

"Bob killed Mary and the kids," he said bleakly.

Natalie didn't pause to notice whether Prince George had done his business or not. She ran home.

"Stan!" she yelled to her husband as she walked in and unhooked the dog's leash. "Bob killed Mary and the kids."

Upstairs, her son Jeffrey heard his mother scream something about the Rowes. He pulled on his coat and headed for the door.

Natalie briefly registered the shock on Stan's face and then she, too, left again, to join the other neighbors huddled in the blustery night, warming themselves in the heat of tragedy. She saw someone pushing a wheelchair down the Rowes' driveway. As her eyes adjusted to the glare of a police car's headlights, she saw that the man in the wheelchair was Bob. His arms were strapped to the chair, his head was slumped forward, and his feet brushed against the snow.

—

Assistant district attorney Michael Gary had given up trying to interview the man, who was apparently overcome by drugs and gas fumes, and had him sent to Kings County Hospital. Gary stayed behind to debrief the detectives on what they'd learned from the neighbors.

Gary had little sympathy for Rowe, whom he saw as yet another suspect, another perpetrator, another "male ego" case—where the man of the
house decides that since life isn't worth living for him, it isn't worth
living for his family, either. Gary's feeling was, Hey, if that's the way you
feel, buddy, take your own life and be done with it! The rest of us will
go on.

Though he was a mild man, he could be biting when so moved. "Very
rarely do you have a woman who plans on committing suicide and takes
out her children or even her spouse beforehand," he would later say.
"Very rare! It's this selfish male ego attitude. 'You couldn't live without
me. You couldn't possibly live without me, so I must take you.' "

However disgusted and tired he may have felt that night, when he
showed up at Kings County at two-thirty in the morning to try to interview Rowe again, Gary was courteous. "Previously I attempted to ask
you some questions and advise you of your rights, but at that time it appeared you were falling asleep," he said to Bob, speaking carefully for a
court officer, who was writing it all down. "I discontinued asking you
questions, and subsequently the doctor here gave you a shot of some
medicine. Presently your eyes are open, you just said you recognize I am
the assistant district attorney. I ask you if you do feel well enough or able
enough to speak to me or answer my questions. More important, do you
understand what I am saying to you? Can you answer that, sir?"

"Yes," said Robert Rowe. "Except for the drug I took . . ."

"It's making your head . . ."

"A little fuzzy," said Rowe.

"Do you comprehend what I am saying?"

"Yes."

Gary routinely advised Rowe of his right to have a lawyer and then
asked him what had happened.

Rowe was confused in some respects. He asked for a cigarette even
though he didn't smoke, and he didn't seem to know what day it was. But
about the crucial matters he was clear.

"About ten o'clock that morning I hit my son's head with a baseball
bat and killed him," he told Gary.

"Which son?"

"Bobby."

"Bob, Jr.?"

"Yes."

The interrogation continued in this terse style until Rowe had confessed to all four killings. There was no hint in his deadened appearance or his blunt answers of the raconteur, the professional manager, the engaging family man.

"I went into the next room and hit Jennifer with the bat first, then I hit Christopher."

"What about your wife, Mary?" Gary asked.

"I waited for her to come home, and I waited for her to take off her coat. She came into the living room, and I killed her with the baseball bat."

Gary continued. "Do you remember if you spoke to Mr. Silverglate that morning?"

Rowe nodded. "To tell him that Mary wouldn't be coming to work."

"Yes," said Gary. "Do you remember having a conversation with him about that?"

"Yes."

"Did you also speak to his wife about that?"

"I can't remember," said Rowe. "I can't remember the chronology of who I spoke to in what order. Risa is his wife."

"Did you speak to Risa?"

"I spoke to her Wednesday night, Risa."

He was confused; Gary saw that. "If you can't remember when you spoke to her, it's not important," he said. "What did you do, sir, with the baseball bat? Did you leave it in the house?"

"I left it next to the chair, standing up," said Rowe.

"Chair in your house?" asked Gary, establishing for the record that they were talking about the same baseball bat. There was no response.

Gary continued: "One question as to chronology: At the time you spoke to your wife's boss, was Mary, your wife, dead already?"

"Yes, everybody was dead."

Gary kept his disgust under wraps. "When you told your wife's boss that she was sick, you lied to him—so what? You could go back into the house?"

"Yes."

"So you could do that? Put a bag over your own head?"

"Right."

"This all came about, sir, because you were having problems with your own employment?" asked Gary, prompted by the detectives' notes.

"Yeah," said Rowe dully. "I couldn't find a job. I was out for months."

"What about the house—were you in danger of losing the house?" prodded the assistant district attorney, trying to focus the groggy man before him.

"Yeah, it bothered me."

"Did you feel it would bring some sort of shame on your family?"

"Right," said Rowe. "Employment outlook was very bad."

Gary was ready to wind up the interview. Rowe had been complaining about pains in his hand and hip, and the assistant district attorney politely asked him about them. Then he left. He had what he needed, and it had been a long night.

CHAPTER 13

Reaction

Irene Wagner picked up the telephone and heard her brother saying, "Lock your doors, don't let anyone in. There's a madman out there—he just killed a family in Mill Basin."

Irene said to herself, Nobody kills anyone in Mill Basin. Nevertheless, she followed her brother's instructions and locked the doors.

When she learned who the killer was from the eleven o'clock news, her shock was all the more potent because of the guilt she felt for having failed the Rowe family. As she listened to the report, which was repeated several times on the radio before she went to bed, her sorrow deepened. Poor Bob, she thought. Poor Bob.

The memory of their last conversation would nag at her. Maybe she should have just gone over to his house and forced him to let her help him. But what could she have done? Never in her wildest dreams did she expect him   a man who had accepted things the way he had—to do what he did.

Edith Patt was home alone. Her husband was out of the country and her son, now grown, was living out west. The television news was providing background noise until she heard something about a lawyer killing his wife and children in Mill Basin and that one of the children was blind. Then she paid attention.

Edith called Ellen Alboher, who had just returned home from an evening out with some friends. Her husband, Al, had already told her the news.

One by one, Edith telephoned the IHB mothers, inviting them to her house the next night. They had come a long way since the group was formed six years earlier, but the ground under them was never really solid. Their fortitude seemed fragile, and they constantly needed reinforcement. Bob's downfall might feel like their own. Edith imagined their distress. If a man like Bob Rowe could end up like this, what about the other husbands, who seemed so much less able? If the Rowes could be so completely obliterated, what might be in store for them?

—

Indeed, Geri Smith was almost hysterical. She and her husband had been lying in bed when the story unfolded on their television. Geri started screaming.

"Calm down," her husband said curtly. "What's wrong with you?"

Without saying a word, she dialed Edith's number. It was busy, so she tried Ellen's. That was busy, too. She kept dialing, thinking that if she didn't talk to somebody right then who understood what was wrong with her, she would go crazy.

Finally, she got through to Edith, and after they'd talked long enough for Geri to calm down, Edith said she had to make some more calls. As soon as Edith hung up, Geri's phone rang. It was Ellen. Geri kept talking, afraid of what would happen if she was left alone—and she did feel alone that night, even though she was in bed next to her husband.

But they couldn't stay on the telephone too long—there were other calls to make. Geri knew she would have to hold herself together until the group met the next night. She was crying as she hung up, and hoping that her husband had been listening to her end of the conversations and that he would be more compassionate than he had been before.

The room was quiet. She looked over at him and saw that he was asleep. Right then she knew that she would have to leave him—and she eventually did.

—

It was a peculiar reaction, she supposed, but when Mary Ann Blaisie hung up the phone after hearing the news, she immediately wondered where she had put the cheesecake recipe that someone in the group had given her. One of the mothers had brought the cheesecake to one of the meetings and it was so delicious, so out of the ordinary, that Mary Ann had immediately wanted to know how to make it, to fill her mouth with that flavor again.

Was it Mary Rowe's recipe? She couldn't remember if it was Mary's or one of the others', but in her mind, the news of Mary's death would always be linked with the extraordinary sensation of that cheesecake.

Where had she put the recipe? She had a strawberry sauce she liked to serve with the cake, and though she wasn't sure, under the circumstances, whether they were supposed to bring something to the meeting or not, she decided to prepare the cheesecake and strawberry sauce. Carrying on was second nature to her by now. That's what she'd been doing ever since she found out, when he was a baby, that her adopted child was legally blind. She and her husband had decided to keep him, even though they'd had the option to give him back, even though she'd been depressed for a year after she learned about his blindness.

By the time Bob killed Mary, the Blaisies had moved from Brooklyn to Connecticut, so Mary Ann couldn't get to the meetings anymore. She felt that nothing would replace them. She loved listening to the IHB mothers talk. Oh boy, could they talk! Mary Ann had a soft, beseeching voice and an elliptical style that made her seem perpetually distracted, so she especially admired those who could be direct. It took her a long time to feel courageous enough to speak up, even softly. Listening to Mary Rowe and Silvia White in particular helped her gather confidence. They told jokes about the blind that would have seemed sick in any other context but helped the group step back from their predicament, made it easier for a shy person like Mary Ann to express herself.

She missed those meetings, but she wasn't looking forward to this one. Before she went to bed, she decided she was going to bring the cheese-cake to Edith's house. No matter what the circumstances, no matter how shocked and sad they were, they still had to eat, and she always found comfort in the subtle texture and sweetness of good cheesecake. Maybe it was Edith's recipe. Mary Ann remembered that Edith was the first one to have a Cuisinart, and then she remembered that the Cuisinart had been a present to Edith from the mothers' group.

Mary Ann decided right then that she wasn't ever going to tell her own son, also named Chris, what had happened in Mill Basin. She didn't want him to think that because somebody had a problem child—no, she didn't mean that, she meant a child with problems—something horrible like this would happen.

When she thought of Bob Rowe, she remembered listening to him talk—so intelligent a man, so nice. Then she pictured him, strong-looking, big, powerful. He must have wanted to make sure he hurt Mary as much as he could, she thought—not that if you hit someone on the head with a baseball bat you think they're going to live.

—

On February 22, Jack O'Shaughnessy had received a call at work from Harvey Sackstein to wish him happy birthday. It was Jack's fiftieth.

Jack had introduced Harvey to Bob Rowe years earlier. Harvey was a lawyer in private practice, also from Brooklyn, and they'd all become good friends. The wives, too. Harvey, whose own fiftieth birthday had been a month earlier, had kidded Jack. "You bum, you didn't call me up for my birthday. Meet me at the office and we'll have dinner."

They got together and were talking over drinks when Harvey asked, "You talked to Bob lately?"

"No," said Jack. "Not for a few months."

Harvey said, "I'll tell Iris to call Mary and set something up for Saturday night—maybe my house, or your place or Bob's. I'll call you and tell you when we'll get together."

"Fine," said Jack. "That would be fine." It had been too long since he and Bob had gotten together.

The next morning, Jack arrived at the insurance company where he worked and where Bob had briefly been his colleague. His boss came into the office holding the *Daily News*.

"Is this our Bob Rowe?" he asked.

Jack stared in disbelief at the headline: SAY DAD KILLED WIFE & 3 KIDS.

Harvey Sackstein heard about the killings on the radio, on Thursday morning. His first thought was to intercept his wife at her office before she found out. As he'd anticipated, Iris fell apart when he told her, and even though she grieved for Mary and the children, she agreed that Harvey should go to see Bob at Kings County as soon as possible.

Harvey had always looked forward to getting together with Bob and Mary. He and Bob liked to philosophize by the barbecue grill, their commentary on life and books and ethics always punctuated with jokes. Bob never discussed how he felt about Christopher, though when he visited the Rowes, Harvey used to think how much easier their lives would be if they had put him in a home. Not that Bob and Mary ever complained. They always talked about Christopher's accomplishments with enthusiasm—bordering on obsession, Harvey felt, perhaps because he couldn't relate to Christopher. He'd been happy when they decided to adopt a third child, because he could relate to Bobby, and he worried that sometimes the family's balance tilted too far toward Christopher, at Bobby's expense. He thought a healthy baby would divert Bob and Mary from being so consumed with Christopher, and Jennifer turned out to be far more than a diversion. She was a pleasurable child.

The day after Harvey heard the news, he visited Bob in the locked ward at Kings County Hospital—more prison than hospital. Harvey was an affable man who could always find something to talk about, but in this alien setting he was lost. The subjects that used to consume him and Bob conversationally were impossible to summon up now. Bob had created a drama too overwhelming to allow for ordinary discourse. But Harvey soon realized it didn't matter what he said. He wasn't sure if Bob recognized him or if he even knew who he himself was, or where he was and how he had gotten there.

Harvey had never seen a man stripped so bare. Bob's vulnerability struck a primal chord in him, a protective instinct, the fierceness of which surprised him. He eventually found himself cast as Bob's champion—or apologist, in the eyes of many friends, especially the wives, who quickly let him know that they considered Bob a pariah. Mental illness may have been part of the equation, according to the gathering consensus, but evil had to have been another. Harvey couldn't understand what had driven Bob to this unimaginable act, but he didn't think evil played a part, perhaps because *evil* wasn't part of his working vocabulary.

—

O nce again Bob Rowe became a touchstone for the people who knew him, only now this paragon of wit, intelligence, and perseverance had been transformed into an object of pity and revulsion and fear. The biblical scope of his action stirred quasi-religious responses in his friends and acquaintances as they tried to incorporate this complex new aspect—killer—into their image of him. The notion of identification had taken an ugly turn.

The women from the mothers' group didn't hate Bob—not in the first few months after the killings—but they had no desire to see him again. Their handicapped children had undermined all their assumptions about the direction their lives would take; their friendship had helped realign their emotions. They had aided one another in altering their expectations and desires, and Bob and Mary had become their partners. Now this meteoric destruction! They were stunned by the violence, and by their own devastating fellow feeling with the killer as well as the victims.

The birth of their children had forged the bond among them; the death of Mary Rowe guaranteed a kind of eternal friendship. The contract was sanctioned by the tears shed together at the funeral, where four white caskets—two large, two small—rolled up the church aisle in a processional of horror.

Silvia White remembered to take the holy card commemorating Mary,

Bobby, Christopher, and Jennifer. She would keep it in the prayer book she took along whenever she went to mass. There wasn't anything she could do for Mary and the kids but remember them, and that she would do—every time she looked at the four names written on the card.

The Mill Basin neighbors felt another kind of loss. The three Sapolsky children would spend years in therapy talking about the deaths—which, in their personal mythology, marked the end of innocence. Alan, the eldest, began systematically going through family pictures and excising Bob Rowe's head.

At first, Barbara Sapolsky tried to alleviate their sense of betrayal. "Bob wouldn't have done this to the kids if he wasn't crazy," she told her children. "He would never have done it." But as she and Natalie Mond and other neighbors talked about it—as if there were anything else that could be discussed—her fury rose.

"Why didn't he just walk?" she would ask. "Mary, believe me, could have taken care of all of them if Bob had walked. She was a strong girl. She would have found a way. Those kids would have been all right without him." As this line of reasoning took hold, she decided it was wrong to ask her children to suppress their anger. Bob hadn't just killed his own children; he'd destroyed something precious in hers.

Natalie felt no compassion for Bob, either, even though she knew "his elevator wasn't going to the top floor," as she described his mental problems.

"I do not believe in taking a life," she said. "But I do believe in the electric chair. You take a life, you deserve to lose yours." No matter how much she'd admired Bob before, this was her verdict. Unequivocally.

Jeffrey Mond, however—her youngest child, one of Bobby Rowe's closest friends, and the unwitting donor of the fatal weapon—continued to believe that Bob was the best father he'd ever known. He felt he understood what the adults and his neighborhood friends couldn't grasp— that Bob had simply flipped. Jeffrey, a high school senior, attributed his insight to his study of Freud and Jung, part of his college-prep psychology course.

His sympathy for Bob didn't mitigate his heartbreak or stop him from maintaining his connection to Bobby through private tribute and ritual, however. He would never relinquish either the toy clown or the baseball bat that Bobby had given him, and for many years on May 10, he lit a *yahrzeit* candle for his friend. Jeffrey, a bar mitzvah—Bobby had been a guest at his passage into Jewish manhood—knew perfectly well that Jews customarily commemorate the date of someone's death with the candle, but he preferred to remember Bobby's birthday, which was four days after his.

CHAPTER 14

The Defendant

On May 3, 1978, Robert Rowe was indicted on four counts of murder in the second degree. Michael Gary, the prosecutor, wanted him to spend the rest of his life in jail. Reading through the witness reports, Gary was struck by the lies Rowe had told the neighbors who were also his wife's employers: *He'd put Mary to sleep, and the children weren't going to bother her because he had taken care of them, too.* Didn't this seem a brazen calculation, a cool piece of subterfuge to hide what he had done? Yes. Unless he was crazy.

The assistant district attorney was troubled, too, by Rowe's decision to kill himself with gas, a method that would take a long time and that was far from foolproof, especially when compared with the quick efficiency of a baseball bat. Gary couldn't shake the thought that the suicide attempt might have been staged. As an attorney, Rowe had specialized in puncturing phony insurance claims. He could have concocted an elaborate scheme to get rid of his own troubles and save himself.

But even as Gary considered this hypothesis, he worried that a conviction wouldn't come easily. Jurors might feel sorry for Rowe when they learned of his boy's disabilities. Over time, the newspaper coverage, initially hostile, had become more favorable to Rowe, casting his story as a parable about society's insensitivity to the plight of families with handicapped children. One of the tabloids ran a sympathetic piece under the headline TORMENTED DAD WAS DESTROYED BY SOCIETY, liberally quoting Irene Wagner, who had called the paper to complain about its earlier reportage, which, she argued, was unfairly judgmental.

On the opinion page of *The New York Times,* a father of a brain-damaged child wrote, anonymously:

> Don't be too hard on Robert T. Rowe, the Brooklynite who is accused of killing his wife and three children with a baseball bat, perhaps because of the struggle involved in helping to rear one child who was blind, deaf and mute since birth 12 years ago.
>
> As father of a 10½-year-old daughter, severely brain-damaged from birth, I can understand how easy it is to commit such a horrible act. My wife and I have often had similar thoughts, separately. It doesn't take much additional stress to commit such an act when a person is under constant stress and fatigue from trying to care for a severely handicapped child, and is drained of all energy and resources.
>
> In addition to the handicapped child, I have two normal children, a girl 6½, a boy 3½. Though we have always tried to provide the best for our children, our everyday life is not "normal" by any means. People constantly admire the "wonderful" job we do and how dedicated we are to the handicapped child. "God surely has a place in heaven for you" is frequently said. And yet, if we committed the act we are capable of, you would hear: "What went wrong? They were such dedicated parents."

Rowe's friends had hired a lawyer, Stephen Scaring, a well-regarded former prosecutor on Long Island, who was now in private practice as a defense attorney. Scaring had entered a plea of not guilty under section 30.05 of the New York Penal Code, "by reason of mental disease or defect," commonly known as the insanity defense.

This was murky territory, philosophically and ethically—politically contentious, obscured by both medical and legal jargon. Jurors who heard such cases were asked to follow difficult and often inexact terminology, to comprehend the difference between a psychopath and a sociopath (there is none), to distinguish between mental illness (not knowing) and moral nullification (knowing but not caring). They were asked to assume the role of psychiatrists, legal scholars, and theologians, to ponder ephemeral distinctions between evil and madness.

The modern insanity defense in Anglo-American law, including the penal code of the state of New York, was articulated in 1843, when a Scotsman named Daniel McNaughtan mistakenly killed the private secretary to Sir Robert Peel, prime minister of England, who was McNaughtan's actual target. McNaughtan, who believed he was the victim of a Tory conspiracy, claimed that he was "driven to desperation by persecution" and entered a plea of insanity. Doctors testified that he was "delusional." The jury acquitted, and McNaughtan was confined in a mental institution.

McNaughtan's not-guilty verdict elicited public alarm (at least editorially, in Britain's major newspapers) and royal intervention (by Queen Victoria), and resulted in the formulation of the McNaughtan Rule, which says: "It must be clearly proven that, at the time of committing the act, the party accused was laboring under such a defect of reason, from disease of the mind, as not to know the nature and quality of the act he was doing, or, did he know it, that he did not know he was doing what was wrong."

New York law modified the rule. It wasn't enough for the accused to *know;* he or she must be able to *appreciate,* as though the matter at hand were a piece of music and at stake was a musician's performance ("technically proficient but soulless"). The distinction was significant, for it put an added burden on the prosecutor, who would have to prove beyond a reasonable doubt that the defendant was sane.

To do that with Robert Rowe, Michael Gary knew he must demonstrate motivation. He had to convince the jury that a rational mind was at work. His job was to make jurors wonder what makes Rowe insane. He may have been angry, overwhelmed, or depressed, but none of that mattered if he *knew* what he was doing, if he *knew* it was wrong—and if he *appreciated* how wrong it was. Then he'd have to face the same punishment as killers driven to crime by poverty, childhood abuse, racism, bad genes, and stupidity.

The prosecutor would be arguing the case before a Brooklyn jury, and he believed this would help him. Jurors were generally less liberal in Brooklyn than in Manhattan, less willing to allow psychiatrists to offer absolution for violent crimes, and the insanity defense was always a hard sell. The defendant claims neither innocence nor self-defense—he simply says he wasn't responsible because he didn't understand that what he was doing was wrong. An acquittal was almost always accompanied by a nagging thought: Did we just let someone get away with murder?

—

Stephen Scaring had given up his position as Nassau County's chief prosecutor for homicide just a few months earlier. He'd spent most of the year working on a splashy murder case in which a Long Island doctor was accused of injecting his wife with a lethal dose of the painkiller Demerol so that he could join his Danish mistress and their two children. The investigation had taken Scaring all over the world, and the trial had lasted three months. He had won the case, but everything seemed boring after that, so Scaring, the son of a police officer, decided it was time to try the other side. He was thirty-five years old.

His first case as a defense attorney didn't reap either the notoriety he'd drawn as a prosecutor or the kind of money he hoped to earn in private practice, but he won an acquittal for his client, a Chinese man accused of murdering his wife, who ended up paying Scaring's fee in shrimp. Then came the call from Bill Campbell, a lawyer who'd been a colleague of Bob Rowe's at Allstate—and, coincidentally, of Scaring's. Years before, while earning his law-school tuition, Scaring had worked in Allstate's legal department and had gotten to know Campbell. He didn't meet Bob Rowe, however, until after the killings.

Scaring drove to Kings County Hospital that first night and found his prospective client semiconscious on a stretcher. Scaring, a tall, skinny man with a quiet voice, introduced himself.

"Am I alive?" Bob asked.

"You're alive," Scaring said.

Rowe started crying. Scaring realized that the man in front of him was no longer psychotic. He knew exactly what he had done, and he seemed to be suffering. The former prosecutor, father of four young children, was surprised at how sympathetic he felt toward this man—this colleague—who had killed his family. He was certain he would never forget the despair on Bob Rowe's face.

After spending several hours talking to Rowe over the next couple of days, Scaring decided to take the case, even though his only option was to plead insanity. It was a lousy defense, Scaring believed, because it was hard to win. He never invoked insanity if he had an alternative, even though he approved of the essential notion of civility that underlay the defense. Society shouldn't punish someone for something he didn't know was wrong. When Scaring taught law students about psychiatry and the law, he would offer two examples of exculpatory delusion: in one, the defendant is squeezing somebody's neck and believes he's squeezing an orange; in the other, the defendant knows that he is killing someone but believes he is doing it for good. Bob Rowe was in the latter category, he believed.

But Scaring had handled a number of insanity cases as a prosecutor, and he knew that juries almost always rejected the defense when they felt threatened. The extreme example was David Berkowitz, better known as the Son of Sam, the serial killer who was being held in the same lockup as Rowe. Berkowitz, Scaring believed, was crazy as a loon, but there wasn't a juror in the world who was going to give a hoot whether he was insane or not. Scaring felt certain that Berkowitz would be in the can for the rest of his life. Jurors felt less threatened when the killing was a family matter—but not much, especially in a case where the killer had returned to a sense of reality almost immediately. The insanity seemed too conveniently timed.

However, these misgivings didn't diminish the lawyer's belief that this was the clearest insanity-defense case he'd ever seen. Scaring would later say that he felt confident he could win the Rowe case in front of a jury filled with police officers. Not that he intended to take the case to a jury.

This wasn't a guy who beat his wife and kids. He was a nice, decent man who adored his family, then killed them robotically. The only motive was his delusional belief that he was protecting them. Besides, Scaring liked Bob Rowe, and he believed everybody else would, too.

———

O n March 3, 1978, the psychiatric narrative of defendant Robert Rowe began when Irwin Brownstein, justice of the Supreme Court, Kings County, ordered an examination to determine if Rowe was mentally capable of standing trial or if he was, in the language of New York criminal law, an "incapacitated defendant."

"Chart #319681," Rowe's case history, was coauthored by Kings County Hospital forensic psychiatrists Richard L. Weidenbacher and Daniel W. Schwartz. Dr. Schwartz's name had recently been all over the papers because one of the hundreds of killers who'd sat on his couch was a celebrity, the Son of Sam.

On March 16, Drs. Schwartz and Weidenbacher offered their first interpretation of Robert Rowe's story in an account of their first meeting with the defendant. "He presents at interview today as a man of generally dour or phlegmatic appearance and manner, who seems isolated or detached emotionally in certain respects," wrote the doctors. "During the course of interview, and as he describes the killing of his family, he expresses surprise or disbelief that he can speak of these matters, or at least that he can speak of them without emotion. He is alert, attentive, courteous and cooperative throughout interview, if perhaps on occasion, a bit impatient. There is, perhaps, something of a buoyant, animated, pressured, or driven quality about his speech; his answers are quick and of an incisive and articulate quality. He is obviously a man of good intelligence. All his responses and all his statements are relevant and coherent, and he made use of no cryptic or idiosyncratic language. He is of robust appearance and he seems to be of good physical health. There are no signs of neurological dysfunction.

"There is no evidence of psychosis at this time. . . ."

When the doctors asked him if he had any desire to commit suicide at that moment, Rowe said, "Strangely enough, no."

He described the killing of his family matter-of-factly, and though he seemed to be on the verge of tears, he didn't cry. His face was impassive when he said, "I feel as though I am in a dream, as though it couldn't possibly be happening."

One of the doctors asked, "As though *what* couldn't possibly be happening?"

"That I killed my family."

They prodded. "Did you in fact kill your family?"

He nodded. "Yes, I killed my three children and my wife."

Without emotion, he offered their names and ages and some details: Jennifer was adopted; Christopher was brain-damaged; he, their father, was preoccupied with pressures, financial and others, connected with Christopher's special requirements.

The interview swept across Rowe's history as details were gathered to be tossed into the analysis. Bay Ridge boyhood. Military service. Law school. Father an electrician (alcoholic but not abusive). Mother, problematic. Religion, Lutheran. Wife, Catholic. Marriage, solid (despite her reticence in bed). Profession, lawyer (successful until no-fault insurance). Children, perfect (except for Christopher).

When the doctors asked Rowe about his plans for a legal defense, for his future, he said flatly, "I don't know. No matter what the outcome, I have no family. I am a family man. Without a family, what would I do?"

DIAGNOSIS: Deferred (1. Adjustment reaction of adult life, with psychotic features? 2. Personality disorder, with obsessional features?)

CONCLUSION: Deferred.

COMMENT: The picture presently is marked by a paucity of emotion, which paucity may bespeak at least in part a defense against intolerable emotion. The picture may also be described tentatively as one of numb resignation. . . .

On April 24, after reviewing Rowe's Gracie Square records and an independent psychologist's report, Dr. Schwartz made the following note:

The psychologist's report has been received. (Rowe) is a rather bright man, with a verbal I.Q. of 120. His performance I.Q. (108) has been affected by the fact that he is considerably depressed. Dynamically, he appears to be vulnerable to emotional pressures and troubled by extremely forceful unconscious homosexual wishes, feelings of inadequacy as a man and feelings of insatiable needs for emotional support, things that his mother had never provided. He somehow attributed the killing of his wife and children to his mother, but in a very confusing, unclear way. The test suggests that unconsciously he may have viewed his wife as his mother when he killed her, and his children as himself. There is a tendency to dissociate, to put off anxiety-arousing thoughts and feelings and therefore his inability to deal with emotional problems in a rational way. He says that he had "a compulsion to kill."

At this time he is not overtly psychotic. The psychologist's diagnosis is borderline personality with episodic psychotic breaks.

On April 26, Rowe showed up for his interview with Dr. Weidenbacher carrying a book of condensed fiction. He told the doctor he had regained his interest in reading and lost his desire to commit suicide, and that he planned to offer a defense of insanity.

"I think that maybe I thought I was killing my mother, whom I hated," he said. He moved and spoke energetically, though his appearance, manner, and speech remained unemotional. "She was interfering with my family, even though she was dead."

He listened quietly as Dr. Weidenbacher suggested that the killings and the 1975 breakdown could be seen as the fallout from his mother's death, the date of which Rowe couldn't remember, a lapse of memory which, the doctor observed, might or might not be significant. The psychiatrist pointed out that the patient's mother had disapproved of his marriage and of Mary, who confirmed her inadequacy by bearing him a defective child.

"He then asked me spontaneously if I thought that the disability and problems of his son (Christopher) may have been an important factor," wrote Dr. Weidenbacher, who agreed that it was possible.

"I asked Mary to put him away," Rowe said, "but she refused to do it." When? the doctor asked.

A very short time before "the incident," Rowe answered, referring to the killings.

Rowe told the doctor he thought he needed further psychiatric hospitalization before he settled the charges against him in court.

"I still haven't sorted out my thoughts," he said. "Every morning I wake up, I still expect Mary to be a visitor here. I wasn't at the funeral. I didn't see her buried. I can't get used to the idea they're dead."

DIAGNOSIS: Adjustment reaction of adult life, with depressive and psychotic features.

CONCLUSION: Not fit to proceed.

COMMENT: From a psychiatric point of view, it appears that the essential problem may be seen as one of pathological reaction to the death of mother, some years ago. Fairly clearly, the relationship between mother and son had been a difficult one, the son feeling frustrated by his mother and harboring strong and mixed feelings towards her. She, in turn, left her estate entirely to his younger brother, disinheriting the defendant, in effect. It seems clear that within a few years of her death the defendant was affected by a psychotic disorder, entailing visual and auditory hallucination of his mother, during which she commanded him to destroy his family. She had disapproved of his marriage and his wife; his wife had borne him one normal child, and one grossly defective child.

He may well also have been affected by delusion, with regard to his conduct. Although the hallucination and the likely delusion with regard to conduct resolved during the course of psychiatric treatment, including medication, there is reason to believe that he was subsequently, and around the time of the reported offense, exercised by delusion regarding poverty. Further, as he himself proposed, he may have been confused, and more particularly, he may, in a sense, have taken his wife to be his mother.

With regard to the question of financial resources and the question of confusion of identity, one notes that his wife apparently "refused" to place their retarded son in an institution, "a very short time before the incident—about a month." In part, his conduct on 2-22 may have reflected a rage felt towards his mother, in part, attachment to her and empathy with her.

Although he is not obviously confused at this time, and although an insanity defense may well prove plausible and feasible in the future, the defendant appears incapable at this time of adequate participation in his defense. He still "hasn't sorted out his thoughts"; he has not as yet truly grasped what has transpired, so that he still rather expects his family to reappear. It would appear proper and wise to arrange for further psychiatric hospitalization, probably over a period of months, with an eye to greater emotional and mental stability and further perspective on the part of the defendant.

On April 27, Dr. Schwartz noted the following on Rowe's chart: "He may be beginning to effectively appreciate the enormity of his crime, for he says that he wakes up each morning with the thought that he cannot accept the reality of the crime, cannot believe it happened."

Rowe told the doctor that his oldest son, Bobby, had been sick too. He had asthma, and for three years while he was in elementary school he had to walk on crutches because of Perthes disease.

Rowe said he thought about the crime perhaps twenty times a day. When Dr. Schwartz asked him which killing haunted him the most, he responded carefully. "That's an interesting question," he said. "Nobody has asked me that before." After thinking for a while, he responded obliquely: "I had a proclivity for my oldest son."

"Intellectualization," Dr. Schwartz observed in his notes. "He guards against emotions."

The doctor was struck by Rowe's readiness to describe the killings again, "in a chillingly unemotional way."

DIAGNOSIS: Psychotic adjustment reaction of adult life.

CONCLUSION: Deferred.

TREATMENT: The patient is being treated with Elavil. He asks to be transferred to the quiet ward because the crazy patients who wake up in the middle of the night disturb him, and we see no reason why he should not be so transferred.

DISCUSSION: We have deferred our legal conclusion because the forthcoming progress of the case is still not clear. We spoke to defense counsel this morning, suggesting that perhaps the trial should be moved forward and that the entire criminal matter could be disposed of before

Mr. Rowe was sent to the Department of Mental Hygiene. . . . If such arrangements can be made we shall deem the defendant, for practical purposes, fit to proceed, for even though he still cannot fully accept what happened, there is no great need for him to "assist in his defense." The facts of the case speak for themselves and, we believe, argue convincingly for acquittal. . . .

———

The prosecutor would need a strong rebuttal from an equally reputable expert. He turned to Stanley H. Brodsky, chief of forensic psychiatry at Elmhurst City Hospital in Queens. Like Daniel Schwartz, Brodsky was a frequent witness—sometimes for the defense, sometimes for the prosecution. After two meetings with Rowe, Dr. Brodsky laid out his conclusions in a single-spaced nine-and-half-page account, delivered to the district attorney's office on June 19, 1979.

As Gary read the Brodsky report he quickly realized there would be no presentation to a jury, not after the psychiatrist's diagnosis, which upended the common perception—and Gary's hope—that psychiatrists for the prosecution (or defense) will automatically support the team that hires them.

It is the opinion of the undersigned that Robert T. Rowe lacked criminal responsibility at the time of the alleged crime due to the presence of a mental illness termed psychotic depression which substantially interfered with his capacity to understand the wrongfulness of his acts. . . .

In his actively psychotic state Mr. Rowe was unable to appreciate the moral implications of his actions. In my opinion Mr. Rowe was so deluded and depressed at the time of the alleged crime that he could not appreciate the wrongfulness of his actions. At present the greatest danger is that he will commit suicide. He will require long-term psychiatric care and will need to be under close supervision for a long period of time.

The frustrated prosecutor told a colleague, "I wanted to take the cop who pulled Rowe's head out of the oven and say to him, 'Goddamnit, of all the times you gotta rescue somebody! Why couldn't you have waited on this guy and let him die?' " Gary had searched to find evidence of rational behavior, a motive for the killings. If only there were something tangible— a single airplane ticket to Acapulco, a girlfriend, an emptied bank account, a million-dollar insurance policy on the lives of the children—he could have said, "To hell with the psychiatrists."

———

The trial was scheduled to take place without a jury—at the defendant's request—in front of Hyman Barshay, a respected judge who had been an accomplished criminal lawyer, perhaps best known for his successful defense of a pharmacist accused of poisoning his pregnant wife and for his tough evenhandedness in the courtroom. No surprises were expected at this pro forma proceeding, which opened on Friday, June 23, with Dr. Schwartz as the first witness for the defense. He had testified several times for Scaring when he was a prosecutor.

Schwartz's credentials were irrefutable: director of the forensic psychiatry service at the Kings County Hospital Center for ten years; associate professor in the department of psychiatry at Downstate Medical Center; psychoanalytic training, research grants from the state, memberships in the psychiatric associations, numerous publications, law school lecturer. Also, he was a lawyer's son, who became a physician as his father advised but couldn't resist the drama of the courtroom. Then there was the critical qualification: He'd examined thousands of criminal defendants and testified hundreds of times.

He would forget most of those cases, but not Rowe. He'd seen plenty of men who killed family members because they hated them or felt overwhelming guilt about something. But Rowe had killed his entire family while he loved them—so he said—and talked about the killing and loving in the same dispassionate voice. It was unnerving.

"I don't believe there were ever any delusions, any involved, paranoid, grandiose system of beliefs that made it necessary for him to do this," Dr. Schwartz told the court. "Yes, he was unhappy over his state in life. He had fears, apprehensions about their financial future, but it was not the kind of situation where he was experiencing commands, hallucinations, let's say, or where he believed that it was necessary to save the world, that he has to do something like that, which we have seen in some cases.

"What's so striking about this case is the period of time. It takes place over a course of eight or nine hours, during which he has no feeling whatsoever, during which he acts like a machine, as it were, delivering these blows. There is no feeling. There is no emotion. There's no real appreciation of what he's doing."

Dr. Schwartz, a small man with a goatee and mustache, was an appealing witness, speaking quietly and in layman's language, bowing his head slightly when listening to questions.

"Had this been a situation of particular frustration, let's say, against one member of the family, where a person might conceivably act violently without any emotion, one would expect that the act would then be the end of the strange mental state. The realization of having actually struck out this way at a loved one, in my experience, will terminate any altered state of emotion if it's a temporary thing, if it's not really mental disease."

Was Christopher the source of the murderous frustration? Rowe's lawyer asked.

"I don't think that in and of itself is the basis for what happened here," said Dr. Schwartz. "Had that been so, we would expect him to kill Christopher first, I think, or in some kind of a rage to strike out at this boy. It's quite possible that he viewed himself like Christopher or Christopher like himself in terms of both being failures."

The details of Bob Rowe's life—heartwarming, mundane, sensational—emerged from Dr. Schwartz's testimony, which lasted throughout the morning. Judge Barshay and the spectators, who included Bob's friends Jack O'Shaughnessy and Harvey Sackstein, heard about his love for his family, his stymied career, his haranguing mother, and his fragile ego. They listened to Dr. Schwartz's vivid re-creation of the killings. A suffocating sense of sadness permeated the courtroom as the lawyers and the psychiatrist tried, vainly, to explain what could elicit such violence from an apparently loving father.

"Was there any indication that the defendant did not have a love feeling for his family at any point in time, either before or after the act?" Scaring asked.

Dr. Schwartz shook his head. "No, the picture I saw was always one of love, love for them which is totally inconsistent with the criminal acts themselves."

Robert Rowe stymied them all—even the psychiatrist who had interviewed thousands of killers.

The prosecutor, Michael Gary, asked Dr. Schwartz to explain the following sentence in his report: "The tests suggest that unconsciously he may have viewed his wife as his mother when he killed her, and his children as himself."

"It would appear possibly that he viewed the two together," said the doctor. "As I said a few minutes ago, there had been a situation with his mother of mixed relationship. She had not left him anything in the will; there had been continued disapproval of him. He described in his therapy his mother repeatedly telling him he was incompetent, but at the same time she expected that he become a judge or senator. It would seem on the psychological test that perhaps there came a time when he viewed his wife, unconsciously, as his mother, as his maternal figure. He was dependent on her and, conceivably, somewhere in the back of his mind he could have been killing his mother."

But, Dr. Schwartz admitted, his analysis couldn't be more than a supposition, a hypothesis, an attempt to make some sense out of the inexplicable. "This is speculative, because these were not conscious delusions that he had," Schwartz said, trying to explain the artful aspect of his science. "What we are trying to do is see if we can understand unconsciously what was happening."

Though everyone felt sure they knew what the verdict would be, Gary couldn't resist asking a final question about the lies Rowe had told his neighbors after the killings were done—how he'd nonchalantly told Risa Silverglate that he'd put Mary to sleep and that the children weren't going to bother her because he had taken care of them as well.

The prosecutor was emotional. "Does that not indicate to you not only an understanding of what he was doing but a good deal of planning and a very well done job of acting to keep from another person the horrendous knowledge that he had just committed those homicides?"

Dr. Schwartz was unfazed. "It indicates an appreciation at that time that, according to society's standard, he had done what was wrong. He had, after the killings, set out to commit suicide. He had failed, obviously. And it was after he returned home, after a night of trying to commit suicide, he returned home with the determination to kill himself in the house, and that he came very close to succeeding. It was in order to keep people away so he could be alone and kill himself that he made those statements."

After Gary was finished with the witness, Judge Barshay asked Dr. Schwartz to stay on the stand to clarify a few things.

"His feelings for his wife were always the same, before he married her and after he married her, and existed until the day of her death?" asked the judge.

Yes.

"Did you ascertain that his opinion of his wife was that she was a very lovable person, never flirtatious and never unfaithful?"

Yes, sir.

"That she was in love with him?"

Yes, said Dr. Schwartz. "In fact, his words were, 'She loved me too much.' "

Judge Barshay asked about Rowe's belief that his family had to be saved from poverty, that he killed them because he saw no alternative.

Dr. Schwartz hesitated. "Yes, I know he said that, but it's not quite that clear. That's not necessarily the total overwhelming explanation. I am not sure how clear his thoughts were at that time at all. At times he's told me simply there doesn't seem to be any reason whatsoever why he did this, and that's consistent with my findings."

The judge probed for a simple answer. "Did you ascertain that he felt it would be better for all of the family members to be dead rather than share his life of total degradation?"

Yes, said Dr. Schwartz and he was dismissed.

After lunch, Dr. Brodsky was called to the stand. Though he was the prosecution's chief witness, his testimony was in crucial ways indistinguishable from Dr. Schwartz's. At the outset he offered his legal opinion, legalistically. "Robert Rowe lacked criminal responsibility due to his inability to comprehend the wrongfulness of his actions due to a mental illness."

But in his testimony, Dr. Brodsky portrayed Rowe's story operatically as well as clinically. The psychiatrist described the defendant's thoughts as he killed his firstborn. "I am killing Bobby, but I am loving him at the same time. I am killing him out of love."

The doctor was impressed by the care Rowe took as he destroyed his family. "Each blow was designed so that it would not cause any pain," he testified. "That was the first blow. A further blow was designed to prevent the family member from becoming brain-damaged, possibly like Christopher. He was feeling what he was doing was necessary, but once he got started, it was almost like an automatic series of acts that propelled themselves independently of him. So that even though he killed Bobby, he for the moment repented that killing, for the moment he felt, What have I done? But this was quickly pushed aside by a kind of mechanical force that was operating on him. He could not stop what already had started, and reassured himself that this is what he had to do."

Dr. Brodsky believed Rowe when he said he wasn't aware of hateful feelings toward anyone in his family. "Even as he was speaking, there was a kind of perplexity about the defendant's delivery, a perplexity in his manner as if to say, 'Could I have done this?' How could he, as he feels now, how could he have done such a thing?"

Gary asked, "Is it your understanding that the defendant's own attempted suicide was part of his overall plan? In other words, did he separate himself from his family?"

The doctor answered, "It was my impression that he was going downhill, into a hopeless state, and he could not separate his feelings about himself from the family. Here was his wife, a happy person, very effective, very well functioning; two of his children—one adopted, the youngest—apparently well able to function. It was only his son Christopher who was severely impaired, as he felt himself to be. He did not separate himself. It was like a fusion between him and the family. They had to go, and he had to go."

Before he excused Brodsky, Judge Barshay asked the doctor if he believed that Rowe had told him the truth.

"I believe he was reliable, although I just don't depend on what somebody tells me," said Dr. Brodsky. "I try to appreciate that in terms of the total picture."

The judge replied, "In context of the entire total circumstances here, are you justified in accepting what he said to you to be the truth?"

Dr. Brodsky nodded. "I believe he was truthful during the interview."

Before court was dismissed that day, Kenneth Rowe took the stand. After he confirmed that he'd identified the bodies of his sister-in-law, nephews, and niece, Judge Barshay asked him if he had visited his brother when he was institutionalized at Gracie Square.

Yes, said Kenneth Rowe. "I visited him almost every day with his wife, because she couldn't drive at all and she insisted on seeing him every day."

That was all. He was excused.

Monday, June 26, was the second and final day of the trial. Testimony from the police officers, the Rowes' tenant, the Silverglates, and Joel and Murray Sapolsky helped complete the re-creation of the night's events for the judge. By the time they were finished, the facts were excruciatingly clear.

Finally, Milton Wald, chief medical examiner for the borough of Brooklyn, offered the autopsy report. The cause of death in all four cases, with minor variations: a compound, comminuted, depressed fracture of the skull with tearing and lacerations of the underlying brain—*compound,* meaning that the skin over the fracture is broken, exposing the bone to the air; *comminuted,* meaning small pieces; *depressed,* meaning the bones were pushed inward.

No imperfection could escape the record; there was no dignity in death for homicide victims. The medical examiner noted that Christopher's skull had a "severe deformity" and that Bobby Rowe's legs were scaly—information that seemed irrelevant to the inquiry at hand but that apparently interested Dr. Wald, who elaborated on the nature of Bobby's rough skin. "What we call ichthyotic—that means dry," he explained. "*Ichthyo* means fishlike, dry like a fish, fish-type skin. That is a skin condition that the child had from the mid-thighs to the toes."

He also observed that Bobby's bladder was full and his stomach empty. He'd been sleeping a long time.

—

That afternoon the lawyers gave their summations.

Michael Gary conceded defeat graciously. "I'm certainly here as a prosecutor and not a persecutor," he told Judge Barshay. "I cannot in good faith make an argument to what defense counsel has said. The people certainly must prove beyond a reasonable doubt that the defendant knew what he was doing when he killed his wife and children, and that he knew it was wrong. The people cannot do so."

Two days later, on June 28, 1978, before delivering his verdict in the People of the State of New York against Robert Rowe, indictment number 538/1978, Judge Hyman Barshay told the prosecutor and defense counsel to sit down because he had a great deal to say. After instructing the court officer to remove Rowe's handcuffs, the judge began to speak of the killings and the history that preceded them.

Hyman Barshay was a judge who rarely revealed either his sense of humor or his compassion in the courtroom. But that day, as he reviewed the testimony and psychiatric conclusions, his tone even more than his words indicated a profoundly human appreciation of the pressures weighing on Robert Rowe. Like Rowe, Judge Barshay came from humble roots—his father had been an immigrant tailor—and reached the professional class after working his way through school. Rowe was a colleague, an equal, a world apart from most of the defendants who appeared in Brooklyn criminal court, who'd been dragged under by poverty or drugs or constant exposure to violence. Rowe had been beset by the travails of a middle-class life: a handicapped child, a stymied career. He may have been a striver who tragically misjudged how high to set the mark.

Judge Barshay gave the verdict: "After a full review of all the evidence in his case on both sides, and each and every exhibit offered in evidence, and the testimony of each and every witness, and after a full consideration of the applicable law, I find the defendant Robert Rowe not guilty of each of the crimes contained in the indictment—count one: the killing of his wife, Mary D. Rowe; count two: the killing of Christopher Rowe; count three: the killing of Robert Rowe; and, count four: the killing of Jennifer Rowe—by reason that at the time of the commission of each of the aforesaid acts, as a result of mental disease or defect, the defendant lacked substantial capacity to know or appreciate either the nature or consequence of such conduct, or that such conduct was wrong."

Judge Barshay committed Robert Rowe to the custody of the state commissioner of mental hygiene and ordered the commissioner to place him in an appropriate institution. After sixty days, under New York law, he could be recommended for release if the psychiatrists attending him determined that he wasn't a danger to himself or to others. However, the law specified that any such recommendation would be subject to challenge by the judge and by the district attorney's office.

Before concluding, the judge added an unusually personal note to the proceedings. "Gentlemen, I am at the bar more than fifty years," said Barshay, who would die, at the age of seventy-seven, before another year had gone by. "I have served ten years as an assistant district attorney, have practiced law, and have been a judge for thirty years. In all that time I have never encountered a tragedy such as I have encountered in this case. I can only say, after reviewing this case from beginning to end, that in 1975 if this defendant had been more competently examined and treated, I am sure this would have been avoided."

The testimony that moved Judge Barshay to his emotional summation revealed a complicated picture, of a man who had failed to live up to his own ambition, which wasn't an unseemly aspiration with impossibly high standards. Robert Rowe wanted to have a reasonably successful career, not a spectacular one, to provide comfortably for his family, not luxuriously. He wanted to be a good father, and this shouldn't have been difficult for him, because he was a natural teacher and he loved children. But what seems like a modest end point in one set of circumstances can become daunting in another.

Before Michael Gary left the courtroom that day, he glanced at Robert Rowe and felt strangely relieved. Everything about Rowe was gray: his face, his hair, his spirit. He looked as though he had died a thousand deaths and might not have the stamina to die another one. He looked at least thirty years older than he was, an old man, barely alive, far removed from his surroundings. Throughout the proceeding, he had sat silently among them, already a ghost. In the end, Gary concluded, it didn't matter whether Rowe received a criminal conviction or not. He would be in an institution for the rest of his life—no doubt about it.

PART II

Like love we don't know where or why

Like love we can't compel or fly

Like love we often weep

Like love we seldom keep.

—

from "Law Like Love"

W. H. AUDEN

CHAPTER 15

The Postulant

Don Cassidy first noticed her after he gave an open-ended assignment to the students enrolled in his English literature class at the Queens campus of St. John's University: Write a theme about something wonderful in your life that has happened to you.

The usual array of subjects considered "something wonderful" by college freshmen eluded Colleen. Sports wouldn't be the thing, though she was a sturdy, athletic young woman, nor would falling in love, since she had never fallen in love—not in the conventional, romantic sense. Had Professor Cassidy told her to write about something devastating, she could have done that, though she wouldn't have, because her cataclysm was a secret. She had spent most of her life trying to cleanse herself, to forget the shame and pleasure she'd experienced innumerable times before she fully understood what had been done to her. There was something wonderful she could write about, however. In her essays, she did theme and variation on the significance of God to the world and to her, Colleen.

It was winter, 1983. She was nineteen years old.

The professor began pulling her aside after class when he realized from her writing that she was an unusual student, nothing like her contemporaries, spiritually empty careerists bred in the recessionary seventies. Though she was thirty years his junior, she shared his fascination with religion, both as solace and as intellectual pursuit. Colleen looked forward to writing papers for Professor Cassidy, because there wasn't anyone her age with whom she could talk about the things that obsessed her. She had been preparing for this outpouring since she was thirteen years old, when she had taken refuge in the local parish. She lived and took meals in her parents' house but thought of herself, increasingly, as a visitor there.

Her world as a teenager was narrowly circumscribed, and deliberately so. She went to the 7 A.M. mass every day and was in school by eight, out by one, and then she went straight to the church on Rockaway Boulevard. While other kids in her section of working-class Queens went to parties and the beach, she painted the fence that surrounded the church. On Saturdays she worked in the rectory, answering phones, writing articles for the parish bulletin, typing the bulletin. On Sundays, during the Liturgy of the Word, she gathered groups of children and took them downstairs, where she translated the mass into language they could understand, using puppets as props. Her diary marked her progress in the spiritual world, not the secular.

Her parents went to Sunday services and placed a statue of St. Jude in their little postage stamp of a front yard. But they didn't wear crosses or attend daily mass. They weren't, her father would say, Holy Rollers. However, they weren't about to object to Colleen hanging around the parish. At least they knew where she was and that she was safe, though they didn't know her secret, how dangerous her life had been.

Colleen was no Holy Roller, either. She wasn't content to let a spiritual tide wash away her anxieties and troubling memories. She was too inquisitive for easy salvation. The bookshelves in her bedroom were filled with theological writings. She tried to comprehend the complex philosophical journey of Augustine of Hippo, the fourth-century priest whose provocative examination of his life, including his emotional and erotic impulses, helped launch his sainthood. Gamely, she tackled (but didn't finish) the thirteen books of *The Confessions,* Augustine's exegesis of his life story, hoping to find some explanation for hers.

But it was St. Francis of Assisi, the pampered son of a rich man, who gave up knighthood and glory to become an impoverished preacher, who would come to preoccupy this adolescent theologian, who felt more at ease in the twelfth century than the twentieth. In the way other girls fell prey to a pop lyric, Colleen was mesmerized by the prayer of St. Francis, the peace prayer:

> Lord, make me an instrument of your peace.
> Where there is despair in life, let me bring hope.
> Where there is injury, let me bring pardon.
> Where there is darkness, let me bring light.
> Where there is doubt, let me bring true faith in You.
>
> Oh, Divine Master, grant that I may never seek
> So much to be consoled as to console,
> So much to be understood as to understand,
> So much to be loved as to love.
> For it is in giving that we receive,
> It is in pardoning that we are pardoned
> In loving that we are loved.
> And it is in dying that we are born to eternal life.

—

Joan Scarlett, the mother of one of Colleen's classmates, recognized the contradictions as soon as the girl joined the lay Franciscans, who met regularly at the church to discuss the teachings of St. Francis. There were a dozen adults and Colleen, a funny kid who dressed in coveralls and chopped her hair short, like a boy's. At fourteen, she was by far the youngest in the group but one of the most articulate and easily the most knowledgeable.

Joan had grown up in a German-Catholic household run with regimental authority by her police-lieutenant father, who believed it was unimportant for girls to be educated, since their destiny was marriage and children. Having fulfilled her destiny by dropping out of high school, marrying, and bearing six children, Joan tried to satisfy her enduring desire to learn with the Franciscans. She marveled at Colleen's easy familiarity with St. Francis and her discerning comprehension of doctrine and history. The girl would have been intimidating if not for the painful yearning she wore so openly on her pixie face. The instant Joan took her seat, Colleen would settle in right next to her, obviously enjoying her warm, fleshy presence. Despite the sophistication of her mind, she seemed like a small child, palpably vulnerable. Joan wanted to hug her all the time.

People used to say, "Why doesn't Colleen dress like a girl? Why doesn't she walk like a girl? Why doesn't she act like a girl?" Joan wasn't certain, but she saw what was lurking beneath those coveralls and had her suspicions. Like Colleen, Joan had developed breasts and a womanly build at an early age, and she remembered how frightening it had been. She guessed—correctly, it would turn out—that Colleen was handling what had been a similarly precocious and unwanted maturity by covering it up.

—

Colleen knew she must have worn her shame on her face, because men felt free to touch her, as if they knew about her. It had begun when she was five or six, when a boy of twelve or thirteen (not a stranger—far from it) taught her secret things to do to him, and he reciprocated. For years, they put their hands and mouths in forbidden places and she didn't know it was wrong. Her father wasn't an affectionate man, so she welcomed the physical intimacy, and then felt confused and ashamed, because the boy made it clear that what they were doing was illicit—and then she felt too helpless and afraid to stop. She would never reveal his name.

When she was ten her breasts appeared, and suddenly it seemed as though her secret was out. One of the neighbors had already been putting his hands on her, and then she became afraid to go into stores, because too often she'd find a suggestive touch or something far more explicit lurking there to unnerve her.

She cut off her hair and covered her body with baggy clothes and occupied herself with tales of suffering and redemption. Though she loved reading tragic love stories like *Romeo and Juliet* and anything by Dickens, her favorite author was Stephen R. Donaldson, a writer of science-fiction melodrama with theological underpinnings. She was especially captivated by the protagonist of the multivolume parables *The Chronicles of Thomas Covenant.*

The character Thomas Covenant is a successful author whose life turns calamitous when he is infected with leprosy. His wife leaves him, he loses a couple of fingers, and a car hits him. *Then* the story starts. Covenant is transported to a new land, where he is hailed as a hero, the reincarnation of a legendary character called Berek Halfhand. As Halfhand, Covenant conducts himself with superhuman bravado through a series of exhausting adventures against many enemies, including Lord Foul, aka Soulcrusher, reluctantly proving his worth with Sisyphean endurance. Even so, after hundreds of pages throughout numerous volumes, he finds only a modicum of peace, but that, apparently, is enough.

Like her literary antihero, Colleen felt compelled to repeatedly demonstrate her righteousness, making do with the good deeds within the grasp of a working-class Irish-Catholic girl in Queens, since she never found herself magically transported anywhere. She volunteered her services compulsively. She cleaned and shopped for elderly people, visited nursing homes, helped the sick at a local hospital, and worked in an ambulance unit.

None of this chronic worthiness eased her adolescent suffering, however, and she wouldn't talk to her parents about her sin, even if she could have. They rarely talked about anything except what they should watch on television. Their house had once been full of life. Colleen was the youngest of five children, chaos enough, and her parents were perennial hosts to their vast Irish families. Then one day Colleen found them sitting in the living room at the bar, the centerpiece for the weekly Friday-night parties. "Dad lost his job," they told her. The parties were over. Her father had worked with his hands for most of his life, as a moving man and then as an electrician, and then he'd put on a white collar and gone into management. But when the recession hit, he was out. He drank his way into depression, and her mother kept him company. Colleen knew better than to lay her problems on them.

After much agonizing, she made an appointment to talk to her parish priest. She woke up that Sunday morning feeling shameful and afraid. What will he think of me? she wondered. Will he understand?

All day she prayed and rehearsed a line: *I feel like the Prodigal Son* . . . That's how she would begin: *I feel like the Prodigal Son* . . .

When she arrived at the church, she felt the pounding of her heart throughout her body, even in her eyes. Her mouth was dry and her hands were sweaty, so she stopped in the kitchen to get a glass of water. She stood there for fifteen minutes, composing herself.

At her confession, she started to tell the priest she felt like the Prodigal Son, but her words sounded tinny. She stopped talking and tried again, and then she admitted that she'd rehearsed her lines but still couldn't find the words to say what she wanted to say.

"Just say it," he said gently.

They were face-to-face in the rectory parlor. Colleen looked at the floor and told him what her heart had been hiding for so long. He didn't reply right away, but when she looked up, she saw mercy and understanding in his eyes.

"It's okay," he said.

Then he told her he finally understood why she had inflicted so much penance on herself for so many years. "I've worried about you," he said.

Colleen felt the heaviness leave her.

"We can wipe the slate clean," the priest repeated, and spoke to her of God's mercy and love. When he finished talking, he hugged her and kissed her, paternally, and told her again that she was loved.

When Colleen looked out the window, she saw it was raining. She decided the rain was a covenant from God, specifically intended for her. For the first time that she could remember, she felt happy. She was fifteen years old.

By seventeen, she felt that she had adequately submerged herself in a life of penance and decided it was time to test her faith. Though she had enrolled at Fordham University, she decided to drop out and join the Sisters of the Atonement at Graymoor, the Franciscan motherhouse up in the Hudson highlands.

Lulled by Graymoor's geographic proximity—it was just a short drive north of the city—she seemed unaware of the distance she was putting between herself and everything she knew. Her Catholic youth group friends were encouraging. They weren't ready to take the plunge themselves, but they were glad to see Colleen fulfill her destiny on their behalf. Young as she was to make such a serious commitment, she emerged from the rigorous psychological trials and was declared mature enough to be accepted into the order.

It all seemed right.

A few months later, Colleen moved to Burlington, Vermont, to begin her postulancy—her trial marriage—a year of observation and adjustment to see if convent life suits the postulant and vice versa. It seemed like a happy match. The work was satisfying. She taught religion to children who had Down's syndrome; she visited a nursing home, where she was assigned to read to a woman who was dying from a brain tumor. The sisters in the convent were kind to her. However, while Burlington wasn't all that much farther from her home in Queens than Graymoor, this time Colleen felt as though she had embarked on a journey as far-flung as Thomas Covenant's. It was one thing to escape from home to the church around the corner, quite another to actually leave. Like many brides who'd advanced to the altar with noble intentions, Colleen discovered she preferred a theoretical marriage to the real thing. After two months she asked for an annulment.

Her decision to leave was motivated in part by homesickness, though she couldn't honestly say she missed watching her mother and father deal with their disappointments by drinking in front of the television every night. There was another reason, however, profound in its simplicity: Before taking on a life dedicated to service, she realized, she needed to be young. She'd taken a bite of the apple far too early and then she'd stopped. Now she wanted to start again.

She returned home and reapplied to college at St. John's, feeling like a failure about her vocation but reassuring herself that the call would come when she finished school. She was certain she would rejoin the religious life when she was ready. Happy to have made a decision that seemed so grown-up, she went to her parish priest to receive his blessing. This time she approached him without fear, because he'd been so kind to her before.

His coldness shocked her. "You've broken a commitment," he told her angrily. With that she lost her confessor, the person she'd entrusted with her secret.

—

Colleen was majoring in theology at St. John's when Don Cassidy singled her out from among his students. He had tried to draw her into apparitional prayer movements, whose followers believed in apparitions of Mary and messages from God, but she had always felt skeptical of charismatics: too much emphasis on emotional prayer, not enough on self-reflection and service. Still, after she completed his class, they remained friends. They'd go to mass together or meet for lunch. She was working in the security office, which helped her pay her tuition, when Cassidy dropped by one day and told her he wanted her to meet someone. She would have no trouble remembering the date. It was September 6, 1984. She was twenty-one years old.

Without hesitation she took a quick break. Though Colleen had left the convent and stopped going to confession, she remained a dutiful young woman, eager to please anyone who had been kind to her. Out in the lobby, the professor introduced her to an old classmate of his. They'd been students together at St. John's in the late 1940s, and the friend had returned for a master's degree in Asian studies.

They chatted for a few minutes. She couldn't remember what they talked about, but she was struck by the glacial blue of his eyes, which happened to match hers. He didn't mention how he had the freedom to become a student again, at his age, and she didn't ask.

She liked him. He was easy to talk to even though he was thirty years her senior, she would discover—the same age as her parents (just a year younger than her mother, to be exact). She liked the way he looked. With his weathered face, disheveled reddish-blond hair, and the blue windbreaker he wore over his tan slacks, he might have just walked off a sailboat.

Seeing how well Colleen and Bob Rowe hit it off, Don Cassidy asked her if she'd like to join the two of them for dinner at Dante's, a popular Italian restaurant for St. John's people.

Sure, she said, and went back to work.

At dinner that night she was mesmerized by Bob Rowe, who seemed to be able to talk about anything. She enjoyed listening to him and Don toy with each other, resuming a battle of wits that had begun decades earlier, when they were her age. Don was a devout Catholic while Bob was Lutheran, and they clearly took pleasure in games of semantics as they argued points of religion and philosophy.

She felt at home with Bob, who was familiar in many ways. His accent, like hers, had been bred in the outer boroughs of New York City. His corny jokes would have gone over well in her parents' kitchen before her father lost his job and her parents stopped telling jokes. But when Bob began to talk about museums in Manhattan, about his own painting, about a trip he'd taken to Greece and Naples and Rome, he seemed unimaginably worldly to Colleen, who had transferred to St. John's from Fordham because the Bronx was too far away from home. It seemed to Colleen that she'd known only gray, whereas Bob talked in colors, weaving disparate threads—representing history, religion, art, nature—into a beautifully textured piece of fabric.

What amazed her most was that he seemed to find her fascinating. When she told him she was studying theology, he wanted to know what she was going to do with her degree. Then he told her she had beautiful eyes.

She would always blush, every time she remembered his words: "Ah gee, you know you have beautiful eyes." She'd blush again, hearing him say, "A man could dive into those eyes and swim away and be lost forever."

It was true that Colleen's eyes were striking, especially when she took off her glasses. But she was also five feet three inches tall and weighed 165 pounds. Her honey-colored hair had been chopped off carelessly. She couldn't tell you what she was wearing without taking a look at herself. Bob's compliments made her feel giddily transformed, as though she had wandered onto the set of a play and suddenly found herself cast as the ingénue.

The evening sparkled. She would have liked it to go on much longer. But after they said good night to Bob, and Don drove her back to campus to pick up her car, she didn't have any expectations. It didn't occur to her that she had become infatuated with this friend of her professor's. She was just happy to have been there, in the charming presence of a man she found to be extraordinarily interesting and unusually happy.

CHAPTER 16

Case Number 092182

Colleen hadn't met an apparition. The unusually happy and interest-ing middle-aged graduate student Don Cassidy had introduced her to was the same Bob Rowe who had killed his wife and children six years earlier. Acquittal under the insanity defense had kept him out of jail, and he had become—in theory—a patient, not a prisoner. But he remained confined in an institution until he had convinced his doctors that he was no longer subject to the "dangerous mental disorder" that led to his crime and was no longer "mentally ill," as defined by New York's criminal-procedure law. This could have taken sixty days or forever. The duration of stay was unrelated to the crime; a killer could be released in two months while a petty thief might remain hospitalized for years.

There are no formulas or tests for "dangerousness," no objective crite-ria. The most instructive predictors of future violence are past and present behavior, and this is reliable primarily in extreme cases, when patients are disruptive, domineering, argumentative. The "good" patient is diffi-cult to evaluate; the intelligent patient even more difficult. Has the quiet man reading a book in the corner been "cured," or is he simply waiting to be released so he can explode again?

Doctors look for signs of a working conscience. Does the patient recognize that he has done something wrong? Does he show "remorse"? But true remorse is difficult to discern. Children quickly learn to say "I'm sorry" because adults want them to (even as they plot how to cover their tracks better the next time). They learn to nod contritely when asked, "Do you mean it?"

Remorse, like love—like the law, in fact—requires interpretation.

On July 3, 1978, a week after the end of his trial, Robert Rowe had been sent to Mid-Hudson, a maximum-security psychiatric hospital for forensic patients (which happened to be located not far from Graymoor, the motherhouse for the Franciscan nuns, where Colleen had prepared to enter her postulancy). Sprawling and ugly, surrounded by a razor-wire fence, Mid-Hudson fit the image of a prison, not a hospital, and its patients, accordingly, tended toward violence and were often transferees from other psychiatric hospitals. Rowe was to be kept there until psychiatrists decided he wasn't "dangerous"—in a technical, legal sense—and could be moved to a hospital closer to home—or what had been home.

Later that summer Jack O'Shaughnessy, Bob's old friend, told Kenny Rowe that he was driving up to Mid-Hudson for a visit. Kenny asked Jack to take Bob some Hershey bars and a carton of cigarettes. Bob didn't smoke, but he wanted the cigarettes to bribe other inmates to leave him alone. Because Jack wasn't the kind to pry, he didn't ask why Kenny didn't go himself, but he'd heard that Kenny's wife didn't want the family to have any more contact with Bob. Jack had also heard that she was afraid Bob would have a relapse, which Jack thought was a legitimate concern, but he also thought she must be bitter. Pat had been close to Mary. She even looked like Mary. He suspected she'd come to some judgment that didn't allow for continued relations with Bob.

Like all of Bob's visitors at Mid-Hudson, Jack was patted down before he was allowed to enter. After passing through several doors he arrived at the cafeteria, where he met Bob, wearing prison pajamas, in the custody of a guard.

Bob spent most of their time together complaining. He was just being warehoused, he told Jack, and he wanted to write about how the taxpayers' money was wasted. Furthermore, the therapy was a joke, he said—he talked to a psychiatrist maybe five minutes a month.

Jack left feeling weary.

It may have been on Jack's second visit that Bob broached the subject of getting his law license back so that he could help other people in his position. He pointed out that he should be able to practice law when he was released, since he wasn't guilty of a crime and therefore hadn't violated the Code of Professional Responsibility.

Jack was glad to indulge his friend in this fantasy, and was encouraged to see that Bob could still muster a provocative argument, even when he was depressed and out of shape and locked up in a mental asylum. Listening to him make his plans, Jack felt sure (as he hadn't before) that the Bob he'd known hadn't disappeared or turned into a devil. Whatever uncertainty he'd had about Bob's insanity vanished. He was now convinced that a profound sickness had indeed come over his friend and now it was gone. As he listened to Bob convincingly spin this wild legal theory, Jack believed that Bob was fundamentally the same man he'd always been, as much as he could be after having his life smashed to bits so unexpectedly. After smashing his life to bits. "If someone had read my future a year before the disaster," Bob told Jack, "I would have laughed at the prophet who accurately told me what was to happen."

Not many weeks went by before Jack began to plan another visit to Mid-Hudson. He'd picked a weekend and made arrangements about the car with his wife, Nellie, and then he had to forget about Bob for a while. Even as he was trying to comprehend the series of events that triggered unfathomable brutality in one of his closest friends, Jack became the object of fate's cartoonish malice. On the Friday night before his planned trip upstate, their youngest child, a junior in high school, was having a pizza with Nellie. The boy handed his mother a slice, she took a bite, and then she was dead. Choked to death. She was forty-nine years old.

Jack didn't see Bob again for almost two years.

———

Whenever Silvio Caso, Bob's old friend and judo partner, came up for a visit, he stopped at McDonald's on the way. Bob had written to tell him how terrible the food was at Mid-Hudson, so Silvio would make a detour off Route 17 and pick up a couple of hamburgers and a Coke, figuring it was the least he could do.

He hated going up to Mid-Hudson. He hated the "nut jobs" he saw walking around there, even though he realized that Bob must be a nut job, too—otherwise he wouldn't be there. They'd meet in the cafeteria, and Bob would immediately start wolfing down the hamburgers.

One time, another patient-prisoner started hassling Bob for one of the burgers.

"No," grunted Bob, and kept eating.

The man took a quick walk around the cafeteria and then asked again.

"No."

This kept going on until Bob finished his food.

Nothing happened, but Silvio couldn't wait to get out of there, and he felt the same way every time he went to visit. The only useful thing he took away from Mid-Hudson were good anecdotes about the thugs and bullies wandering around the cafeteria in pajamas, like the one about the man who had to wear boxing gloves all the time because he had a habit of punching his fellow inmates.

Silvio visited Bob out of loyalty, but he was troubled by the outcome of the trial. He'd known Mary Rowe a long time and felt loyalty to her, too. He'd always thought she was outgoing and funny and a perfect match for Bob, and he admired the way she had handled Christopher. Right after the killings, Silvio hadn't known what to make of the situation. Bob was his friend and he wouldn't abandon him, but he hadn't yet formed a final opinion about whether the killings were deliberate or the product of illness. On his first long drive up to Mid-Hudson, he kept replaying the trial in his mind, adding evidence from his own dossier of memories. He thought about the times that Bob and Mary had joined him and his wife at his in-laws' place up in the country. Bob would place Christopher on top of a guitar and would watch him stroke the strings for hours and laugh—at the sound or the vibration; they weren't sure which. The kid was a mess, but Silvio could see that Bob loved him anyway. Could that love have been perverted into a rage so powerful it altered a man's character and turned him into a cold-blooded killer?

Then Silvio remembered something. Bob used to take Christopher on kayak rides in Jamaica Bay—just the two of them. If he had wanted to kill the boy, it wouldn't have been a problem to just drop him overboard and say that there had been an accident. Who would have argued with him? So Silvio concluded that Bob had been ill when he killed his family.

Like Jack, Silvio was usually so eager to leave that he couldn't concentrate on what Bob had to say. But he did remember one conversation. Bob told Silvio how angry he was at the assistant district attorney, who had complained to the judge that Bob showed no remorse.

"What did they want from me?" he said bitterly. "To feel remorse. What remorse did I have? I was sick. I didn't do this on purpose. They want me to get on my knees and show some kind of repentance or remorse, Silvio. I could not show any remorse, because I was sick when I killed my family. What the hell do they want from me?"

Bob Rowe stayed at Mid-Hudson for almost a year. In the spring of 1979, he was transferred to the Creedmoor Psychiatric Center in Queens, a mental hospital just a few miles from Mill Basin. Though Creedmoor had a small forensic unit for patients who had been acquitted of crimes under the insanity defense, it was a low-security institution, for patients who weren't considered dangerous.

At Creedmoor, Bob's keepers—nurses, medical doctors, psychologists, social workers, and dietitians—kept close track of his eating, sleeping, and bathing habits. The diligent note-taking was remarkable considering how understaffed Creedmoor was, but there was a legal concern as well as a therapeutic interest behind such scrutiny. Most of the insanity acquittees were likely to press for release, and Creedmoor's administration wanted to have a record that would support its institutional decision, pro or con. While the handwritten progress notes were often cursory and impossible to read, they can offer a narrative, however fragmented, of a patient's life.

Excerpts from the daily progress reports for Rowe, Robert, case number 092182, Creedmoor Psychiatric Center Forensic Unit, Queens, New York:

April 3, 1979. Mr. Rowe is a 49-year-old lawyer transferred to Creedmoor Psychiatric Center from Mid-Hudson Psychiatric Center where he was held on a 330.20 CPL charged with the murder of his wife and three children. Mr. Rowe remembers his Mother as "a lousy personality—cranky and standoffish with people"—his father as "happy-go-lucky" and a good male figure. He alleges to have heard his mother's voice telling him to kill the family in 1975. Oddly enough, he states he was not hearing these voices when he committed the crime several years later.

Examination reveals several elevations indicating some personality dysfunctioning at this time; mainly of a sociopathic and depressive character. The latter would appear to be mainly situational in nature. Mr. Rowe can be expedient and disregard conventions. He does not always feel a strong obligation to others believing he is entitled to his own opinions regardless of what they think. He has some mistrust of those in authority and may close his mind to well-meaning suggestions from people. Yet he is intelligent enough to be controlled and socially correct before putting forth an argument. Thus the impression that he gives is one of being cooperative and accommodating. . . .

He feels unable to work productively due to impaired judgment and concentration and cannot understand what he reads as well as he used to. His memory often drops facts and he has difficulty in starting to do things due to fear that he will be unable to complete them. He sometimes feels as if things are so strange as to not be real and experiences occasional alienation from his own environment and surroundings. Some of these depressive feelings may be due to bona fide "guilt" but some is also due to resentment at the current predicament in which he finds himself vis—alone and incarcerated without family and financial resources and virtually friendless.—*James J. Audubon, psychologist II*

May 14, 1979. It remains a mystery to me how he managed to commit the crimes he allegedly did. . . . It has been difficult for me to observe signs of depression because he never brought this out when I communicated or listened. He has been somewhat friendly after the initial introductory process. He tries to be cooperative.—*G. Phillips, psychiatric social worker*

August 13, 1979. Robert has proven to be an excellent teacher's aide. His intelligence, patience and even temperedness has resulted in increased learning in my students.—*M. Wolf, teacher*

Sept. 9, 1979. Patient is receiving a regular diet. Appetite is somewhat poor-fair. Tends to omit meals, especially breakfast. He should be encouraged to eat a well-balanced diet in effort to acquire and maintain optimum nutritional status. Since 3–29–79 Pt. has lost 15 lbs. He is somewhat within normal weight range. Weight noted. 183 lbs. Ht. 5′10.″ *[indecipherable signature], diet. tech.*

Sept. 15, 1979. Patient continues to discuss his remorse in somewhat inappropriate manner. In discussion of his family relates only his *deep* affection for them all, including the family members whom he killed; & his brother whom he feels abandoned him. He claims to be w/o hostility or anger.—*Gerald M. Gall, M.A. candidate, therapy volunteer John Jay College*

Sept. 20, 1979. Pt. takes medication willingly. Pt. sits alone, reading a book or newspaper. He doesn't seem to want to socialize with the others here on ward. He seems to have a gloomy disposition. Appetite, sleeping, cleanliness are good.—*R. Byrd (MHTA)*

Sept. 20, 1979. The past several weeks Mr. Rowe has seemed largely unavailable for interaction in the daily life milieu. This is not to imply that Mr. Rowe is not skilled at normal interpersonal communication. He does in fact display facility in this function. Nonetheless Mr. Rowe has often not been seen in the day hall or as a participant—some of the time due to sleeping (observed on 5–6 occasions doing so since 9–4–79.) Since Mr. Rowe does not have many relatives, his lack of "presence" in the day hall area indicates there may be a degree of loneliness in his life. Speaking to him supports the impression that he does feel some loneliness.—*G. Phillips, psychiatric social worker*

Oct. 6, 1979. 6 P.M.–12 midnight Mr. Rowe went to NYC musical and the behavior of this patient and sign of motivation was outstanding.—*Kevin Price, recreational therapist*

Oct. 15, 1979. As of this date, Kenneth Rowe has visited 1–2 times in last 6 months, last visit in July 1979.—*G. Phillips, psychiatric social worker*

Oct. 16, 1979. Mr. Rowe continues to reside in the Forensic Unit under mandated admission by CPL330.20. He has escorted ground privileges at this time. A major activity is his teaching assistant position as a helper to Mr. Michael Wolf, instructor. Mr. Rowe assists Mr. Wolf 2 days a week, Tuesdays and Thursdays.

As noted above, Mr. Rowe's brother Kenneth seldom visits having only come 2X since Mr. Rowe has been at Creedmoor Forensic Service. Mr. Rowe is accepting of this although he would like more frequent visits. There is no phone communications either.

Mr. Rowe appears to be managing his confinement reasonably well, considering the extent of his problems, and the losses resultant. He is not too active but participates in some activities. The teaching assistant job seems to help him during his confinement as it is something he enjoys doing.

Mr. Rowe continues having his hope to be able to settle in Hawaii one day in the future. He said the relatives there know of the homicides committed. One relative, a cousin, has corresponded with him and has reportedly tried to be "understanding."—*G. Phillips, psychiatric social worker*

Oct. 19, 1979. I asked who Rowe admired—e.g., Gandi *v.* Hitler. He said Lincoln and Gandi: "they didn't abuse power." I pointed out Hitler and Gandi were both mothers boys—maybe they had more in common. He seemed very annoyed at my suggestion. I asked about Roosevelt. RR said he did what had to be done. I said he mistreated the Jap-Americans. How did he feel about that as a part Polynesian. He said the Jap-Amer [indecipherable] and deserved some of what they got; yet he admired them. Related that Rowe's background was Hawaiian and Scandinavian. Saw himself as easy-going and loving like the former. Now thinks he is more "cold-blooded" like the latter. Doesn't have all the "positive" emotions of a Hawole [*sic*]. I feel the man may be a multiple personality.—*J. Audubon, psychologist II*

Oct. 23, 1979. 12–8:30 shift. Resident is no problem. His sleeping and eating habit are good. Most of the time is reading when we come on duty.—*E. Garcia*

Oct. 28, 1979. Monthly progress note. Pt. is guarded, distant, secretive, interested in denying mental illness. He is grandiose and interacts poorly with staff and other patients. Does not seem as depressed as in the past.

—*[indecipherable signature]*

Oct. 30, 1979. On arrival to the ward at 6:30 P.M. Ms. Pride stated Mr. Rowe was not accounted on 4 P.M. count. Apparently pt. escaped.—

Althea Newkirk, rehab II

Creedmoor was a three-hundred-acre campus, containing seventy buildings, located in the middle of a residential neighborhood in Queens. The forensic unit was small. It housed about forty patients, or less than 3 percent of a patient population of about 1,700. Though these "insanity ac-quittees" had committed homicide, arson, and assault, they were no longer considered dangerous enough to require the extra security measures available at fortified mental institutions such as Mid-Hudson. They were always referred to as "patients" or "residents," not "inmates" or "prisoners." The forensic unit at Creedmoor was a locked ward, but upon demonstrating their reliability, patients could receive grounds privileges, which allowed them to move freely to other buildings for therapy, work, or classes.

The main gate at Creedmoor wasn't kept locked, and the fence surrounding the property was riddled with holes. Some patients with grounds privileges routinely slipped out to the diner across the street or to the movies. They could do this without attracting attention because they weren't prisoners—they were patients, dressed in street clothes, provided either by their families or by the state of New York.

Bob fled because he couldn't stand it anymore. Creedmoor had become unbearable, like Bedlam. "Nuthouse, madhouse" were the words he recorded in his journal. In the forensic unit, men and women were locked up together, and so were the very psychotic and the merely disturbed. There was little supervision. The patients slept in cubicles, eight beds to a cubicle, and nothing separated them from one another, not even a curtain. There was no place to be alone. Bob couldn't take refuge on the porch, because it had been taken over by druggies who openly smoked marijuana, which he found offensive. Sometimes on his way to the bathroom, he'd step over people having intercourse, which offended him even more. The place disgusted him.

Nights were terrifying, especially after three inmates began to threaten him. "We can do anything with you at night," they would taunt. "We can kill you at night when you are sleeping."

He wanted to get away, to be with people—normal people—to see families with children. His entire life had revolved around his family, and he had done away with them. For months he'd been trying to face this horrendous fact, to understand what had happened, to contemplate the future, to decide if he deserved one. He was still drawn to the idea of suicide, at least as a hypothetical course of action.

It was surprisingly easy to leave. He called his friend Harvey Sackstein, the lawyer, who was taking care of his money (he had about $60,000, which included proceeds from the sale of the Mill Basin house, the family's savings, and Mary's life insurance). Bob told Harvey he was bored and had started gambling a little with some of the other patients and needed cash. "It's your money," Harvey said, and brought over $400. Harvey was pleased with Bob's progress at Creedmoor. He seemed completely different from the wrecked man he'd been at the trial—himself again—though Harvey had to admit that no one, including Bob, understood who that really was.

With cash in his pocket, Bob made a detour on his way back to the ward from the class he helped teach. He slipped through the fence and made his way to the subway. He arrived at the Port Authority bus station near Times Square and checked to see what bus was leaving next. It was heading for Las Vegas.

Las Vegas was as good a place to go as any; in fact, it made him feel as though he hadn't completely bamboozled Harvey: He would be gambling—in more ways than one. He didn't really care where he was going; he just wanted some quiet, to get away from the forensic unit. He wanted a long trip, to see that the world hadn't disappeared just because he had.

He checked into a motel near the Golden Nugget casino and settled into a routine: walking around during the day, gambling a little, dropping himself into the bathtub at night. It didn't take long—maybe three days—for him to conclude that he didn't want to kill himself and that he didn't want to stay in Creedmoor. With the lucid thinking of a rational man, he decided to return and find a legal way to get out of the institution.

He called Harvey and asked him to send money for a plane ticket home. Harvey agreed to wire Bob a ticket—he wasn't going to get scammed again.

If Harvey was angry, he didn't let Bob know it. He picked his friend up at the airport, took him for lunch at the Pan American Motor Inn on Queens Boulevard, and then returned him to Creedmoor.

—

The record keepers expressed little curiosity about Robert Rowe's sudden exit—or his reappearance a week later. Escapes, referred to as "elopements" by the psychiatric staff, were part of the routine at Creedmoor, though not common in the forensic unit. The overworked staff could barely keep track of the patients who were there. When they were gone and the police were notified, they became somebody else's problem.

Nov. 7, 1979. Pt's relative, administration, regional office, 105th Precinct, DAs office notified of patient return.—*[indecipherable], RN*

Nov. 7, 1979. Expresses no desire to work in workshop. As far as he is concerned there is no rehabilitation in mental institutions. Stated the teaching program is not rewarding. He did this for the last 20 years before his crime teaching his retarded kid.—*[indecipherable], RN*

Nov. 7, 1979. Assistant DA Audrey Vitola informed about pt's return to unit.—*R. [indecipherable], ORT[?]*

Nov. 7, 1979. Resident is watching TV this evening. Ate a good meal, smiling and laughing with peers. Body clean, looking for a bath towel. Cooperative with staff.—*M. Price [?]*

Nov. 8, 1979. Resident appeared to have rested well. He awakens early, friendly with staff, washed up in bathroom, ate a good breakfast. Walked around smiling. He stated is feeling fine. No problems at this time. *[indecipherable signature]*

Nov. 8, 1979. Robert in good spirits this A.M.—*[indecipherable], M.D.*

Nov. 8, 1979. 4–12:30. Resident cooperative, calm and friendly. NO management problem. Kept to himself most of the evening—watching TV or sleeping on and off in front of TV. Did not converse very much with any residents. Appetite good. Personal hygiene good. No visitors this time. Offers no complaints.—*T. Race*

Nov. 9, 1979. Resident was quiet this PM. Spent most of (if not all) the afternoon sitting in dayhall asleep or looking at television. Appetite seemed to be good.—*R. Beetle*

Nov. 9, 1979. 8 A.M.–4:40 P.M. Resident spends most of the day after awakening in the morning sitting or lying down in the day room on chair and hassock and appears to be contented with no complaints. *[indecipherable signature]*

Nov. 10, 1979. Resident returned from escape on 11–6–79 and has been no problem. Appears less depressed since the return but continues his old habits of lying down in front of the television with his eyes closed or apparently sleeping. His personal hygiene still needs improving and his appetite still appears good.—*[indecipherable signature]*

Nov. 11, 1979. 8:30. Resident stayed up until about 2:30 then went to bed. He is still in bed. He did not get up for breakfast. He still remains quiet and friendly with staff. No problems at this writing.— *J. France*

Nov. 11, 1979. 8–4:30 P.M. Resident spent most of time staying to himself, sleeping at long intervals in dayroom on sofa near TV. No management problem but refused lunch.—*D. Montgomery, LPN*

Nov. 13, 1979. Pt is not delusional but he is depressed and withdrawn. Sleeps during the day. Will attempt to get patient more attune with group therapy.—*[indecipherable signature], M.D.*

Nov. 14, 1979. Saw RR on 11/9. I asked about his running away and how that might affect his reputation. He said nothing revealing. . . . —*J. Audubon, psychologist II*

Nov. 15, 1979. Pt. arrested.

Charged with "escape in the first degree," a felony—an unusually punitive charge for "elopement" from a mental hospital—Rowe was taken to the Queens House of Detention, where he was interviewed once again by Daniel Schwartz, the psychiatrist who had examined him before his trial, eighteen months earlier. Once again Dr. Schwartz was asked by a judge to determine whether Robert Rowe was mentally competent to undergo a court hearing on the charges.

The psychiatrist's assessment this time:

He is alert, pleasant and cooperative, perhaps a little too jovial or casual about his present legal situation. His cheerfulness is in striking contrast to the absence of emotions, which he had following the murders. On questioning he seems unable to state when he regained his ability to emote. Moreover, he does not seem very interested in when this happened or why. As before, he shows very little interest in understanding or searching within himself.

He readily acknowledges having committed the present offense and explains, "I was confined to Creedmoor and I just couldn't stand the confinement and I walked out one day." He states that he flew to Las Vegas, where he remained in a small, downtown hotel for a week, walking around, doing very little gambling and thinking a lot about committing suicide. Finally he arrived at the conclusion that his wife would not have wanted him to kill himself, whereupon he decided to return. He called up one of the lawyers who had represented him on the murder charges; he, in turn, wired Mr. Rowe the plane fare.

He complains that the psychiatric and psychological treatment he received in Creedmoor was minimal and certainly not to his liking. He says he would spend most of his time talking to people who gave him no suggestions as to what to do. In the hospital there was "nothing to do!" He wants some kind of work. For a while he taught twice a week but, he points out, one of his sons was retarded, and teaching such people was too oppressive.

Now he would prefer Creedmoor as the lesser of two alternatives. In QHD [Queens House of Detention], he complains, "the disco music goes on from 8 A.M. to I A.M. and the inmates are horrible."

DIAGNOSIS: Mixed personality disorder.

CONCLUSION: Fit to proceed.

COMMENT: Even though Mr. Rowe now demonstrates emotion that is of a positive quality and much more intense than it was eighteen months ago, there is something strangely hollow about him, something which defies diagnostic terminology. Nevertheless, he certainly understands his present legal situation and should have no difficulty whatsoever in working with counsel.

Rowe's lawyers negotiated a deal: He agreed to a guilty charge for escape, but in the third degree—a misdemeanor. On December 14, he returned to Creedmoor.

Over the next few weeks, his progress reports indicate a new seriousness about the vow he'd made to find a legal way to leave the facility. On his first day back he engaged his psychologist, James Audubon, in a discussion of the penal code's intention toward mental patients. He complained that he didn't receive treatment at Creedmoor, "just diagnoses—not help." In his daily notes, Audubon wrote: "He was sure he could never get a job and his real concern is that he sees any kind of work as futile anyway. Admits he thought of suicide when he ran away but couldn't complete the act."

There was an obvious change in Rowe's behavior and manner. He no longer simply slept and watched television. Though he still remained aloof from the other patients, he began to open up to his counselors, as they wanted him to.

Jan. 11, 1980. Saw RR on 12/28. He rotated the discussion to the current
world situation. I said thinking too far ahead can increase depression.
Admits he was very busy—preoccupied with job and family—at one
time. His family gave him happiness—novelty, stimulation, etc. Very
few patients went as far as him, i.e., home, family, children. He has had
to make a bigger adjustment to the "nothingness" of ward life, confined
to other patients. He has lost everything! Does not know how to recapture happiness.—*J. Audubon, psychologist II*

Jan. 31, 1980. As noted in above notes, Robert feels troubled. He appears
to feel unhappy at times more so than others. He does appear to feel the
loss of his family. He was worried about his job, though at first he did
not seem to realize himself the extent to which this bothered him. One
reason it troubled him so much is he eventually had come to lose his
belief in his ability to succeed in a job and this lack of belief in himself
was present up until the time of counseling at least. When given some
ego support and guidance, he seemed to regain a little confidence, at
least momentarily, improving his mood, and allowing him to think a
little constructively. Vocationally he's considering some type of sales

work but more counseling is indicated before a final choice is made. We have been asked to submit a Medical Psychiatric Summary to the Bureau of Disability Determinations for the purpose of determining his eligibility for Social Security Disability Benefits.—*G. Phillips, psychiatric social worker II*

By spring, the Creedmoor staff was introduced to the old Bob Rowe, the man who had impressed his friends and neighbors as a "take-charge" kind of guy, who hadn't hesitated to challenge doctors and teachers he found to be inept. On March 8, 1980, he sent a handwritten letter to James E. Prevost, the state mental health commissioner, in which he explained (in lawyerly detail, complete with case citations) the shortcomings of his treatment at Creedmoor. He complained that during his year there, he had never been given a treatment plan and that he had had individual therapy—at his insistence—with a psychiatrist only five times.

"I would like you to direct the Director of this institution to provide me with a treatment plan and with some more relevant therapy on a regular or continuous basis," he wrote. "At present, I am sitting in a day room 16 hours a day trying to kill time by reading and looking at T.V."

Several lower courts have decided that involuntarily confined mental patients have a right to treatment. Wyatt vs. Stickney 325 F Supp 781, 344F Supp373, 344 F Supp 387 (MD Ala. 1971) Kessellrenner v Anonymous 33 N.Y. 2d 161, 305 N.E.2d 903 (N.Y. 1973). There are numerous other citations.

Even persons who are dangerous to themselves . . . Lynch v. Baxley 386 F. Supp 378 (MD Ala 1974). Wyatt v. Stickney supra.

I again request that you aid me to receive the treatment I am legally entitled to.

My psychologist says his tests indicate I am not psychotic and he could testify before a jury that I am not mentally ill at this time. My attending psychiatrist says I am not psychotic at the present time.

I therefore request that I be allowed to go through my chart with a professional MD to determine what has been written about me on the issue of "dangerousness." If I am not psychotic and not dangerous what am I doing in this institution? If I am dangerous what specific remarks have been placed in my chart?

Rowe sent copies of the letter to the director of Creedmoor and the head of the forensic unit, to Steve Scaring and Harvey Sackstein, and to an organization called Concerned Citizens for Creedmoor.

The response came quickly. The New York State Department of Social Services asked the Creedmoor administration to respond to Rowe's complaint. On May 22, 1980, Robert W. Damino, a psychiatrist in Creedmoor's forensic unit, did just that. Dr. Damino, who was both a doctor and a lawyer, was in a delicate position. In the early 1980s, the prevailing attitude in New York toward mental patients was more liberal than it would become ten years thence. The operating dictate among psychologists and psychiatrists working in state hospitals was CYA—cover your ass. So the director of an institution like Creedmoor would feel compelled to offer a thorough, legally unchallengeable answer to Rowe's question "If I am not psychotic and not dangerous, what am I doing in this institution?"

Dr. Damino wrote:

He has been continuously hospitalized since July 1978 and at no time during this hospitalization . . . has he been considered mentally well enough to be released from the hospital without being a danger to others. This has been the opinion of psychiatrists and the Treatment Team at Mid-Hudson and it has been the opinion of psychiatrists and the Treatment Team at the CPC Forensic Unit.

His being considered too dangerous to live outside the hospital includes his being too dangerous to work on a regular basis at any substantial gainful employment. Indeed, he could not be away from this hospital (CPC Forensic Unit) more than two days without Court permission, and he has not been, nor is he being considered for, recommendation at this time to a Court to be away for more than 48 hours. As of the present time he does not even have the privilege of going alone on the grounds of Creedmoor. In short, he has not been able to engage in any substantial gainful employment while hospitalized, and his condition has existed for more than one year and is a mental impairment.

He is considered a danger to others outside the Hospital on a long term basis (as more than two months) because when he became psychotic he committed serious crimes. If he were not considered dangerous on a long term basis he could not be legally hospitalized. He would have to be released. Moreover, in order for him to be hospitalized in a mental hospital his dangerousness must be by reason of a mental illness as defined by the Mental Hygiene Law. (This matter was stated clearly by N.Y. Court of Appeals in the case *Matter of Robert Torsney, NY2nd*—opinion No. 203, July 9, 1979).

To state the matter another way, and, more simply: If he could engage in substantial employment he would have to not be considered a danger to others (or himself) functioning outside the hospital. That has not been so since he was first hospitalized July 1978 in Mid-Hudson. His status here is that of patient, not prisoner.

Apparently, Rowe got the message. On April 9 the patient sent his résumé to Creedmoor's department of education and training, asking for a job. "From 1969 to 1975 I was licensed by the State of New York's Board of Education to teach a night adult education course entitled 'Law for the Layman.' The course consisted of topics such as: evidence, how to buy a house, semantics, criminal and tort law, accidents and traumatic medicine, installment loans, contract law, leases and the law of wills and estates. There were thirty students per class. If the attendance dropped below thirteen, the course was discontinued. My class was never discontinued."

Then, while he waited for a response, he asked Dr. Audubon to explain once again the rules concerning release—what, exactly, he needed to do to get out. On May 27, the doctor wrote: "I explained rules of evidence and proof needed for release. I told him a longer stay doesn't make a patient less dangerous."

By summer, Robert Rowe had become a model patient, displaying a satisfying combination of industriousness and remorse, which was dutifully recorded.

July 21, 1980. Bob interacted well and showed interest in group process for the first time.—*J. Livingstone, psychiatric intern*

July 24, 1980. Discussed his future plans . . . Ecology, race relations and urban renewal have caused a revolution. Where does he fit in? Quality of different schools were examined. I recommended application to joint psychology-law program at the U of Maryland. How he could combine his interest in the law and psychology. He will write to them for further information.—*J. Audubon, psychologist II*

Sept. 4, 1980. JOB DESCRIPTION OF MR. ROBERT ROWE

1. Do mental health related literature search for the clinical research department. This work entails spending time in the hospital library and going through reference books and journals.

2. Assist in identifying authors who can contribute articles to the Creedmoor Journal of Urban Psychiatry. This work also entails spending time in the hospital library and going through reference books and journals.

Sept. 9, 1980. Saw pt. who is excited about his appeal for release. Says that doctors on staff agree that is not psychotic and believe he should be released. Spent much time discussing a book he was reading on Africa.—*[unsigned]*

On September 10, Robert Rowe's attorney, Stephen Scaring, filed a petition for writ of habeas corpus, asking for his client's release from Creedmoor. In summary, he wrote:

Petitioner's medical prognosis has been one of constant improvement and stabilization—to the point of achieving a solid and time-tested reputation for being as sane as "anybody on the street." Since January 1980, Petitioner has not needed to receive drug-related treatment. His days are spent immersed in books, helping those on the ward who are substantially impaired and contributing to group therapy sessions in a positive and constructive fashion. Since January, Petitioner has read 113 works, ranging from political treatises in colonial history to modern trends in medicine and the law. His attitude and adjustment—universally recognized by those who have observed him over a succession of months—continues to be positive and praiseworthy. It is a strik-ing contrast to see Petitioner conversant with members of the Creed-moor staff—doctors, psychologists and attendants engaging Petitioner in friendly banter as if he were a peer—and then to observe the true ill-ness, which exists among others on the ward. Admittedly eligible for release upon the observations of professionals, a lucid, coherent, soft-spoken, non-dangerous, articulate, illness-free Petitioner is yet sub-jected to the frustration and degradation of being cast among 45 profoundly disturbed persons—locked on a ward with no hope of re-lease. Petitioner has been exhibited to visiting teams of practicing psy-chiatrists and medical school classes as a fundamental—if not sadly amusing—example of the dilemma of warehousing an ostensibly "nor-mal" individual.

—

On September 16, four months after assuring the Department of Health that Rowe required institutionalization, Dr. Robert Damino changed his mind. Rowe had demonstrated that he could play the game, admirably. On cue, he'd transformed himself into an involved, socially active patient—not a loner. That he could do this so quickly was seen as further proof of his sanity. Writing with another psychiatrist, Ashwin Pandya, Dr. Damino declared:

It is our opinion that this patient does not suffer from a *dangerous men-tal disorder* in that

A. He does not suffer from a mental illness as defined in subdivi-sion twenty of section 1.03 of the Mental Hygiene Law and
B. He does not appear to be a danger to himself or others.

He has been non-psychotic since at least May 3, 1978—a period of more than twenty-eight months. While at Mid-Hudson and while at CPC he took part in many activities such as group therapy and various forms of occupational and recreational therapy. He has spent a great deal of time reading and writing. In general he has been a cooperative, well-behaved patient (with one exception—he escaped while on unescorted grounds privileges at CPC Forensic Unit, was gone about one week Oct.–Nov. 1979, returned voluntarily). He has had individual therapy. During his hospitalization he had frequently expressed remorse for what he had done, and, he had "relived the situation" many times in attempting to cope with severe feelings of guilt. During his hospitalization at Mid-Hudson and CPC Forensic Unit, a period of more than two years, he had not shown any aggressive tendencies towards others.

He indicated that if he left the hospital he would get his own apartment and attempt to work and go to school. He had not been disbarred. He indicated that he is temporarily suspended from the bar (2nd Dept.) that he has not been convicted of any felony (only conviction was for the escape in 1979—guilty (found) of a misdemeanor) and that he would seek to have his membership in the bar reinstated if he were released.

On December 18, 1980, Judge Leonard Yoswein ordered that Robert T. Rowe be discharged from in-patient psychiatric care, but the judge required him to visit a state-approved psychiatrist once or twice a week until it was determined that he could go less frequently.

On December 30, Rowe's progress notes at Creedmoor came to an abrupt close. "Discharged today. Left the forensic unit at 10 A.M."— *[indecipherable signature]*

CHAPTER 17

A New Person

Often when the nurses and psychologists and night attendants at Creedmoor observed "pt. Rowe" slumped in front of the television set in the day hall, he wasn't sleeping at all. He was dreaming about Puccini. He had once loved settling into his seat at the Metropolitan Opera House at Lincoln Center, under sparkling chandeliers, surrounded by prosperous, well-dressed people. He had enjoyed having become an educated, upper-middle-class professional man who could afford to pay exorbitant prices to hear beautiful music. His adolescent ambition to move out of his social class had been fulfilled. But this sense of propriety and achievement was an ancillary pleasure. Bob Rowe genuinely loved the music, and his pleasure in it was heightened when he transmitted his appreciation to his son Bobby.

It would have made a perfect collage for the photo album: orchestra, grand hall, father, and son, pasted together as a panoramic reminder of a superb moment, when life seemed unassailable.

What would become of all the Rowe family photos, actual and

imagined—the catalogue of their existence? Only Bob was left to re-member how it really had been, the stories behind the smiles. But how could he dare to remember any of it?

—

O n December 30, 1980, at the age of fifty-one, Bob Rowe left Creed-moor determined to make a fact out of the legal theory about him—that he was a free man who had done nothing wrong. Not *willingly*. With the verdict of not guilty, he had received the imprimatur of the state. Yet he understood that there was a vast distance between theory and reality, between legal forgiveness and public acceptance. He was determined to spend the rest of his life, if it came to that, trying to convince society at large, and himself, that he was not a monster and that he was entitled to recapture everything he had achieved and then destroyed.

On the morning of his release, he checked into the Pan American Motor Inn, the nondescript hotel on Queens Boulevard where Harvey Sackstein had taken him to lunch after he returned from Las Vegas. It wasn't much—just somewhere to live until he found something better. That evening he planned to go to the opera to reassure himself that every-thing he loved wasn't gone, that there was still beauty left in the world. But first he had other desires to satisfy. He spent the afternoon with a prostitute on the west side of Manhattan.

He would describe that day in writing, in a tone that was confessional yet coy. "If Satan exists, I'm sure he was sitting next to me on the F train that took me to mid-Manhattan that afternoon," he would recall. "He must have been smiling in glee. Come to think of it, we were both smil-ing.

Some moralists out there will now be clucking their tongues or wag-ging their collective fingers. So be it. I have found out only recently that I am a terribly human person. I have passions. As a young single man who served in the American Army overseas in two separate en-listments, I did not live a promiscuous life. To me, sex implied a rela-tionship of some type. I equated formal marriage with proper living.

However, I found that being locked up for three years made a difference. Sometimes to be around women is in a (minor) sense satisfying in itself. I guess that is why co-education is so much more sensible than "boys" or "girls" schools. But there was no exposure to women at all in most of the penal institutions that I had recently been exposed to. In the Creedmoor Psychiatric Center which I include under the rubric "penal institution" we did have a mixed ward: forty-five patients, nine women and thirty-five men. The women in the forensic unit were not my cup of tea. Some of them were degradingly promiscuous, some were delusional, some were generally unappealing and some were terribly ugly—or worse, stupid.

Homosexuality was no viable alternative. I'm sorry fellows, I like girls, Thank God I had little exposure to homosexuals in the prison and the mental health system and when certain aggressive types showed up, I had no difficulty fending them off.

So release day was also sex day. . . .

Afterward, it was also opera day. At Lincoln Center that evening, he bought a ticket without finding out what was being performed. It didn't matter to him that it was a rather obscure French work by Poulenc, with a libretto by Georges Bernanos, called *Dialogues des Carmélites,* about an aristocratic young woman during the French Revolution who becomes a nun to escape the chaos of the secular world, only to find that there is no escape. Bob wouldn't record how he felt about the opera's contemplation of fear and the heroine's struggle to find grace through religion and self-sacrifice. He registered only one thought as the music began: "Yes, I am really outside."

—

Bob Rowe hoped to write a book someday. Among the titles he rejected: *Snowflakes, Red Snowflakes, A Snowy Morning, One Snowy Morning, Beyond All Reason, The Solution.* He experimented with dedications, all of them to Mary, several of them quoting her description in her high school yearbook: "Capable, considerate, gracious." However, he never proceeded beyond the introduction, which he would rewrite repeatedly. In one draft he tried to explain the man he had been. "I would marry,

of course. I would have children. What is life without children? The trust
and admiration that shine out of the eyes of a fulfilled child is more precious than any value except perhaps the love of a good woman. I hoped
to give away a daughter in church, to visit a son at his college dorm. If I
died in bed, I would naturally be surrounded by grieving loved ones
mourning the passing of a faithful husband and a responsive father, a dad,
a loyal friend. This was not an idle dream. It was built into my nature by
my religious background, my schooling, and by my culture. The culture
of the Depression, World War II, Korea. Things did not work out that
way."

In another draft, he quoted from the *Rubaiyat* of Omar Khayyam, mistakenly attributing the lines to Oscar Wilde. Bob loved movies, so it is
possible that he remembered the opening credits from the 1945 film version of *The Picture of Dorian Gray,* which conclude with the passage
from the *Rubaiyat.* He was considering these words as an epigraph for the
book he would never write.

> I sent my soul through the Invisible,
> Some letter of that After-life to spell,
> And by and by my Soul returned to me,
> And answered, "I Myself am Heav'n and hell."

———

Jack O'Shaughnessy often worried that Bob was going to kill himself
when he got out of Creedmoor. He believed this was distinctly possible, even though the last time he'd seen Bob—up at Mid-Hudson, before
Nellie died—he'd been reading psychology books and talking about
switching over to criminal law to defend people with mental problems.
But Jack had suspected Bob's talk about the future was a ruse to fool the
psychiatrists so that he could get out and finish the job he'd begun the
night he killed his family.

Not long after his release, Bob called Jack and asked if he could come
over. That was fine with Jack. He was alone and could use the company,
and he'd always felt bad about not going to see Bob again after Nellie
died. They stayed up all night talking. Jack felt as if they were in college
again, the two of them alone together, arguing politics and religion and

the future of the world without a glance at the clock. Bob mentioned that he'd like to go back to practicing law. He said that while he was at Creed-moor, he'd worked with some of the doctors and had written an article about the rights of mentally ill patients. Jack realized that Bob's pro-fessed desire to be readmitted to the bar hadn't been a ruse at all. He re-ally thought he could do it.

As Bob explained his plan for getting his license back, the words rushed out of him like a surging creek after a spring thaw. Yet the torrent didn't carry a single mention of his family or what he had done. That didn't seem strange to Jack. He didn't talk about Nellie's dying, either.

By morning, Bob was ready to prowl and Jack was up for anything. Just as they had when they were students, they trekked into Manhattan and ended up at the Marble Collegiate Church on Twenty-ninth Street, where Norman Vincent Peale had drawn crowds of thousands with his optimistic sermons back in the 1950s. Bob couldn't stop exclaiming how beautiful it was as they admired the church's stained-glass Tiffany windows and awesome chapels. In this confessional setting, Bob re-vealed that he had intended to kill himself as soon as he got out, just as Jack had suspected. But he said that when he was being transferred from Mid-Hudson to Creedmoor, shackled, waiting for the van to leave, he began leafing through a magazine someone had left there. Even when contemplating suicide an insatiable reader can be distracted by the writ-ten word. In this case, it was a religious publication distributed by the Unitarian church.

He wasn't really paying attention, was just thumbing through the mag-azine while he was waiting. But he was stopped by a short poem entitled "A New Person."

> Father, I am willing to be born again;
>   to be a new person, unstained by
>   old clichés worn out with use.
> The new beginning is what You ask of me.
>
> You will no longer let me cling to what is
>   over—finished—no longer wanted by
>   You, my soul, or by others.

> I will let go—
> I will to let it go:
> The old person passes, and the new has come!

He was so struck by the poem's possible meaning for him that he began to read it again. This time, he saw the author's name under the title and a chill went through his heart. The author was named Mary Rowe. He knew it wasn't his Mary, but that didn't undermine his belief that the poem was a message from beyond. Revelation, too, is in the eye of the beholder.

He tore out the poem and sent a letter to Mary Rowe, care of the magazine. In it, he explained the circumstances that had brought him to her poem, and how reading it had made him change his mind about killing himself.

She answered, saying she was happy to have been instrumental in saving him from suicide. Reinforcing his sense that his finding the poem was a fated event, she told him she, too, was a Lutheran, a deaconess. She was an old woman and had been toiling in the vineyard of the Lord for many years and hadn't been sure that she'd accomplished anything. Now, finally, she'd been rewarded by saving him.

The next time Jack saw Bob, after he had settled into an apartment, Jack saw the poem by Mary Rowe, framed, sitting on Bob's desk, not far from a picture of Bob's Mary. Later, when Bob would remarry, the framed poem would hang on the living room wall.

CHAPTER 18

Father, Mother, Sister, Brother

As Colleen and Don Cassidy drove back to St. John's from the dinner with Bob, Don said quietly, "I want to talk to you about something."

His sober tone surprised Colleen after such a spirited evening. He began by telling her that Bob had been a successful lawyer with a wife named Mary, a lovely woman, who had also been a friend of Don's. There were three children; one of them was handicapped. Don told her how Bob had had a nervous breakdown and left his job and stayed home with Christopher, the handicapped child, and began to feel like Christopher— helpless, useless, unable to function.

Colleen had spent much of her life playing tag with sorrow. She understood what it meant to feel like an outcast. Her natural empathy did not, however, prepare her for the punch line.

Her sigh must have come across like a gasp of horror, because Don immediately apologized. "I shouldn't have told you," he said.

"No," she said. "You should have."

Don explained that he had wanted Colleen to meet Bob because of her spiritual depth and sensitivity. He thought she could help Bob deal with "the tragedy." That's how Bob's friends would always refer to the deaths, never as homicides or killings or murders and never in the plural—as four individual events—but as part of a greater whole that included Bob: the tragedy.

Don asked Colleen to pray for Bob, and she readily agreed. Unlike many people who would hear Bob's story, Colleen didn't feel deceived by the warmth and intelligence and humor that had drawn her to him, or revolted by his past. She met the nightmare with mercy.

Bob was furious when he found out that Don had told Colleen.

Upon learning from Don how angry Bob was, she went to his apartment to tell him not to worry, that she wanted to be his friend.

Over and over, Bob said, "I told him he shouldn't tell you—who else did he tell?"

Colleen was distraught as she tried to think of how to make him understand that she wasn't going to judge him unfairly. Speaking impulsively, she distracted him from the spilling of his secret by telling him hers. Without hesitation, she offered him details of the shame that she'd entrusted only to her parish priest. Her mortification was the greatest gift she could offer.

Once she pulled out the stopper, the revelations poured out of her. She told Bob about her father, who had lost his job, having worked his way into management after starting off as a moving man. She told him how her parents had started drinking and didn't stop for years, or so it seemed to her. She told him she wasn't a leper like Thomas Covenant but that she felt like one.

Just as he had once succumbed to Irene Wagner when she told him that she too had a handicapped child, Bob responded immediately to Colleen's story. With protective tenderness, he began to ask her questions. Colleen felt as though Bob were trying to piece her together from the inside out, as if he wanted to see the connections among her mind, heart, and soul.

They talked for fourteen and a half hours that night. Somewhere in the middle, at around three in the morning, they went out into the cool October night for air. Bob insisted on walking by the edge of the curb. With exaggerated gallantry, he bowed and said, "In case a man with a lance should come by, I can save you." Exactly the right thing to say to a girl who lived in the distant past and longed to be saved.

They walked for a while in a silence that was comfortable despite the outpouring that had come before. Bob stopped and pointed at the sky. "That's Orion, the great hunter," he said with great emotion in his voice as he helped her find the points of the constellation. He told her that when he had shown Orion to his son Bobby—born the same year as Colleen, 1963—he had told the boy, "Whenever you see Orion, you'll know that I am thinking of you and loving you."

Bob looked at Colleen and said, "Now you are part of that."

Most of the stories he told that night were about Christopher, though he also talked about Mary, Bobby, and Jennifer. Colleen, who had spent much of her life absorbed in the lives of the saints and their suffering, readily consumed Bob's grief. She had no trouble reconciling his sorrow about the death of his family with the part he had played in it. She understood that it was Bob who had killed them, but she believed he wasn't responsible. He couldn't have been.

One of the books Colleen held dear was called *The Wounded Healer*. In it, theologian Henri J. M. Nouwen argues that personal suffering enables people to help others. That's how Colleen thought of herself and Bob—two wounded healers helping each other.

Later, she would respond to those who questioned their relationship with a question of her own: "Are you a person of faith?" She would insist that she told him her awful secrets because her religious beliefs required her to reach out to him.

That may have been true, but she was also smitten. A few hours after she returned home from their night of confidences, she wrote him a letter decorated with drawings of little happy faces.

"You helped me so much," she wrote. "Actually I think we helped each other. It's good to know you're not alone in your hurt and suffering. I know for me, I couldn't bear it without other people. Now I have a special person: You. . . .

"Tonight, when I look up at the stars and see 'the Great Hunter' I'll think of you. Think of me, the funny-looking one. . . ."

In the letter, she began mapping their future together, with the immediacy of someone who has made a decision, conscious or not, to make a commitment. She promised to help him find a teaching job, admonished him not to work too hard, and encouraged him to call her whenever he wanted to talk. "Bob, do you know what we have now? A beautiful friendship, signed, sealed and delivered," she wrote. "Know that I am always here or there for you. Somehow I know I can always count on you."

They slept together a week later.

Many people, Colleen realized, would think that Bob had, to use the old-fashioned phrase, taken advantage of an inexperienced and troubled young woman. She expected there would be those who said, derisively, that she was looking for a father figure. That was true enough, but wasn't a lover supposed to be a father, a mother, a sister, a brother? Bob would say that to her: "I'm your father, I'm your mother, I'm your sister, I'm your brother." She felt the same way toward him.

She didn't care what anyone said, because she didn't expect anyone else to understand what a happy sexual encounter could mean to someone like her, who had only unhappy associations with sex and who had assumed that her life would be a celibate one.

They were in his apartment, surrounded by his books and the seascapes he'd painted, when their hands touched. When Colleen, usually a careful and articulate storyteller, would describe this encounter, she would become so flustered that she would find herself in metaphoric overdrive. "There were fireworks I had never seen before, and they were there for him and for me. It was really like this, it was almost like a magnetic force. We didn't know how it all happened. This attraction, for both of us. I think at one point we just touched hands and the hands were like, for him and for me, like phew! Like electricity. We always used to say, 'Remember the hands! Remember the hands!' "

With the passionate tenacity of a new lover, she recorded her feelings in minute detail in letters to Bob. In the beginning, the correspondence was voluminous, at least from Colleen's end. Bob's pull was so powerful that she needed to write to him the instant she left him.

Oct. 8, 1984

My dear Bobby,

I'm sitting here in my little 2 × 4 boiler bedroom writing to you after 10 lovely hours of uninterrupted sleep. I was tired.

I went to that retreat meeting last night. Luckily I had three hours of sleep before I involved myself deeply in what was going on but all my thoughts kept coming back to you, you beautiful man. So I have been thinking.

First of all, I have to say you'll never lose me. Never be afraid of that! I said yes to you and to us a long time ago. I love you so very much. Where do we go from here? Let us size up the situation. We are two lonely and hurt people who shared our deepest suffering, who wanted to help each other and want to love each other. You've taken my loneliness away Bob.

Now let's talk about the romance aspect. First with what happened. You made me feel so beautiful, like a whole woman for the first time in my life. I wanted to give all of me to you and I know you wanted to give all of you to me but I had to think. If we are going to have this kind of relationship I think I have an answer for myself, which is part of my belief system, but I just had to sort it out.

Sex for me involves a commitment. I know it does for you, too. It's a sign of that commitment and it fosters and deepens that commitment. Of itself it is empty and shallow. In some strange way I know we are committed to one another and I know the bond we share is deep and powerful.

Now, back to your question of the other night. Can two people of the opposite sex share in a relationship without being sexually involved? The only example I can think of to date is St. Francis and St. Clare, they were two celibates who loved each other very much but were not sexually involved.

However, they were sexually attracted. The story goes that Francis once, in a heat of passion for Clare, threw himself in a thorn bush to suffer pain for his desire and came out unharmed and freed of his desire. Anyway, the saints had their problems, too.

What if we decide not to continue in a sexual relationship? Will we have to look for thorn bushes or take cold showers?

I know that I am physically attracted to you. You're beautiful. (I love the word beautiful.) You're a gentle and passionate lover, your gentleness means so much to me. I haven't met up with many gentlemen, as you well know. You are every bit an artist Bob Rowe. Lovemaking is a beautiful work of art filled with tenderness and soft passionate colors.

What about you Bob? Is your attraction for me as great? Would you have difficulty living without a sexual relationship for me? A question for both of us: Do we want to live without a physical relationship.

Love and people are complicated aren't they? At least we can never be bored, for every question there is another question.

The other night when I didn't sleep I just wanted to look at you. I love looking at you and thinking of you. It was good to see you at rest without all your troubles. I wish I could take them all from you but perhaps my love can make them bearable. You have opened a door in my life that I thought would not be open for me, Bob. I never thought I would be capable of loving any man, and I wanted so to love someone. Your love opened the door for me. I was a person who didn't trust anyone, not even myself. I trusted you completely.

I risked that trust and you didn't let me down. You are a lovely, beautiful man and I love you so very, very much. That's part of my thinking. I'll think some more and you know, we'll talk! Boy, can we talk!

I'll be looking forward to Saturday and I know we'll talk before that. Don't worry about anything, Bob. You've made me so very happy. I hope I've given you some happiness no matter what we decide.

We'll always have each other. I need you. I know you need me. Let's just love each other, you are special Bob Rowe.

Love always,
Colleen

Bob was far more circumspect than Colleen, for many reasons, among them his ongoing relationship with another woman. He had told Colleen about the woman, whom he had met shortly after his release from Creedmoor, and Colleen accepted Bob's description of the relationship—that he was drawn to the woman's children and the prospect of re-creating a family. Also, he appreciated the woman's tolerance of his history, which he had revealed almost immediately. But, he said, the woman was short-tempered and he was repelled by her frequent outbursts, which didn't conform to his notions of a happy family life.

Colleen was too young and too infatuated to fully consider the complex currents of Bob's emotions. He treated her as a protégée as well as a lover, and she was receptive to that, too. Though he wrote sparing responses to her outpourings, he studied her letters as an editor might, responding to them with extensive commentary in the margins. She regarded this as a sign of devotion, though it was his habit to annotate everything he read, a technique he'd picked up from *How to Read a Book,* a self-improvement classic by Mortimer J. Adler and Charles Van Doren. Bob read Colleen's letters more than once, and then composed his marginalia in different colors, dating each comment. Even in romance he retained his lawyerly style.

One theme emerges clearly from his annotations: He felt enormously guilty about having sex with Colleen, though he didn't specify whether the source of his guilt was the other woman, Colleen's youth, his past, or something even more elusive: salvation of his soul. Ever accommodating, she assured him regularly—and unreliably—that the sexual part was over.

She wrote to him on October 8, 1984, that his love "opened the door for me." He responded, several months later, in the margins: *What do you mean for love? The Greeks have seven, eight meanings. The English word is a dangerous abstraction.*

She wrote, "I trusted you completely."

Why? Why?

She wrote, "Let's just love each other, you are special, Bob Rowe."

And so are you and so are you. Your objectivity, solid common sense and caring suffuses all you do, distinguishes you from all other women I have ever met, but you are for someone or something else. I am sent to try and heal you. You are on your way.

Okay, great, I need you. . . . What do I do? A woman desirable comes along. I love this woman truly in a Christian way. But when she offers what she shouldn't, complicated syndrome here, I collapse like a cheap cigar box.

They would continue to debate the propriety of their involvement, though their determination to make their relationship strictly platonic never moved beyond the hypothetical.

Oct. 14, 1984

[Colleen to Bob]:

It's now 11:10 P.M. I'm sitting at my very organized desk with my thorn bush across from me. It's a very funny and happy present for me.

You're going to laugh at what I did. I attached a little note to it saying, If Francis and Clare can do it, so can Qan Wan Lo [Bob's name in Chinese, a lover's nickname] and Colleen. . . .

In the margins, Bob to Colleen:

Five months later and we can't and it is bothering me.

Same letter, Colleen to Bob:

I'm looking upon this as a very positive and memorable experience. Just think, now I know what the power of love is, how very awesome and beautiful that bond between a woman and man can be. I would have never known this had I continued the way I was going.

It's funny Bob, now I know without a doubt, one thing I want in my life. I want a lover and I want to be a lover and I want children, as many as I can have. This is one thing in my life I am sure of and you have helped me to discover this. You better believe that one of those many kids is going to be named Robert Thomas. Thank you.

In the margins, Bob to Colleen, five months later [March 5, 1985]:

Possibility of someone else is there. But today she has changed. Recently she has said she does not need children. She is giving up a family for me.

It's not a question of guilt. It's what I did. Me. I owe service to God . . . I cannot serve God carrying on an illicit relationship with Colleen. I cannot. It is hypocritical. But this is what lies below the surface.

Mary was 48, my God, what I took from her. She was rushing to the end with no rest, no rest. . . . What pressures she must have absorbed. But at the end of her life, at 60, 65, she could have rested perhaps.

Bobby was an exceptional person. I took everything from him. Everything. I took the best thing I ever created or met or experienced.

Jennifer, a beautiful flower, a little doll crushed like a bug.

Christopher, Christopher, Christopher.

Nov. 21, 1984

Dear Bobby,

Do you know what? We solved something. You know, from the beginning before we shared our stories and before we began, shall we say, our extracurricular activities, we tried to find a name for what we were to each other. Well we've got a name for us. We're family! And we have a future.

Do you know something else? We are special people. Not many people would be willing to accept the alternative we have accepted. We must be very special in our love; we are united in the fullest way in our infinite love for God and our Lord Christ Jesus.

The love we shared was so beautiful and I will never forget those precious moments we spent together. Orion will always make me smile at this memory. The affection we gave to each other was founded in a deep love. We wanted to express our love and compassion and express each other's hurt. I would have married you in a minute had life been fair. We are compatible in every way except for age. We do have each other and I thank my God for that. We are lucky.

. . . You keep mentioning when we struggled to solve this thing that you realized how weak you really were while I've learned a tremendous amount. Don wasn't the only one who thought I was a religious icon. I also had the same ideas about myself. I thought I was a pillar of the church, able to do without temptation with a single bound. Look! Up in the sky. It's a bird! It's a plane! No, it's Saint Colleen.

Saints are not made by withstanding temptation. They're human with all the same weaknesses and problems. I even began to doubt whether I was a sinner. But you see my dear friend I was a spectator in life. I only stood at the sidelines of life and wouldn't involve. My, have I gotten involved, myself in the action. I probably would have been safe from getting hurt but I doubt that salvation would have come to me because I wasn't testing out my Christianity. I wasn't living up to the potential the Lord God placed within my being. A test of our Christianity is the struggle we're going through in this very human situation.

Bob, dryly, in the margins: *We both get zero.*

—

Even after Bob made a complete break with the other woman, a few months later, his romance with Colleen continued to be a secret. But eventually Colleen wanted Joan Scarlett to know about Bob and to approve of him, and he consented. Joan was glad to hear that Colleen was seeing someone. She knew Colleen had had a difficult time readjusting when she'd returned from the Franciscans and that a lot of people at church had been happy to see Colleen get her comeuppance. They'd been jealous of her for the responsibility she'd been given by the priest and gloated when she dropped out of the religious order. Joan was just glad that Colleen was home, and wanted her to be happy.

She knew that the man Colleen would bring over would be somebody special, but she couldn't have anticipated the nature of Bob's uniqueness. The first surprise was Bob's age—mid-fifties, the same as Joan. That threw her a little, but she knew plenty of people who had married a generation up or down, and not all of the senior types were old lechers. But when Colleen revealed Bob's history, Joan felt sick. She would never do anything to hurt Colleen, so she didn't tell her not to bring this man into her home. But she couldn't shake the fear that settled on her. Though she was someone who believed in absolute honesty, she decided not to tell her husband, also named Bob. They'd been married thirty years, and she thought she could anticipate his every reaction, but this was a new situation. She'd have to see for herself whether Colleen had lost her marbles.

As Bob Rowe sat talking at her kitchen table, Joan's fear evaporated. She was surprised at her own reaction. As a police lieutenant's daughter, she was a law-and-order person and believed in the death penalty. But here she was, with no high school education, no college education, and this man engaged her in conversation as if she were his equal, or even his better. She liked him.

She liked him more and more as she saw how Colleen was blossoming. All of a sudden she was wearing makeup and showing up in capes and berets. Now she walked like a girl, talked like a girl, and dressed like a girl. She was planning to go to law school. More significantly, she had overcome the numbing shyness that she'd used as a barrier between herself and the men who leered at her or worse. She'd been afraid to talk to strangers on the telephone or to enter a store alone. Now she seemed self-reliant, even confident.

—

Five years would pass before they married. It was a period of meta-morphosis for both of them. Bob converted to Catholicism, of his own volition and without Colleen's urging, surprising old friends like Jack O'Shaughnessy, who remembered Bob's youthful skepticism. But neither Jack nor Colleen nor any of the many psychiatrists who had examined Bob could explain the profound inconsistencies in his past behavior—any more than Bob himself could. His new religion was part of a necessary reinvention, a process that was not unfamiliar to him. In his earlier life, he and Mary and the mothers from the IHB had made similar alterations in perception and sense of self in order to deal with their children's handicaps. Now, he was the nonperson who had to adjust to his new circumstance.

Colleen was crucial to this unstated plan. Though she was willing—eager—to join Bob on his unusual journey, they proceeded cautiously toward marriage. Colleen believed they knew everything about each other: Bob had confessed to her his whorehouse escapade after his release from Creedmoor; he'd told her all about the woman he'd lived with before he met her (all of which was insignificant measured against the tragedy). Even so, there were many consultations with priests and friends, as well as with Bob's therapist, Stephen Teich, who would become Colleen's doctor as well. While he didn't consider their relationship to be an unhealthy one, exactly, he acknowledged that it took root in trauma. "They both had pain, they both had damage," he would say cautiously, "and they fit in a way that helped each other to heal."

Colleen would be Bob's only family. His brother, Kenneth, had made it clear that he wouldn't be part of Bob's second life. When Bob was about to be released from Creedmoor, he had been disappointed that the date was set for after Christmas. He'd looked forward to being with Kenny and Pat at their annual open house on Christmas Day. Bob often said that his family was everything to him and that the only family he had left was Kenny. Kenny told Bob later that it was just as well his release had been postponed, because it would have been difficult to be together on Christmas. One of his friends' wives, part of the regular group who came every Christmas, had told Ken and Pat, "If Bob is there, we're not showing up."

"That's an interesting reflection of 'the Christmas Spirit,' " Bob wrote in his journal. "If Christ returned to earth today he would probably be summarily destroyed—probably in the electric chair."

Kenny also told his brother not to count on restoring their old relationship. "Patricia doesn't want to have anything to do with you," he said.

Bob wrote that down, too. "It was good to get these views candidly from Kenneth. He does have one aspect that is appealing—to me at least. He is terribly frank. Sometimes that can be very helpful. I shouldn't put it in such a way that might indicate he doesn't have any other strengths. He has many. Actually he has potential to be a much more human person than he is. I love my brother very much."

Harvey Sackstein felt obliged to broker a reconciliation. He had met Kenneth and Pat Rowe through Bob and Mary and had become their friend and attorney. As he watched many of Bob's friends abandon him (though they may well have felt he abandoned them when he killed his family), Harvey began calling Kenny, urging him to renew contact with his brother. Kenneth agreed to meet Harvey and Bob at a diner in Bayside, Queens. The brothers didn't embrace, but they weren't hostile. Harvey didn't pay attention to the conversation, just to the tenor of it, which was friendly enough. Afterward, Harvey asked Kenny whether he planned to get together again with Bob, and he said, "I'll give it some thought." Though they would speak again by telephone, that was the last time the Rowe brothers saw each other.

———

Colleen and Bob were married on December 30, 1989, nine years to the day after Bob's release from Creedmoor, at a Catholic church in Brooklyn—an old German church that they had helped refurbish. Bob repainted an old statue of the Virgin Mary, and he and Colleen cleaned the altar's large wooden panels with Murphy's Oil Soap and then varnished them. As they worked, Colleen sang "Ubi Caritas," a Latin hymn—"Where There Is Charity."

She loved her wedding, even though of the eighty people who came to the ceremony in Brooklyn and to the reception at a Chinese restaurant in Queens, only a handful were from Bob's previous life. Harvey and Iris Sackstein and Jack O'Shaughnessy and Don Cassidy were there, but Cassidy's wife was busy that day, as she always was when Don got together with Bob and Colleen. Many other former friends had dropped away—including Bill Campbell, the lawyer who had hired Steve Scaring for Bob.

It was the wives who kept their husbands away from Bob, according to Silvio Caso, who didn't go to the wedding for that very reason. His mother-in-law, who had played host to Bob and Mary and their children on many occasions in upstate New York, referred to him as "the murderer." Even Silvio's wife, who had herself spent plenty of time in mental hospitals as a patient, told him she was afraid of Bob. Silvio would say, in front of Colleen, "If I died, Robert Rowe would have been the last guy in the whole goddamn world she would marry because of the fear he would do it again."

Silvio was loyal to Bob, but he understood that fear. Not long after Bob was released from Creedmoor, the two of them took a trip to New Orleans. They rode an Amtrak train called *The Crescent*. Silvio packed a little overnight bag with fresh shirts, clean underwear, toiletries—the ordinary things people take with them on trips. Bob brought these things plus a huge suitcase filled with textbooks, which he read all the way down and during every minute they spent awake in their motel room in the French Quarter. This was characteristic of the Bob he had always known, but it didn't stop Silvio from feeling apprehensive about staying in a room alone with a man who had just been released from a mental institution after killing his family. He wouldn't say it to Colleen for a long time, but he always wondered what had prompted her to become friendly with Bob, to fall in love with him, and then to marry him, all the while knowing what he had done. He didn't understand Colleen, but he thought she had guts.

At least Bob was truthful, which is more than many men could say.

"He was up-front with Colleen," said Silvio, who didn't know that Don Cassidy had made it impossible for Bob to be secretive. "He never lied. He was an honorable person."

—

Colleen and Bob settled into routine with remarkable ease. Friendly notes on the refrigerator documented their preoccupation with laundry detail, getting the car fixed, back problems, house pets, dieting. "Bobby, I need you around for a long time," wrote Colleen. "Think thin."

He responded in kind. "Colleen my Queen. I couldn't finish this article. Read it. It seems to have some info on your back problem. Let's solve the back situation. I left the cats in the bathroom. I will call you."

Though their written correspondence naturally dwindled after they moved in together, Colleen continued to express herself most fluidly in letters. "I wanted to tell you how much I love you and how much I appreciate your helping me to develop into the woman I've become," she wrote. "Thank you also for helping me make it to law school and through law school. I would have copped out without you.

"I can't believe how much I've changed. I can talk to others without being afraid. I can disagree, take a position, reason, not allow people to step all over me and most of all I can love a man. You. You, Bob, are all important to me so long as we both exist in this world. I want to be together in good times and in bad times. When I look at a baby I think how precious the life of each person is . . ."

Colleen was in awe of Bob's energy and breadth of interest. She often found him awake and busy at three in the morning, usually reading or painting. He serenaded her on the ukulele with Rudyard Kipling's "Gunga Din," which he had set to music. He wrote stories in different styles and voices for the parish magazine. One month he'd write a meditation on the prison system, then he'd do a funny piece about a memory-improvement course, then he'd write a story about a man with a handicapped brother. In two years he produced more than fifty articles and short stories. He pushed her relentlessly through law school, more intent than she was on her obtaining her license. She was happy to be one of his projects, a subject for his pen. She loved his elegant script, developed in an era when students were trained in the Palmer method and fine handwriting was a mark of distinction. She kept every note, every poem.

> Dear You,
>> As I stood on this crest cold and alone
>> I was suddenly joined by a dog named Bone
>> We two looked into the swirling mist
>> To see our friend approach.
>> To see Colleen the velvet fist
>> Arrive in a Christmas coach.
>> It was loaded with gifts and goodies
>> And all kinds of things
>> We hurried to greet her
>> On our six little feet
>> I was a wonder but all Bone did
>> was eat eat eat.
>> Finally alone on Christmas Eve
>> I looked into your eyes of blue
>> And we started to swim
>> Because I realized I was a man who had everything.
>
> (I'm also intoxicated.)

The past lived with them, comfortably and uncomfortably. Colleen had assumed this with her wedding vows. Bob took her to visit Mid-Hudson and Creedmoor. She stood with him across the street from the house on East Sixty-fourth Street and listened to him reminisce about his life there with Mary and the kids. When they bought a kayak, they named it *King Kamehameha II*.

Bob groomed her as he had groomed Bobby. To encourage her to read, he left notes for her in the margins of books. He introduced her to Puccini and van Gogh and Monet, and charted her career with a fond determination that seemed more fatherly than husband-like. In a letter to a lawyer friend, he observed, "Colleen is better prepared to go through law school than practically anybody I have ever known. She has tremendous exposure to the law through you, me and her volunteer work—but basically she does not have the confidence she ought to have.

"I'm trying to get her into Moot Court but she is resisting. I want her as experienced as possible when she graduates so she can be thrown right into the court grinder immediately. Try to emphasize the importance of being able to get up and talk on your feet without telegraphing. (You know, she has a quality which she shares with both of us and most Irishmen; the English called it 'obstinate perseverance.')"

When they examined old family albums together, Colleen would search for a hint of the pressures that had led to catastrophe, but they were invisible. She saw only a happy family, smiling and vibrant. By the seventies, Mary had let her hair grow long; she looked exuberantly exotic sitting on the deck of their sailboat in a bathing suit, her hair blowing back. There was little Jennifer in her princess dance costume; there were funny pictures of Bob clowning around, dressed as Santa Claus, working in the garden. There was Christopher as a beautiful baby with red hair, and Bobby on ice skates, not a hint of the disease that put him on crutches for a couple of years and which Bob always feared might return with a crippling vengeance.

One day Bob showed her a note that had fallen out of his Encyclopedia Britannica. "To the senior trial attorney. Best wishes for the future and great expectations for a book written about you. Love, the family of the senior trial attorney." By then, Colleen recognized Mary's handwriting.

Like many married couples, Colleen and Bob repeated anecdotes so often that their memories sometimes seemed merged, so it didn't seem unusual to Colleen to fondly recall something Mary had done. She might refer to the time Bob came home to find Mary holding a broom while the cleaning lady was sitting on the bed telling her life story. "The woman needed someone to talk to," Mary had explained to Bob when he asked her what had been going on.

Colleen came to love Bob's family because it was his, and she participated in both his hagiography of them and his grief, though she never accompanied him to their graves. They were buried in the plot Bob and Mary had bought for themselves, which remained unmarked. Whenever she pressed him about buying headstones, he deferred, though he frequently visited the graves—always alone.

"You shouldn't see me there," he told Colleen. He rarely spoke of the killings, but sometimes she would find him alone in the middle of the night, clutching photographs of his children and sobbing.

He found the past waiting for him everywhere, often unexpectedly. What seemed like a harmless piece of pop culture could carry a terrible reminder. While watching *The Untouchables,* Brian De Palma's Chicago gangster movie, Bob and Colleen were holding hands enjoying the operatic action when Robert De Niro as Al Capone gathers his henchmen around a huge table in a lavish banquet hall. With good-natured swagger and an exaggerated smile, he exhorts the men to work together as a team, holding a baseball bat as a prop. Then, without warning, he lifts the bat over his head and with stunning violence cracks open the head of one of his lieutenants and splatters the white tablecloth with blood.

Bob took his hand from Colleen's and covered the lower part of his face.

"Are you okay?" she whispered, ready to leave.

He nodded, but she could feel the tension throughout his body as they watched the rest of the movie.

That was life with Bob. Ordinariness mingled with horror.

He established a number of businesses that required little more in start-up expenses than the cost of printing stationery and business cards: Motivational Outreach; Management Recruiters; Rowe Investigations. He volunteered as a hospice worker, a literacy teacher, a tutor for college interns from a criminal-justice program on Long Island. He helped prison inmates get in touch with lawyers and medical services. But he lost his job at an investigations agency after someone remembered who he was, and the New York City Board of Education rejected his application for a teaching license because of his history. He tried to become a teacher at private schools, which didn't require Board of Ed certification, sending out hundreds of résumés, and then left two months after he got a job at a parochial school because he couldn't adjust to the early-morning schedule (or to being the only man on the staff or the low pay).

"I have felt for many weeks that nothing I can do will work out," he told Colleen in a letter written at five o'clock one morning. "It is a loss of faith. I feel as though I am being sucked into a vortex and that I am helpless. It can only end in a public institution. This is like going to hell again."

A small incident had instigated his panic: He'd lost Colleen's camera and a leather case he loved. When he told Colleen, she shrugged it off. "They are only things," she said.

Not to Bob. "Their loss is symbolic to me," he told her in a note. "It has become a focal point: nothing seems to go right. I go one step forward and three steps back." He continued:

> It was terrible. I tried to pray. Nothing. I prayed to the Virgin Mary. Even to Damien [the nineteenth-century priest who lived among Hawaiian lepers and who was Bob's favorite saint]. I tried to read. No good. I read the Bible, the Lives of the Saints, but nothing helped. It is a terrible feeling. Like you are going over a waterfall into a black hole. This is when I need God but I do not have a good relationship with him.
>
> Then I take out all your pictures and look at them one by one. You are such a cutie pie and such a fine person. God was very good when he sent you to me because I need you very much. I will never leave you . . . I am looking at your picture now. Even though you are sleeping, I know that there is someone who cares for me above everything else. Isn't it wonderful to be loved like that? Thank you very much.

Colleen would write Don Cassidy a letter to thank him for introducing her to Bob. He called her immediately to thank her for the letter because, he told her, he had often wondered how she felt about how it had all turned out. He assured her that when he'd decided to introduce them to each other, he had hoped Bob would find in Colleen a sympathetic ear, someone eager to grapple with the most profound moral questions. He had never expected their relationship to become anything more than a friendship. Don told her he had often wondered if she resented him for being the catalyst for their romance. In her letter, she said that she never regretted a moment of her life with Bob, even though it was difficult—and Colleen, who was precise in her language, was deliberately understated in her assessment of her life with Bob. When you lived with someone with Bob's past, she observed, you became acutely aware of the difference between difficulty and calamity.

CHAPTER 19

Real Life

The mothers from the IIID thought they understood why Bob Rowe had done what he did. It had occurred to more than one of them that the only way out was through death. If Bob had killed himself too, they might have felt sympathy. Instead, they felt horror. As they saw it, having erased fate's mistake, Bob proceeded to rewrite his story, positioning himself as a victim of insanity entitled to start over again, then generously giving himself a new, young wife. When they heard that he was released from the mental hospital less than three years after the killings, they felt the world was judging them once again: Were children like theirs—and their mothers—expendable?

"I suppose if you really follow Christianity, you're going to say, Okay, we've got to give the guy another chance," Silvia White told the group. "But I have a little bit of conflict with this. I really don't feel this way."

She felt that insult had been piled on top of horror, and the others agreed. But they were stronger than they had been. They'd been knocked flat by God, by providence, by the failure of medical science—lay the blame where you will—and they had picked themselves up. Bob Rowe and the judicial system were trying to flatten them again, but they understood more about themselves and their children now. So what if they were undervalued in the human marketplace? They had come to know that self-worth was subject to daily fluctuations, inflated and depressed by the events of a particular day in an individual life.

There were questions of guilt. Could they have helped prevent Mary's death? Worse, had their own occasional fantasies of destroying themselves or their children somehow filtered into Bob Rowe's consciousness? But there was also the unspoken satisfaction of realizing that they, the lowly mothers, had been the Darwinian victors in their small chapter in human evolution. They had adapted better than the men.

Mady Gaskin could have said good riddance to Leonard, Jr., when he ran away from home. Instead, she realized how much she loved him. He hadn't known what to do with himself after he got out of high school, twenty-two years old and technically an adult, still neither here nor there. He had grown up to be tall and slender, an imperfect reproduction of his father, with strong traces of Leonard, Sr.'s, good looks and charm but all of it slightly off-kilter. When Mady called the police and they laughed and told her that's what boys his age did, she didn't feel like explaining that he wasn't like boys his age.

Mady was frantic. She'd get in the car and cruise up and down Forty-second Street, in the Times Square area, where in those days depravity was distilled to its terrifying essence, one peep show after another, the whole mess avoided by anyone with anything to lose. Which is why she thought Leonard, Jr., might be there. But she didn't find him there, or at any of the programs for the blind that she called, thinking he might take refuge somewhere he'd been before. She tossed aside her precious privacy and told her colleagues at the Board of Education about him, ordering them to get in touch with her wherever she was if her son called, even if she was with the chancellor. But Leonard, Jr., never called.

It was the worst time in her life, even worse than when Leonard, Jr., was born, with all his troubles. At least then she'd been able to put her arms around him and try to help him. Now he was telling her she couldn't help him, that he had to do it himself.

And he did. For three years he didn't speak to his family at all, he just wandered and hung out. Even at his lowest, Leonard, Jr., found people he could think of as friends for a while, especially in bars where the standards were low. He'd always been taken care of and didn't know how to take care of himself. People stole his things if he turned his back for a second. He was filthy.

But gradually, he became surprisingly competent. Slow as he'd been at math and reading and history, on the street he found his subject. He could parse the language of the homeless; he snapped up the geography and the sociology. He used his old connections at the Lighthouse for the Blind to hang out there when there wasn't anywhere else to go; he learned how to watch out for the cops at Penn Station when they'd come around to chase him and his buddies. He adapted. He learned how to play chess, and it turned out he had a knack for the game, so he hung around the clubs in the Village, hustling games. But one day he decided he'd had enough. He'd accepted the fact he wasn't going to have a life like everybody else's, but he wanted something better than this. He went home and let his mother help him.

—

Adaptation took many forms. In 1981, when Elyse was ten years old, Ellen and Al Alboher sued Parke-Davis, the manufacturer of Dilantin, the anticonvulsant drug Ellen had been taking to control her "shakes" when she was pregnant with Elyse. Since Elyse was a baby, attorney friends had urged Ellen and Al to sue, because at the time of Ellen's pregnancy, Dilantin carried no warnings about possible adverse effects on pregnant women. Back then, Ellen wasn't prepared to get on a witness stand and relive her pregnancy and the birth of her child without eyes. But as Elyse grew older and it became clear that her problems were neurological as well as visual, Ellen began thinking about the future. Elyse was too bright to spend her life in workshops, but she would not be capable of competing with blind college graduates (and half of *them* wouldn't be able to find jobs).

She took Elyse to one pediatric neurologist after another, none of whom could diagnose the girl's mental condition. But one of these doctors, upon hearing that Ellen had taken Dilantin, pulled out his copy of the *Physicians' Desk Reference* and pointed out that there had been a change. The PDR now warned that the medication could cause birth defects.

The trial lasted two weeks. The jury awarded Elyse $7 million, but the Albohers settled for much less, afraid they would lose on appeal. Like everything associated with Elyse, the outcome was bittersweet. Ellen was happy to know that her daughter would be provided for—the payments would come steadily throughout her lifetime—but the money wouldn't give Elyse eyes or normal neurological functioning. Ellen's child was still blind and always would be, unless there was a miracle. That was Ellen's secret hope—that one day there would be a miracle and with the settlement money Elyse would be able to afford to buy it.

—

Silvia White had always expected her blind daughter, Liz, to be self-sufficient, and Liz met that expectation. When she was sixteen she was traveling alone on the subway, and was injured only once, emotionally, when a stranger dropped a quarter into a ceramic cup she was carrying because her backpack was full. At eighteen she went to college, right on schedule. Liz wanted to be treated like everyone else, which didn't mean she wanted to be the *same* as everyone else. She didn't necessarily want to see, because wanting the impossible was a waste of time. Like her mother, she was a pragmatist.

But in 1983, when she was twenty years old (the same age Bobby Rowe would have been had he been alive) and a slight, pretty young woman, Liz read an article about an ophthalmologic surgeon who had found a way to successfully reattach retinas in cases that sounded similar to hers. Without hesitation she decided to fly to Memphis, where the operation had taken place, to find out if the doctor could do the same thing for her.

"I've got this great idea," she told her roommate. "I'll take Shawna [her dog] and we'll go to Memphis, and who knows! Maybe I'll come back and be able to see."

The immediacy of her reaction surprised her. It wasn't as though she had ever fantasized (much) about waking up in a hospital recovery room and having the bandages on her eyes removed and receiving the miracle of sight. Yet, like many blind people, she had always used the language of sight. "Can I see that?" she would say. "Show that to me." And the idea of color had always fascinated her, especially when she was little. Red was a special favorite. She just liked to say it: red. But like Professor Milligan, the blind philosopher, she didn't miss the pleasures of sight nearly as much as she felt the dislocation of living in a sighted world.

Still, when she read about the Memphis ophthalmologist, she felt the stirrings of hope—a disturbing yet exhilarating sensation. Once hope came into the picture, she felt she had no choice but to try.

Much as she didn't like to, she turned to her family for help. She knew they would oblige and that would always be both incredibly comforting and irritating, because it would turn into an obligation for her. She left the dog with her parents and went with her sister Judy, next oldest to her and Madeleine. Judy lived in Washington, which was more or less on the way. They drove to Tennessee, stopping at Graceland to pay homage to Elvis.

The visit with the doctor was brief.

"I can't do a thing," he told Liz. He explained that he had only operated on infants and very young kids—up to seven years old—who still had retinas to attach. In Liz's case, there was nothing left. Cataracts covered the front of her eyes; her corneas had decomposed. There was no retina to attach, only scar tissue marking the spot, like a lake in a volcano crater. As he talked, he showed pictures to Judy to illustrate. Liz got the idea.

It was terrible to hear. She hadn't expected to be so disappointed. Hoping had made her vulnerable in a way she hadn't anticipated. If she had been only wishing, it wouldn't have been any more devastating than, say, not winning the lottery—you didn't really expect to win the lottery. But reading about the successful operations, Liz had allowed herself to believe that hope was warranted. And hoping had led to wanting—desperately.

Yet, before going to Memphis, she'd said to her roommate, "It would be cool if the operation worked, but would I be crazy if I said no?"

Her roommate, who could see, looked at her and said incredulously, "You'd say no?"

"I might," Liz said. "Who wants to shake their world?" Did she really want the bandages to come off and be flooded by sensations that had no meaning to her? She was a competent blind adult. Did she want to become a child again?

She always wondered what she would have said if it had been offered. She really believed she might have said, "No, I think I found what I came for."

But she wasn't given a choice. After the hurt wore off, she began to wonder what disappointed her more—being told that she wouldn't be able to see or being told there was no hope.

—

In 1980, Edith Patt left the Industrial Home for the Blind after twenty-two years. She wanted to try something else before it was time to retire, and she was almost certain that her decision was not related to the guilt she carried about recommending the Rowes as Jennifer's adoptive parents.

The killings had been a transforming event for her and for a number of the women from the mothers' group. Now Edith felt the power of a blood tie with the women—because of proximity and because of blood spilled—that she'd previously thought of as a fraternal bond (you never heard of blood *sisters*). They were no longer clients and counselor but friends, still together even though the mothers had completed their ten-year fund-raising commitment to the IHB and their children had all gone their own way. When one of the women had something she needed to discuss, she would call Edith or one of the other mothers, who would pass the word along, and within a day they would arrange a time to get together.

Now Edith understood why, decades after World War II, her husband, Ray, never missed the annual reunions of his army battalion, even though most of the other men were from the South or the Midwest, and not Jewish—and Ray tended to divide the world into Jew and Gentile. He felt this powerful link to his army buddies even though he had become legal counsel to B'nai Zion, an organization whose bottom line was Jewish solidarity and whose ranks began to fill with Holocaust survivors after the war.

Edith liked joining Ray at those army reunions, and felt more at home with the Gentile women than she did with the Holocaust survivors at B'nai Zion. She found she had a great deal in common with the wives from Tennessee and Kentucky. Many of them were, like her, also in the helping professions, and they worried about the same kinds of things she worried about: how their children were doing in school, what they liked to cook. *Weibishe zachen*—wives' matters—she called their conversations, using the Yiddish expression with deliberate irony.

She could have discussed these homely matters with the B'nai Zion women as well, but she didn't. She preferred the company of the platoon wives, because they aroused no conflict in her. Because their husbands had fought together, she felt (accurately or not) that they regarded her as just another American wife. They didn't delve into questions of religion or philosophy; their commonality was taken for granted. This camaraderie and acceptance thrilled Edith, for whom being Jewish had almost no religious meaning. It was just another way of feeling alienated. With the platoon wives, the subject never came up.

With the B'nai Zion wives, being Jewish was *the* subject. Edith was in awe of the Holocaust survivors, who were struggling to become American, but she couldn't identify with them. She studied American history, not the Torah; she ran an experimental kitchen, not a kosher one. But these differences didn't reach the core of the matter. She didn't think she had it in her to survive what they had survived. They made her uncomfortable, because she didn't need another reminder of her own weakness.

It would occur to her that the mothers' group had more in common with the camp survivors than with the platoon wives. Like the survivors, the mothers were bonded by a common sorrow that Edith couldn't really be part of. She admired their resolve, but she didn't identify with it. She thought of herself as too lazy to do battle with fate.

To herself, she admitted that she would probably have kept away from the mothers' group if it hadn't been her job to make a connection. It wasn't necessary or appropriate for her to be friends with them. They needed her help, not her friendship. She could direct them to schools and social-service agencies and could listen to their complaints and yearnings, but she felt that because of her professional role—she was their social worker—she couldn't be their friend no matter how close she got to them. So the friendships she developed with them after the killings surprised her more than anyone.

After leaving the IHB, she became the head of social work at the New York Institute for the Education of the Blind in the Bronx, which operated a boarding school for blind children Mondays through Fridays. On weekends, the children went home to their parents. Many children who had gone to the nursery school at the IHB would continue their education at the Institute, among them Elyse Alboher and Anne Mauro and Phyllis Roth's two daughters.

Not long after she arrived at the Institute, Edith became aware of a persistent friction between the teachers and the parents. The teachers complained frequently about how the parents were interfering and how the parents didn't really grasp what was going on with their children. "We have them all week; they have them only on the weekends" was the theme of the complaints.

Edith would think, Yes, they have them only on the weekends—and for a lifetime. She decided to give the teachers some insight into the pressures weighing on the parents. For the first time in years, she brought out the Rowe tape—the recording that had so impressed the mothers' group when they first heard it.

The voices of Bob and Mary Rowe hadn't lost their power to grab an audience. The teachers at the Institute listened guiltily as Bob Rowe talked about the insensitivity of doctors and teachers, thinking perhaps of their own insensitivity in dealing with the less articulate parents who regularly appeared before them with similar complaints. They were impressed by the couple's perceptiveness and candor. Edith could see on the teachers' faces that Bob and Mary could still help other people realign their thinking about handicapped children and their parents.

There was a buzz of excitement in the room after the tape ended as the teachers began the process of self-evaluation. As they planned how to modify their reactions the next time they were confronted by an unhappy parent, Edith walked among them passing out pieces of paper.

When the teachers read what she had given them, the mood in the room changed swiftly from receptiveness to revulsion, as though they had bitten into a lovely cake and found it crawling with worms.

"How could you do this to us?" one of them asked angrily, waving the photocopies of news articles.

There was the *Daily News* headline that had brought the news to Bob Rowe's old friend Jack O'Shaughnessy: SAY DAD KILLED WIFE AND 3 KIDS. There was the follow-up feature in *The New York Times:* A BROOK-LYN FAMILY'S LONG STRUGGLE ENDS IN TRAGEDY.

"I wanted you to know that people suffer—that you never know how much they suffer," Edith replied calmly. "This was a model family."

"How could you use such an extreme case to make a point?" someone asked. "These things don't happen in real life."

CHAPTER 20

The Leper

In 1873, the Belgian-born missionary who called himself Damien (after an ancient physician saint), the man Bob Rowe would look to for guidance, took up residence in the Kalawao leper colony on Molokai, a sparsely populated and remote island in the Hawaiian chain. Kalawao had been settled after Hawaii passed a segregation law in response to a decades-long leprosy epidemic. The colony was built on a natural prison—a stony promontory squeezed between the sea and the base of a fifteen-hundred-foot-high cliff. In the winter, the surf was so rough that boats couldn't land for a month at a time. At other times of the year, the water was treacherous even when it appeared to be calm, because sharks swam there.

Father Damien would spend the last sixteen years of his life among the lepers of Kalawao—organizing schools, cleaning and dressing wounds, overseeing the replacement of makeshift shacks with sturdier buildings. Finally, he himself contracted leprosy. Four and a half years later, he died at the age of forty-nine.

In his biography of Father Damien, Gavan Daws described life on Kalawao: "The simplest things, the liveliest and most harmless of pastimes and entertainments, were touched with horror. The musicians for whom Damien made flutes out of old coal-oil cans played with only two or three fingers. Boys running in friendly competitive races toiled along on stumps of feet. Damien said of one young runner that he had failed to toe the mark; and it was true, the boy had no toes. At Kalawao, all jokes were black."

The same year that Damien moved to Kalawao, a Norwegian scientist, Gerhard Henrik Armauer Hansen, would discover *Bacillus leprae,* a breakthrough in the study of bacterial disease. Hansen's studies refuted the centuries-old notion that leprosy was hereditary rather than contagious, making the disease much more frightening to Western colonialists. "If leprosy was in fact contagious, and if—as Damien's life and death among the Hawaiians seemed to show—the contagion was capable of passing between races, from dark-skinned man to white-skinned man, then perhaps Western imperialism was creating an empire of leprosy, in which Westerners themselves might be consumed," observed Daws.

Bob Rowe became obsessed with Damien's story, looking for congruity with his. He handily found geographic unity with his own parentage: a *Hawaiian* leper colony; a *Scandinavian* scientist. He found a physical resemblance, though Damien was dark and he was light, because Damien too had been stocky and athletic (before he withered). He found significance in the fact that Damien had died at forty-nine, almost the same age Bob had been when he'd destroyed his family. He found spiritual parity in his metaphoric and Damien's actual leprosy. "I feel like a leper," he would tell Colleen.

Yet he was well aware that no one was likely to nominate him for sainthood. He knew there were plenty of people who regarded Robert Rowe as the man who had cracked under the pressure of raising a handicapped child, killed four people—his own family—and then beat the system. He knew there were those who asked: How could he get away with this?

But with his unswerving sense of self-preservation, he would rephrase the question: How could this have happened *to me*? He had asked the question before, when Christopher was born, but then he was incontestably a victim, even if only of an accident. He didn't acknowledge that it was one thing to be struck by lightning but quite another to be the lightning bolt.

He looked for answers everywhere, but mainly in the books he bought even when there was no money. Colleen once counted the books that he'd crammed into the apartment just to see how many there were. There were 3,500, and Bob had read almost all of them. It was easy to tell when he'd finished a book; with his habit of vigorously underlining text and scribbling marginalia, he left the physical imprint of intellectual struggle on everything he read—letters, novels, reference books, the Bible. These fragments of thought and emotion reveal a soul in turmoil but only hint at the nature of the turmoil.

Along with the story of Damien the leper priest, the Book of Job was a perhaps unavoidable focus for Rowe's restless mind and his equally restless pen. "Who among us has not been tempted to ask Job's questions?" the writer and scholar Cynthia Ozick asks in an essay about the Bible's righteous sufferer. "Which of us has not doubted God's justice? What human creature ever lived in the absence of suffering? If we, ordinary clay that we are, are not equal to Job in the wild intelligence of his cries, or in the unintelligible wilderness of his anguish, we are, all the same, privy to his conundrums."

Imagine Bob Rowe, with *his* conundrums, reading the story of Job, identifying with this very human soul brought to thundering life by an ancient poet, sustained into perpetuity by theologians, academics, and ordinary souls, all of them trying to come to grips with tragedy, whether universal or particular, the Holocaust or the death of a child or—in the case of Robert Rowe—a wife and children, killed by the father and husband who professed love and adoration for them.

The story of Job is believed to have been recorded 2,500 years ago, in the section of the Bible called the "wisdom books"—didactic literature that could be looked at as instructional manuals for the soul. The subject of Job is suffering; its question, Why does God allow it?

Job is a decent, successful, and God-fearing man chosen to be the guinea pig in an experiment organized by Satan, who, observing Job's good fortune—his wealth, his ten children, his charity—throws out a challenge to God. "Is it for nothing that Job is God-fearing? Have you not surrounded him and his family and all that he has with your protection? You have blessed the work of his hands, and his livestock are spread over the land. But now put forth your hand and touch anything that he has, and surely he will blaspheme you to your face."

Intrigued, God agrees that Satan should test his hypothesis. Does Job's righteousness hinge on his prosperity? Satan deploys the fury of man and nature to rip Job's life apart, with calamitous result: Marauders steal Job's working livestock and kill his herdsmen; lightning strikes his sheep and shepherds; and, most cruelly, a tornado destroys his ten children.

Despite his anguish over these dreadful events, Job proves Satan wrong. He remains faithful to God. "The Lord gave and the Lord has taken away," he cries out, after cutting off his hair, tearing his cloak, and falling to the ground. "Blessed be the name of the Lord."

The irritated Satan tells God the test wasn't severe enough. "Skin for skin!" he snorts. "All that a man has will he give for his life. But now put forth your hand and touch his bone and his flesh, and surely he will blaspheme you to your face."

God gives Satan permission to up the ante. Job is covered with boils "from the soles of his feet to the crown of his head." Though his wife rails at him, "Curse God and die," Job remains steadfast. "We accept good things from God; and should we not accept evil?" But he also implores God, "Why then did you bring me forth from the womb? I should have died and no eye have seen me."

Thus begins an elaborate, poetic, and unresolved inquiry into the nature of God and justice. Did Job do something to provoke God? And if not, then why is he being punished? (There is no answer. "The ways of the true God cannot be penetrated," writes Ozick. "The false comforters cannot decipher them. Job cannot uncover them.") God does, however, try to compensate Job for his suffering. "Thus the Lord blessed the latter days of Job more than his earlier ones. For he had fourteen thousand sheep, six thousand camels, a thousand yoke of oxen, and a thousand she asses. And he had seven sons and three daughters. . . . In all the land no other women were as beautiful as the daughters of Job; and their father gave them an inheritance among their brethren. After this, Job lived a hundred and forty years, and he saw his children, his grandchildren, and even his great-grandchildren. Then Job died, old and full of years."

Bob Rowe didn't regard the story of Job as an instructional exercise but as a personal message. He recognized himself in both incarnations of Job, as the man who had everything taken away from him by forces beyond his control and also as the man to whom life was restored. When Job laments, "I shall not see happiness again," Bob replied in the margins of his Bible, *"Not true."* When Job asks, "Why did I not perish at birth?" Bob asked, *"Or in Korea?"* When Job cries, "The Lord gave and the Lord has taken away," Bob demanded, *"By what rationale?"*

By law, he believed, he was no more responsible for the deaths of his wife and children than Job was for the decimation of his family. Mental illness was the culprit—his Satan. He wasn't guilty of anything. But he'd lost enough jobs and had been shunned by enough friends for him to realize that most people apparently didn't agree with him. (In fact, in 1984, the insanity plea in New York was changed from "not guilty" to "not responsible by reason of mental disease or defect.") He believed that he would be denied total absolution unless he could practice law again.

Certainly, financial considerations also played a part in his quest for reinstatement to the bar. His gross income in 1984 was $9,093.55, and it had been a struggle to earn that. However, the primary propellant was his desire to be welcomed back into society as a person of consequence, and with a clean moral slate. As he saw it, the state had exonerated him of murder because he was mentally ill and then the state declared him free of mental illness. He wasn't a criminal, yet he'd been stripped of his profession, like a criminal.

He needed his law license to convince himself as well as the world that he wasn't blameworthy for what he'd done. He'd realized this early on, at Mid-Hudson, when he told the indulgent but disbelieving Jack O'Shaughnessy that he wanted to get his law license back.

———

In 1985, there were 78,956 people licensed to practice law in New York State. A few years earlier, as part of a massive overhaul of the court system and in response to the boom in the law business, the regulation of attorneys had been transferred to the state from local bar associations—voluntary organizations that had been swamped by complaints against lawyers. The four appellate divisions, which made up the second tier of the state's court system, were put in charge of admission, suspension, disbarment, and reinstatement of attorneys. Each appellate division has a "character and fitness" committee, which interviews law graduates who want to become members of the state bar. There are also eight "grievance committees," which handle complaints and disciplinary proceedings against lawyers.

The grievance committee for the second and eleventh judicial districts oversees the behavior of lawyers practicing in the boroughs of Brooklyn, Queens, and Staten Island, and there were 7,188 lawyers in those districts in 1985. Many of the cases are petty—complaints against lawyers who file papers late, who charge too much for their services, who don't answer clients' phone calls. The more serious complaints usually involve lawyers accused of stealing from their clients. Most of the cases are dispensed with on paper, so the eight lawyers on the grievance committee for the second and eleventh districts rarely make an appearance in court.

It is an unglamorous job carried on in dingy headquarters on the twelfth floor of the Municipal Building in downtown Brooklyn, where the worn blue carpet is littered with scraps of paper, rubber bands, and dirty Band-Aids. Someone once tried, vainly, to brighten the grimy beige walls with worn posters of Impressionist paintings, the Gauguins and van Goghs competing with official exhortations against smoking and in favor of recycling. The staff refrigerator carries a hand-lettered plea on the door: PLEASE DO NOT HIDE YOUR FOOD IN BAGS SO WE FIND IT COVERED WITH MOLD TWO MONTHS LATER. LABEL YOUR FOOD WITH LITTLE POST-IT NOTES INSTEAD. (THANK YOU).

Working in these conditions, it was understandable that Mark DeWan, the thirty-five-year-old staff lawyer assigned to handle Robert Rowe's application for reinstatement, might become a little obsessive about Rowe. He had never seen anything like this case, and wasn't likely to again—not while processing claims of professional misconduct.

If DeWan had been a student of the Book of Job, he probably wouldn't have assigned the part of Job to Robert Rowe. The grievance-committee

lawyer more likely would have given Rowe the role of Satan, a provoca-
teur bent on undermining a system of belief. Instead of unleashing the
fury of nature to carry out his will, conjuring lightning and tornadoes and
bodily invasion to test man's faith, this contemporary Satan was attacking
the modern way: in court. The man who had killed his family had decided
to push the system's capacity for compassion to a previously unheard-of
limit.

DeWan didn't buy Rowe's basic assumptions: that a successful insanity plea was the same thing as innocence and that an insanity acquittee's
future should be unencumbered by his past; that there is no debt owed because there was no crime and there was no crime because there was no
volition; that legally, the four corpses must be seen as irrelevant. For
DeWan, the corpses were far from irrelevant. They hovered over this stew
of ethics, law, and psychiatry like the ghost of Banquo in quadruple. In
DeWan's view, Robert Rowe was a murderer. He had killed his wife and
three children, and that alone violated disciplinary rule 1–102(A)(6): "A
lawyer shall not engage in any other conduct that adversely reflects on his
fitness to practice law." But in the law, nothing was that simple, especially
when the defendant was a lawyer.

———

On October 27, 1978, the five justices of the appellate division had
suspended Robert Rowe's legal license under section 691.13 of the
Rules Governing the Conduct of Attorneys, which says, "Where an attorney subject to the provisions of section 691.1 of this part has been judi-
cially declared incompetent or involuntarily committed to a mental
hospital, this court . . . shall enter an order suspending such attorney from
the practice of the law, effective immediately and for an indefinite period."

As soon as he was released from Creedmoor at the end of 1980, Bob
believed that the suspension should be lifted. He was no longer confined
to a mental hospital and, according to his psychiatrists, he was no longer
mentally ill. But he was under court-mandated psychiatric supervision at
Creedmoor's outpatient clinic and would remain under supervision until
a judge ruled otherwise. Bob was aware that his case for reinstatement to
the bar would be much stronger when that happened.

At first he willingly went to the psychiatric sessions, but it wasn't long before he wanted to stop his biweekly visits, because he had little regard for his therapists. As an inpatient at Creedmoor, as part of his therapy, he had written an article in which he argued that state-appointed psychiatrists overmedicated patients in lieu of therapy. (The article, called "The Right to Refuse Treatment: Therapeutic Orgy or Rotting with Your Rights On," was published in *The Journal of Urban Psychiatry,* an in-house publication written primarily by Creedmoor doctors.) He had stopped taking psychoactive medication in 1979, a year before his release.

He didn't hide his disdain from the clinic doctors. He complained that they rotated in and out of the clinic frequently—even though he had seen one doctor consistently for more than two years. One of his therapists recommended that Bob continue treatment but with a psychiatrist of his own choosing, because "unless Mr. Rowe feels that he is a full partner in his own treatment rather than a victim upon whom psychotherapy is imposed, the benefit of treatment will be minimal."

Finally, in 1985, Bob called a legal adviser at Creedmoor to find out what steps he had to take to remove himself from state-mandated psychiatric care. He was told that his treating psychiatrists would have to recommend his release, and then the state commissioner of mental health would file an "application for discharge" on his behalf with the supreme court in Queens, where Creedmoor is located. The Brooklyn district attorney's office would be given the opportunity to contest the application, just as it had when he applied for release from the hospital. The process was arduous and could take several months, because the state hospital administrators would be reluctant to risk cutting the cord with a patient with Bob's history.

He knew he should wait to be discharged before he filed for reinstatement, but as months went by and the paperwork didn't come through, he grew impatient. He told himself that his being in treatment wouldn't matter, since so many people, including lawyers, are under psychiatric care (ignoring the fact that the *reasons* most people are under psychiatric care weren't nearly quite so dramatic or dangerous as his). On November 27, 1985, with the discharge issue unresolved, he filed his application for reinstatement.

Three months later, on February 28, 1986, the five justices for the Appellate Division, Second Department, Supreme Court, State of New York, followed the recommendation of their grievance-committee attorney, Mark DeWan, and rejected the Rowe application without a hearing. This was not unusual but rather the way that most grievances are handled. It is also where most grievances end. The Rowe case, however, was just beginning.

Bob immediately appealed the decision to New York's highest court, the Court of Appeals, which agreed to review whether he had been entitled to a hearing. Meanwhile, the discharge proceeding was limping along. In December, while he had been waiting for a decision from the Appellate Division, he received a telephone call from a lawyer at the state's Mental Hygiene Legal Services, offering his services, which would be free because of Bob's status as a quasi-ward of the state. Bob accepted the offer and then took an immediate dislike to the lawyer because he wore sneakers to court and his clothes were always mismatched.

Their relationship didn't improve as Bob became impatient with what he regarded as the lawyer's insufficient diligence. But who could match Bob's passion for his cause? He was a relentless advocate on his own behalf, working on three fronts: the reinstatement proceeding, the discharge case, and an appeal to the Board of Education's refusal to give him a teaching license. (All this legal maneuvering consumed the time and energy he might otherwise have devoted to a job. His annual income in 1986 dropped to $2,329.16.)

The Brooklyn district attorney's office objected to Bob's discharge from state psychiatric supervision—not surprisingly. So, once again, a judge ordered yet another psychiatrist to evaluate Bob Rowe's mental condition, by interviewing him and reading his psychiatric history, now as thick as a medical text.

On March 24, 1986, Dr. Lawrence Siegel concluded that court-mandated treatment should be continued. "Defendant continues to use somewhat maladaptive defense mechanisms in his day to day living," wrote Dr. Siegel in his report for the court.

Psychological testing done in May, 1985, revealed that the defendant's defenses were fairly rigid and that he used primarily repression and denial. Such defenses are not the most adaptive defenses.

Continued mandated out-patient treatment is recommended for two reasons. The first, and most important, is for continued surveillance of this defendant's mental condition. Individuals who have suffered psychotic breakdowns have an increased incidence of subsequent psychotic breakdowns. If the defendant has indeed suffered from a major depressive episode in the past (this diagnosis seems more consistent with the clinical facts than the diagnosis of schizophreniform psychosis given in the Creedmoor record) then he will have a thirty to forty percent chance of suffering a subsequent major depressive episode. While he does say he will seek psychotherapy in such a situation, it is not unusual for individuals who suffer from recurrent major depressions not to be aware that they are [in] need of help, even when they express a desire during a period of remission to seek psychotherapy should they become ill again.

The second reason that court mandated out-patient psychotherapy is recommended is for continued psychiatric treatment of the defendant. He makes it abundantly clear during examination that, were he not mandated to attend a clinic, he would not. This is consistent with his strong need to see himself as a well individual, and an inability to allow that he has underlying problems or difficulties. This is, further, consistent with the above-mentioned rigid defense mechanisms of the defendant. Although I would concur with Creedmoor that he is not likely to make full use of the therapeutic potential of such court mandated therapy, nonetheless, some progress might be made. One suggestion is that he be asked to attend group therapy where other individuals in the group would be more able to confront him about his personality characteristics, as opposed to an individual therapist, to whom he would be more able to deny that such characteristics exist.

In reviewing the record one finds that the instant offense occurred several months after his prior discontinuation of psychotherapy. He stopped seeing Dr. Distelman on October, 1977. The instant offense occurred in February, 1978. At the time of his stopping therapy, he and his wife both reported that he was doing well. At this time, although he appears to be doing well on the superficial level, it is recommended that he continue in therapy nonetheless.

The Siegel report infuriated Bob, who angrily refuted it by page and paragraph in a testy letter to his lawyer.

"As to Dr. Siegel's report," wrote Bob:

Page 2, Paragraph 1: My daughter was not adopted because of "fear of another defective child being born." It was to insure that all chance of that happening would be negated. Dr. Siegel seems to be implying a congenital defect in my family. The geneticist found just the opposite but Siegel left that out.

Page 2, Paragraph 2: I worked for Allstate 20 years and was a manager for 16 years. I did not have to change my job. I chose to change my job. He implies I was forced out of Allstate. Not true.

Page 2, Paragraph 4: Distelman was discontinued because I had complained innumerable times that the medication was too heavy; I was falling asleep on the job and at home. I am not surprised if that is not in his record.

Page 3, Paragraph 4: "While in the hospital, he was generally distant from others, however, he presented no management problems on the whole." Dr. Siegel apparently doesn't realize that in a forensic, locked unit you keep your distance if you want to stay alive. And I presented no management problem, period.

Page 3, Paragraph 5: Siegel keeps making gratuitous remarks: I am not "generally" cooperative. Actually, I have been completely cooperative. If there is anything in the Creedmoor record to the contrary, it is incorrect.

Page 4, Paragraph 4: I do not have great difficulty estimating my income. I, frankly, did not consider this item relevant to my mental condition. I made this quite clear to him and he reports it as though I am a mathematical birdbrain.

Page 4, Paragraphs 5, 6: I had told Dr. Siegel that Christopher's condition, his effect on my wife and the rest of my family was a unique stress. If Christopher had not been born, I would not have had the breakdown. I was particularly sensitive to sick children. When I worked as an orderly in a hospital while in school I had difficulty in pediatrics, or in handling sick children. He conveniently left all of this out and the many details I gave him on stress with Christopher, i.e. the patterning, the physical therapies, the work on weekends and holidays—and a lot of other details regarding Christopher he conveniently left out. However, he puts in his report a completely prejudicial gratuitous phrase, "Oh yea, murder."

Page 5, Paragraph 3: "I don't think I was in my right mind when I did it?" Is Siegel kidding? I said I wasn't in my right mind—period. It is little "Siegel" touches like this that make this report really malicious.

Page 5, Paragraph 4: is a masterpiece of scientific bullshit. Here I am—again (gratuitously) generally cooperative. The inference being, I am a little uncooperative. Then he does a job on me: "He denies feeling nervous or depressed." He denies . . . He denies . . . The good Dr. Siegel leaves you with the impression I am denying but infers—negatively—those things can all actually exist behind my denials.

Page 5, Paragraph 6: Where does he get the Recurrent major depressive episodes? It was one illness. This "Personality Disorder." Is that an illness in D.S.M.III? I think you should really go into this aspect.

Page 6, Paragraph 2: I do not express a degree of remorse for my past actions. Siegel makes me sound like a murderer who is only a little remorseful. I took great pains to explain to him I have NO remorse for the killings because my ethics, my morality, my legal training and my religion all scream at me that I was not acting voluntarily with full freedom of my will. I am remorseful as to whether or not I could have done anything to prevent this from happening. I sought medical advice immediately.

Page 6, Paragraphs 3, 4, and 5: I cannot discuss with you intelligently since Dr. Siegel is again playing around with semantics and psychiatric jargon, e.g, "maladaptive defense mechanisms"—"rigid defense mechanisms" "repression and denial." (These describe most of the lawyers and judges I have known!) He mentions a study but does not provide a footnote so we cannot follow up on his blatant unverifiable speculation. How dare he come up with this 30%–40% estimation without providing the study, conditions, sampling, etc., etc., etc.

Page 7, Paragraph 2: Dr. Siegel leaves out material: He talks of my not attending a clinic voluntarily. He does not mention my criticisms of pub-

lic psychiatry, the fact I wrote an article regarding the abuses of psychiatry, the chemical abuse of patients by psychiatrists, the fact that I use 2 priests and my religious sacrament of confession to let off steam.
Page 7, Paragraph 3: I stopped seeing Dr. Distelman because he was botching me up chemically and I told Distelman so and Siegel also.

I know that you have a heavy case load but I do hope we can work together to attack Dr. Siegel's testimony and his report.

Please get me these medical records as quickly as possible. Dr. Siegel is so rigidly an advocate and so prejudicial, I am sure you can neutralize him.

Bob followed up the letter with numerous telephone calls to his lawyer, suggesting strategy, urging him to expedite the case by pushing the Creedmoor psychiatrists to file their reports. By July, the lawyer was fed up with his unauthorized co-counsel's advice and haranguing. He called Bob a "smart-ass" and told him to find someone else to represent him.

By November the case had fallen apart. Bob's new lawyer dressed appropriately but had little experience with mental-health law. The psychiatrist who had been treating Bob for more than two years had left Creedmoor and Bob didn't like or trust his replacement. Mental Hygiene Legal Services withdrew its support of Bob's application, and the court ruled that he should continue seeing the state psychiatrists for another year and then the case could be reviewed again.

Meanwhile, Bob had received a hearing date from the Court of Appeals. He was scheduled to appear before the panel of seven judges in Albany, the state capital, on January 12, 1987. After the fiasco with the clinic lawyers, he'd decided to argue the case himself.

On January 11, 1987, he and Colleen took the train to Albany. Bob passed the time reading newspapers, history books, and law books and consuming boxes of small doughnuts blanketed in powdered sugar. Colleen spent the entire trip worrying about him, but she paused occasionally to snap a photograph, as though they were on vacation. When they arrived, before checking into the Albany Hilton, Bob pulled out a map. "Always get a lay of the land," he told Colleen. They stopped by the

Court of Appeals building, where they photographed each other on the front steps.

That night, after she and Bob checked out the Jacuzzi by the hotel swimming pool, Colleen fell asleep the same way she had for the last several nights: lights ablaze, with Bob surrounded by books and papers. A few hours later, long before dawn, she woke up to find Bob already dressed in a navy blue suit and a white shirt and conservative necktie, ready to rehearse. She had come to know his case almost as well as he did. It had been an extraordinary internship for a first-year law student.

He was brilliant that day, she thought—composed and self-possessed. The only visible sign of his nervousness was his tendency to touch his nose whenever one of the judges asked a hard question.

Coincidentally, Rowe's twenty-two minutes before the Court of Appeals was immortalized on videotape. The New York State Commission for Cable Television had been considering whether to allow cameras in state courtrooms. January 12, 1987, had been picked as the day to record, as an experiment, every argument conducted in front of the Court of Appeals.

The camera captured the image of a solid middle-aged man with fair hair and a high forehead and an easy smile, confirming Colleen's impression that he was poised, articulate, and personable. He was even jocular, as if he routinely sparred with New York's most powerful judges. When one of them asked him what, exactly, his status was as a psychiatric patient, he laughed.

"I'm out among the living, moving around, doing all kinds of things," he said lightly. "There is no incompetency. I am under a court order to go every two weeks to be monitored."

Later, he would try to assure the judges that this shouldn't pose a problem. "Your Honor, there are many lawyers practicing law who see psychiatrists. I'm taking the position that even though someone is taking therapy, he can practice law. My own treating psychiatrist goes regularly to a psychiatrist!"

But this aplomb became jarring when Bob calmly referred to himself in the third person as he described the killings. "On February 22, 1978, the appellant killed his wife and three children . . ."

Colleen had worried about his dispassionate presentation of the killings when he'd rehearsed for her in the middle of the night. It sounded so cold. He told her she was wrong. He was presenting the case as a lawyer, and that's how a lawyer would say it.

"On February 22, 1978, the appellant killed his wife and three children after a period of two and a half years of a slow mental deterioration," he said in a steady voice. "Because Mr. DeWan has gone back into the history, I should say there were two very ill children involved. One was a deaf-mute, blind, retarded boy who could not walk until he was about seven years of age."

Then he slipped into the first person, without altering his tone or expression: "This put tremendous pressure on the family, my wife, and myself. My other son was sick; he was on crutches for three years."

Colleen watched the judges carefully. They still seemed to like him. As he continued, they smiled on cue when he wanted them to. When he was finished testifying, Sol Wachtler, who was then the chief judge, turned to Mark DeWan. "Why shouldn't there be a hearing? I'm hearing convincing evidence. What is the danger of allowing a hearing?"

This was the grievance-committee lawyer's first appearance before the Court of Appeals, too, and he looked as nervous as he felt. His voice was thin and uncertain, and he looked even younger than he was—thirty-six, by then—his pale, earnest face framed by red hair and a red beard, both neatly trimmed. He kept interrupting himself to clarify, which wasn't easy, because the judges kept cutting him off mid-sentence.

Judge Wachtler repeated sternly, "What must he do to get a hearing?"

DeWan replied, "I can imagine that the Appellate Division would take into account a current psychiatric evaluation . . ." He trailed off, then began again. "I can't characterize . . . there is no certainty."

Yet DeWan was certain that he was right. It had been infuriating to sit there and listen to Rowe talk about the killings as though someone else had committed them! After a few false starts, he managed to articulate his case. "It is my position that as long as Mr. Rowe remains under court-ordered psychiatric care, that should be an effective block to his reinstatement. At this point, Mr. Rowe attempts to categorize court-mandated psychiatric care as mere therapy, and I would submit that it goes well beyond the mere therapy that millions of Americans indulge in and that it is not merely for the purpose of bettering one's self-image."

"How do you know that?" asked one of the judges.

DeWan took a breath. "In 1978, Judge Barshay said he was not guilty by reason of mental illness or defect, and that was based on a great deal of psychiatric evidence. Mr. Rowe has also consistently misrepresented the implication of Judge Yoswein's 1980 decision as a judicial finding of competency. It was merely Judge Yoswein's decision that he remain in psychiatric care as an outpatient, because the district attorney had failed to show that he was still dangerously mentally ill and in need of further inpatient psychiatric care. It merely changed [the] location of his treatment. It did not state that disability had been terminated."

The judge asked, "Would discontinuation of all treatment entitle him to a hearing?"

The grievance-committee lawyer was impassive. "That would raise the next question: Is he fit to resume the practice of law? There are two issues: Has the disability been terminated? Is he fit to resume the practice of law?"

—

On February 10, 1987, the Court of Appeals issued a unanimous opinion, one paragraph long: "In view of the fact that the petitioner was found not guilty by reason of mental disease or defect, as a result of which he is still receiving court-ordered psychiatric care, and the additional fact that the affidavit of his own psychiatrist is not sufficient to raise an issue of fact in support of his mental fitness to practice law, the Appellate Division did not abuse its discretion in denying the application without a hearing."

Bob was devastated. Three days later, he described his reaction in a letter to a lawyer friend:

It came as quite a shock. Colleen was hit twice as hard, because the Court was so friendly and was asking me and DeWan all the questions we wanted them to ask. I really don't understand it myself. They do not answer the two questions we pose. 1) immediate reinstatement or 2) a hearing. They only answer number two although number one was in the original motion. Can they choose to ignore an issue like that? As to number two, they say my psychiatrist does not raise an issue?? I assume they mean Dr. Jacques. Does he have to say—or any future medical person—that I am fit to practice law?

What is "fitness to practice law"? What do I have to prove to get a hearing? What is the standard? How can I guess what they want? I really am thrown for a loss here because I do not understand the decision and frankly I couldn't explain it to Colleen.

Since it is a 7–0 decision, my first reaction was to forget any further appeal. Would the Supreme Court even consider certiorari under these circumstances??

On the other hand, the resolution seems so entirely weak that I can't understand what or why they have done what they've done.

Is it because they just don't want to open up a can of worms? There are a lot of poor and mentally ill people around. I can't believe that they are up to that.

He signed the letter by drawing a cartoon of a uniformed man lying on the ground, his body pierced with arrows. "Love and kisses, General George Armstrong Custer."

Bob Rowe, however, was still far from making his last stand.

CHAPTER 21

The Final Appeal

Still acting as his own attorney, Bob went back to the Appellate Division on April 29, 1988, triumphantly brandishing his unconditional discharge from outpatient treatment, which had been ordered two months earlier by Judge Allen Beldock. He was sure he'd cleared the path to reinstatement.

His new application was even more thorough than the first—seventy-five pages of argument, affidavits, and other documentation—and even more assured. "This application is made pursuant to 22A NYCRR 691.13 subdivision (e) with the confidence that this court will dispense with the taking of any further evidence and reinstate in the light of the incontrovertible medical proof presented," he declared.

The affidavits vouching for him were impressive, not just for their effusiveness but because many of them were written by lawyers, members of the bar that Bob wanted to rejoin. DeWan dismissed the affidavits as inconsequential because most of them came from Bob's friends. But it could be argued that in Bob's case, the fact that old friends—who had known and liked Mary—were willing to testify on his behalf made the affidavits even *more* impressive.

Dr. Alvin Kahn, director of medical education and vice-president for medical affairs at the Brookdale Hospital Medical Center in Brooklyn, had met Bob and Mary through Harvey Sackstein and liked them both very much. After his release from Creedmoor, Bob was suffering from angina and began seeing Dr. Kahn as a patient as well as socially.

"I have seen him periodically, both as a physician and as friend since September, 1981," wrote Dr. Kahn in his statement. "He has followed my medical regimen and advice carefully, has reduced his weight and has acted optimistically with regard to his physical condition. Moreover, I have been able to discuss, observe, and evaluate his present lifestyle and the manner in which he handles stress. At no time have I observed any sign of mental difficulty or even a negative attitude toward the myriad problems his new life has presented.

"Prior to the tragedy Robert Rowe had a fine reputation as a teacher, business executive and lawyer. He has picked up his life again, is developing a business and has gone back to volunteer work. In my opinion, he possesses the requisite skills and moral character to be a practicing attorney in New York State."

Bob's old friend Harvey Sackstein and his daughter, Ellen, also an attorney, weighed in. So did Don Cassidy, the English professor who had introduced him to Colleen, and John O'Shaughnessy. His priest vouched for his character, and so did Colleen, though she described herself only as a second-year law student who had been tutored by Bob.

His new psychiatrist, Dr. Stephen Teich, who had been seeing Bob every week for several months, declared, "It is my professional opinion that he is psychologically fit to resume the practice of law."

They all vouched for him, though many of them secretly believed that their friend was on a quixotic mission. Silvio Caso certainly wanted Bob to get his license back so he could earn a living, but Silvio was a lawyer and he knew in his lawyer's heart that because of the enormity of Bob's actions—killing four people—he would not get his license back, not ever, even though he had been found not guilty by a judge, by reason of insanity. Yet he didn't want to hurt Bob's feelings, so he too dutifully

composed a thorough and heartfelt endorsement of his friend and colleague.

Mark DeWan wasn't touched by this abundance of loyalty. He was fed
up with Rowe's persistence and with anyone who encouraged him. In his
answering papers, he argued that the discharge from mandated care
didn't prove that Bob was cured. "The mere fact that two psychiatrists
and a Supreme Court judge have concluded that petitioner no longer has
a 'dangerous mental disorder' or is 'mentally ill' (as defined by CPL
330.20) does not mean that petitioner is currently fit to resume the practice of law. Especially in view of the fact that petitioner murdered his
wife and three children in 1978, this Court should take every available
precaution to ascertain petitioner's current fitness."

Then he moved in for the kill. He asked the court to authorize a disciplinary proceeding against Robert Rowe on various charges of professional misconduct. He was tired of haggling over the suspension issue.
He wanted Bob disbarred.

First, argued DeWan, Rowe had violated his suspension by writing the
article for *The Journal of Urban Psychiatry* at Creedmoor. He was ille-
gally acting as an attorney, because in the article he cited case law, offered his opinion, and called himself "Robert Rowe J.D." without a
footnote explaining that he was a suspended, nonpracticing attorney.

Tutoring Colleen was another infraction of the suspension order, another
example of Bob practicing law without an active license, DeWan said.

Then there was the escape from Creedmoor. Even though it was a misdemeanor, DeWan argued it should have been reported to the Appellate
Division, and that failing to do so constituted "professional misconduct."

These petty charges were mere garnish, but the gatekeepers for the bar
wanted to do everything they could to keep an acknowledged killer from
practicing law. How would *that* look?

DeWan wrote: "It is beyond cavil that petitioner's murder of his wife
and three children, which he freely admitted to a New York City Police
Department detective and a Kings County Assistant District Attorney, violated Disciplinary Rule 1-102(A) (6): 'A lawyer shall not engage in any
other conduct that adversely reflects on his fitness to practice law.'

"Because petitioner was suspended by this Court pursuant to Judge

Barshay's declaration of petitioner's incompetency and petitioner's involuntary hospitalization, a disciplinary proceeding was never authorized to ascertain the facts surrounding and to impose sanction in relation to petitioner's killing of his wife and three children."

The paper-sparring went two more rounds. Bob accused DeWan of "employing a 'shotgun' approach" and refuted his arguments, one by one. He was especially rankled by DeWan's use of the words *killed* and *murder.*

"It ill behooves an officer of the Court to recklessly accuse someone of 'murder' and 'killing' knowing full well that there has been a competent legal finding of innocence after trial," Bob huffed.

He concluded by accusing DeWan of responding "with sophistry and personal value judgments. There is an undercurrent one senses that the Petitioner is a criminal who got away with something and must now be punished. The Respondent's opposition attempts to discriminate against the insanity acquittee ignoring the applicable law and seeks to impose personal opinion in place of law."

DeWan huffed back. "It must be noted that there is no provision in the CPL for such a verdict of 'innocence.' . . . Judge Barshay found petitioner 'not guilty by reason of mental disease or defect,' a substantially different determination from a finding of 'innocence.' "

His final jab: "Petitioner has himself used the word 'killed' to describe his conduct on February 28 [*sic*], 1978, during a video-taped psychiatric examination with Dr. Azariah Eshkenazi on January 14, 1988. Also, on January 12, 1987, appearing before the New York State Court of Appeals, petitioner stated, 'On February 28 [*sic*], 1978, appellant killed his wife and his three children.' Under these circumstances, petitioner's objections to affirmant's use of the words 'killing' and 'murder' are clearly baseless and should be disregarded."

On October 7, 1988, four months after DeWan's final papers were filed, the Appellate Division ruled tersely: "The motion is denied."

Bob realized he needed help if he wanted to appeal again. He contacted the New York Civil Liberties Union, where a lawyer gave him some advice on how to introduce a constitutional issue into the case, which would encourage the Court of Appeals to grant a hearing.

Then he referred Bob to William Brooks, who ran the Mental Disability Law Clinic at Touro College in Huntington, New York, and taught constitutional law at the Jacob D. Fuchsberg Law Center there. Brooks specialized in mental-health cases and had appellate experience.

Brooks, who was thirty-five years old, had a long thin face, basset-hound eyes, and a full head of shaggy hair. He struck Bob as a sober young man who knew his stuff, but that was about it. Bob prided himself on being able to win over people he wanted to win over, but Brooks eluded him. They just didn't connect.

The truth was, Brooks didn't want to get too close. In college, he had done volunteer work with retarded children, and that experience sparked his later interest in the constitutional rights of the mentally ill. It would occur to him that in another scenario, he might have been an advocate for Christopher Rowe. So he thought it would be easier for him if he didn't know too much about Bob's past, especially when his wife and colleagues started teasing him about hanging out with a family killer. "Am I next?" Brooks's wife needled him. He laughed at the jokes, but without mirth, because there were so many layers to this disturbing case, which began to seem more and more like one of those hypothetical situations law professors dream up to confound their students.

So Brooks never examined the trial record or asked any questions about what had happened. Better to focus on the issue at hand. That was much easier, because he believed that Bob Rowe's reading of the law was correct. The only thing to be decided was whether he was mentally fit to practice law—period.

Brooks would later admit that he was perhaps naive to think a case like this would be decided on a literal reading of the law. Most of his experience was in civil cases, dealing with the constitutional rights of mentally ill people who had been hospitalized against their will. Only later would he come to realize that Bob Rowe's culpability wasn't the issue; nor was his mental competence or his ability to practice his profession. What concerned the grievance committee was public perception. Lawyers had enough public relations problems without welcoming back into the ranks someone who had killed his family.

But Brooks was a purist, so he didn't worry about public perception as he worked out his strategy, because he felt that was completely irrelevant to the question of Bob's ability to practice law. For the appeal, Brooks wanted to keep the focus on the suspension itself. He believed that Bob's motion for a hearing couldn't be denied under the due-process clause of the Constitution, under the theory that an attorney's license is his property and it can't be taken away from him permanently if he is suspended for a medical disability rather than because he did something wrong. If the lawyer provides enough evidence that the disability is gone, then due process requires a hearing to see if his "property" should be returned.

The Court of Appeals bought the argument.

On April 6, 1989, in a unanimous opinion, the court explained that a first-time application to the bar couldn't be rejected without giving the applicant a hearing, while a lawyer disbarred for professional misconduct or a felony isn't entitled to a hearing. But an attorney suspended because of mental disability doesn't fit into either category.

The suspension is not a punishment or sanction; it is a necessary precaution taken by the court to protect the public and further its confidence in and reliance upon the integrity and responsibility of the legal profession. In addition, unlike a disbarred attorney, an attorney suspended because of medical disability retains a protected property interest in his license during the period of suspension.

Inasmuch as petitioner was suspended because of his disability and his application for reinstatement presents prima facie proof, by clear and convincing evidence, that the disability has been removed, due process requires a hearing to resolve that question of fact, and to enable the court to determine on the whole record whether he is fit to practice law.

Bob was jubilant when he got the telephone call about the decision. Then the phone rang again. He didn't pick it up—he and Colleen always screened calls—but he heard an unfamiliar voice from the speaker of his answering machine say, "Mr. Rowe, congratulations on your victory in the Court of Appeals. We'd like to interview you." A few minutes later, the doorbell rang.

The *New York Post* had them boxed in. For a couple of hours, Bob and Colleen sat in their apartment trying to ignore the repeated ringing of the telephone and doorbell. Finally, when she couldn't take it anymore, Colleen decided to take a look, figuring that whoever was waiting outside for Bob wouldn't know who she was. She walked quickly past two men leaning against a car parked out front. One of them was holding a big camera. Feeling both scared and a little silly, she pretended she didn't notice them and went to a pay phone to call Bob. Then she went back home.

After a few more hours of playing cloak-and-dagger with the reporters, Colleen and Bob started to get the giggles. At the time, they were living in an apartment above a Chinese restaurant in Ozone Park, Queens, where the world seemed tilted because the floor was so steeply slanted. Now the fun-house view matched their reality: exhilarating yet frightening and, somehow, absurdly funny. They called their friends the Scarletts, who lived nearby, and asked if Bob could stay with them for a few days. After dark, when the reporters had given up and gone away, Bob slipped into a long military-style trench coat and wrapped a scarf around his head, and he and Colleen went over. The Scarletts began laughing hysterically when they saw their friend looking like a pulp-fiction hero.

The *New York Post* recovered from its failure to ambush Bob with SE-QUEL TO SLAUGHTER, a story spread across five columns, illustrated with exquisitely tasteless photographs of Bobby's baseball bat, of a body being carried out of the Rowes' house, and of Bob, wearing a coat and tie and satisfied smirk.

Replete with fiery language and lurid detail ("he slowly turned into a deranged killer who had dreamed about massacring his family for years before he actually went on his bloody rampage"), the article was a classic of its kind, simultaneously capitalizing on the tragedy and professing righteous indignation at Robert Rowe's temerity for wanting "to pick up where his life left off."

There were few repercussions from the article. Bob briefly became a target for Bob Grant, the conservative radio commentator, and Colleen spent a lot of time wondering if her family was ever going to ask her about Bob's past. They didn't.

Three years passed while they waited for a hearing. Colleen graduated from law school, and she and Bob got married, and a few months later, in

September 1990, they spent their honeymoon in Ireland, at an inn in Killarney, on Lough Lein (the Lake of Learning). The innkeeper warned them to be careful because an Irish fertility god was hanging on the wall of their room, and had inspired many babies. By the time Bob's case finally worked its way to the top of the pile at the Court of Appeals, Colleen was two months pregnant.

—

A retired judge with the appropriately biblical name of Moses M. Weinstein was chosen to be referee at the fact-finding proceeding, which began on March 5, 1991. His job was to compile a record to help the Court of Appeals reach a decision in the Robert Rowe case—which, after more skirmishing, had evolved into a high-stakes legal combination platter: His application for reinstatement to the bar was merged with the grievance committee's disbarment proceeding against him on charges of professional misconduct.

Judge Weinstein, approaching his eightieth birthday, prided himself on his ability to keep his personal opinion about a case out of it. In fact, he tried very hard not to even think thoughts that had the ring of opinion, because that could interfere with the legal process. He had been the referee in a great many cases involving disciplinary actions, and they came and went quickly, rarely lasting more than a few days. So even though the Rowe case, with its gory backdrop, was highly unusual, a few years after it was over, Judge Weinstein would have a hard time picturing Robert Rowe, whom he would remember only as "a very nice man who seemed to have his feet on the ground." Strange things would stick to your memory when you have heard so many cases. For example, Weinstein did remember William Brooks, the constitutional-law professor who represented Rowe—not for his legal acumen or lack of it, but because, as the judge would recall, "That man had a very bushy head of hair."

It wouldn't have bothered Judge Weinstein had Robert Rowe gotten his license back. More accurately, he didn't have a strong feeling about it either way. He did feel strongly about other grievance-committee cases for which he'd been the referee. "I have a feeling when people steal money from their clients as to whether they should practice law," he would say. "But this case, it was a question for the psychiatrists. I only presented the facts. If the Court of Appeals ruled that this man should practice law again, I wouldn't have a problem with that. If he had appeared before me in court, I would have treated him like any other lawyer."

Above all, Judge Weinstein wanted to keep what he called "an emotional element" out of the hearing, which took place on three separate days in March, April, and May. He became annoyed with the grievance-committee lawyer, Mark DeWan, who insisted on repeating that Robert Rowe had killed his family, one by one, with a baseball bat, and who, as often as possible, inserted into the record the words *killed, baseball bat,* and *murders.*

A witness testifying during one of these occasions was Henry Pinsker, the psychiatrist who both sides agreed should be the expert witness regarding Rowe's mental condition. Dr. Pinsker, whose lengthy and impressive curriculum vitae was submitted into evidence, was the associate director of the department of psychiatry at Beth Israel Medical Center in Manhattan, a professor of clinical psychology at Mount Sinai School of Medicine, and the author (or coauthor) of thirty-six published papers on diverse psychiatric problems, whose titles included "Don't Play Parent to Your Patients"; "Musical Expression of Psychopathology"; and "A Study of Whether Uniforms Help Patients Recognize Nurses," among others.

Dr. Pinsker was sixty-two years old, a slight man with wild, wiry hair and a sly sense of humor. He was slightly bemused by the question—the *only* question—he was asked to address: Is Robert Rowe fit to practice law? The question reminded him of his days as an army psychiatrist, when he'd been asked to evaluate soldiers' suitability for Antarctic duty. There was no standard for that, either. He was fascinated by this case. He'd never known of anyone in this kind of situation who was released from a mental institution as quickly as Rowe had been. Insanity acquittees almost always spend at least as much time in mental hospitals as they would have in prison had they been convicted—and the crime in this case was particularly disturbing. He supposed it was because Rowe was a white attorney and not a black street-person.

Dr. Pinsker didn't have the faintest idea whether Rowe stood a chance of reinstatement. He didn't know what the procedures were, what the law was, what the regulation was. But he believed the man should be allowed to practice law. He would describe his position like this: "Nothing about recovery from depression means you can't be vice-president of the United States or practice law. I might question whether a person who became depressed should have certain kinds of responsibilities—not because he couldn't execute them, but because it might be too much for him and might predispose him to a recurrence of depression. That's a treatment issue. In terms of fitness to practice law, one of the things we believe most strongly is that depressive illness, certainly later in life, is an isolated illness, perhaps recurrent, but when it's over, it's over—not like schizophrenia, which has residual effects for a lifetime for many people. Depression is depression. When you're over it, you're over it."

Not that he would recommend Bob Rowe for all kinds of law. He would have to practice his profession in the way that suited him. "Being admitted to the bar does not subject somebody to automatic pressures," Dr. Pinsker testified. "Yes, there are occupations within law that are tremendously stressful, and there are occupations within law that are very easy. Being admitted to the bar makes it possible for somebody to work. It doesn't mean that he'll immediately be thrown into every conceivable work situation that exists in the legal profession."

Mark DeWan wanted Dr. Pinsker to evaluate how Rowe could cope with the unpleasantness and stress that would inevitably arise in the daily practice of law. "Let us say Mr. Rowe had a client who Mr. Rowe did a great deal of work for and they got into a dispute over his fees. Do you think Mr. Rowe could handle a fee dispute with a client?"

Dr. Pinsker replied, "I think so. I see no reason from what I have observed that he would be unable to handle this."

DeWan continued, "Did Mr. Rowe explain to you that in 1978, prior to the murders, that Mr. Rowe—"

Judge Weinstein interrupted to make a correction. "Prior to this *incident.*"

The lawyer seemed puzzled. "Prior to this incident?"

"Let us not keep calling it murders," the judge said tersely.

DeWan went on. "Did Mr. Rowe explain to you that he had feelings that he was not able to support his family and that he experienced financial pressures?"

"Yes."

"Do you feel that—in your opinion, how would he react to a similar situation?"

"I think that the whole episode then, the whole illness involved—that period of being unable to work and the concern that he couldn't support the family and the suffering [that] was coming to them—then became the manifestation of the illness," the doctor said. "His life is very different now. And I think that if he were to be engaged in some form of legal activity, and became unemployed, but let us say he's no good—because I can't answer that—let us say he's an incompetent lawyer—I can't address that question—and works for somebody and is fired. I think his position would be that of any sixty-year-old man who is fired from a job because he didn't do it right, which is a discouraging, depressing thing to happen, but I have no reason to be concerned from what I know of him, or mental disorder generally, to be concerned that his response would be anything other than the usual unhappy response to not being able to work."

In his written evaluation, which had been submitted into evidence, Dr. Pinsker described Robert Rowe's illness as "Major Depressive Episode with mood-congruent psychotic features," and provided a description of the disease:

> Severe delusional depression is a condition quite different from the mild or moderate depression that may affect almost anyone. It is not a product of moral or intellectual weakness. The condition is characterized by physiologic changes as well as disturbances of thinking and feeling. Once established, the condition is autonomous. The depressed mood cannot be altered by willpower or by distraction. When delusions are present they cannot be rebutted by reason. From the record, and from my own observations, I conclude that Mr. Rowe's condition was a classical case of this disease, shaped, as it always is, by the circumstances of his own psyche and life. Suicide is a frequent complication of this illness. Murder is not. When it occurs, the vic-

tims are invariably immediate family, the rationale is invariably to spare them greater suffering, and the murder is prelude to the patient's suicide.

Once an individual has recovered, there are no continuing manifestations of mental disorder. This is quite in contrast to schizophrenia, in which a variety of emotional and psychological dysfunctions may be observed following apparent recovery from an episode. It is not like alcoholism or substance abuse disorders for which recurrence is a daily danger. In general, a person who has had a major depressive illness is vulnerable to having it again, but in this case, since ten years has elapsed since his recovery, it is clear that there is no pattern of recurrent episodes of illness.

At the hearing, DeWan zeroed in on Pinsker's description of Rowe's psychiatric history as "a classical case" of a major depressive event.

"Can you explain what that phrase meant?" he asked. "Does that have any significance in the psychiatric field? Why would this be considered a classical case?"

Dr. Pinsker answered: "I use the term 'classical case' because it's characteristic. The manifestations of illness that he had as described there are those described by writers in the psychiatric field over the course of many years.

"In a way, I think I was rebutting the unspoken proposition that what he did was simply wrongful behavior, motivated behavior, by a nasty person. I think this is why I use the term 'classical case,' to underscore that this is a manifestation of a well-known psychiatric illness, and with this—this is where the idea of classical comes in.

"Sure, if a person does something horrible, the question is, is he doing it because he's a horrible, dangerous person or because of illness? The more we look and find that there is an illness behind it, the more comfortable we are in saying that if he recovers from the illness, that takes care of the problem."

DeWan pressed on. "Would you say that Mr. Rowe recovered from the illness?"

"I would say so," said the doctor.

Though he didn't mention it at the hearing, Dr. Pinsker actually thought that Rowe had a kind of "funny thinking," which the doctor would describe as a "rigid" way of looking at his story. By that, Dr. Pinsker meant that Bob Rowe seemed to have a way of thinking about his situation that didn't allow for contradiction. He lacked some mental flexibility. But Dr. Pinsker believed this was a minor impairment, a small reservation. At worst, it meant the man was operating at 92 percent instead of 100 percent—and no one had asked the doctor to consider if Rowe was 100 percent or not.

—

In the end, the psychiatric testimony seemed irrelevant. Judge Weinstein concluded that Robert Rowe had violated disciplinary rule 1-102 (A) (6) with each crack of the baseball bat. He agreed with the grievance committee that Bob's escape from Creedmoor was a "serious crime" and that his failure to report it was a professional failing. He said Rowe's authorship of "The Right to Refuse Treatment: Therapeutic Orgy or Rotting With Your Rights On," was unauthorized practice of law.

On January 15, 1992, five judges of the Appellate Division, Second Department, confirmed the report submitted by the special referee, Judge Weinstein.

Robert Rowe was disbarred.

Almost immediately, he filed an appeal.

Bob's friends began to think of him as Jake LaMotta, the middleweight boxing champ who was unable to stop punching even when he was bloated and beaten. Wasn't it enough? Bob had a new baby daughter and a young wife and he *wasn't* young—he was sixty-two years old. By the time his case came up for a hearing at the Court of Appeals in October, he'd undergone triple-bypass heart surgery and almost died when postsurgical complications caused his liver to malfunction.

The Court of Appeals was having its own problems. On November 7, 1992, one week after hearing Bob's case the second time, chief judge Sol Wachtler, who had been suffering severe depression and behaving erratically since his mistress broke off their affair two years earlier, was arrested on charges of harassment after he sent her teenage daughter a condom in the mail. Three days later, in his twentieth year on the Court of Appeals, he resigned. (He pleaded guilty to harassment and spent eleven months in federal prison.)

On November 18, 1992, in a unanimous opinion, the Court of Appeals put an end to it. The judges agreed with Bob that he shouldn't have been disciplined for writing the article for the Creedmoor psychiatric journal. Otherwise, however, the opinion simply put a legal gloss on Silvio Caso's analysis, which he'd computed long before the special referee spent three days inquiring about Bob Rowe's mental condition. As Silvio put it, succinctly, "Who the hell thinks they're going to readmit a man who killed four people?"

The Court of Appeals was conclusive if not succinct. "A disciplinary proceeding is concerned with fitness to practice law not punishment," wrote acting chief judge Simons in his seven-page opinion. "Its primary concern is the protection of the public in its reliance on the integrity and responsibility of the legal profession. Thus the inquiry is not directed to the attorney's subjective mental processes, but to the objective and qualitative nature of the conduct, for it is the acts themselves which the public sees and which guide its perception of the Bar. Although respondent was not criminally responsible for his acts, they tended to undermine public confidence in the Bar and, as such, they properly provided a basis for disciplinary action."

It should have been over. But Bob urged Brooks to file for certiorari—a final appeal—with the United States Supreme Court, even though he knew it was a long shot. The Supreme Court was inundated with requests for "cert," and Brooks, whom Bob had begun referring to as Abraham Lincoln, told him the application was a waste of time. But Bob insisted. With his single-mindedness—which could also be called optimism or narcissism or myopia or "funny thinking"—he felt he could be a modern-day McNaughtan, a champion for the rights of the mentally ill who had been released from institutions. He understood that he might not be the ideal poster boy for the mentally ill, but that didn't stop him from pressing ahead.

On January 27, 1993, he made a note in his journal: "1) focus 2) consolidate 3) regroup 4) prioritize 5) retreat 6) retrench 7) attack."

Even if the Supreme Court didn't come through, he had one more outlet for vindication. Shortly after the disbarment, a reporter from *The New York Times* who wrote about legal issues had called Brooks about Bob's case. Though Bob was leery of reporters, the *Times* wasn't the *Post* and the reporter, David Margolick, had struck Brooks as a serious man who would be fair.

On May 13, the night before Margolick was to interview him in William Brooks's office, Bob wrote: "Three hours sleep. Too much excitement. The die is cast. Colleen has interesting ideas about photographers. I agree. I will get him to sign. No photos except rear. No photos profile—or three-quarter. No photos of car or of the baby.

"Thought: Why then am I going to Bill's office?"

On May 14: "The session goes well. I think we will get a fair run but no great help."

Later that day, Margolick called. The article was scheduled for the next day's paper. Bob made a list: "1) Get papers 6:30. Are we published? Is it a little positive? 2) Go to church no matter what happens 3) Get diapers 18–25 lbs. 4) Start collecting books on Criminology, Martial Arts, U.S. Colonial War and Korean War."

Margolick's piece appeared on the front page of the Saturday Metro section under the headline HORROR'S STIGMA STILL CLINGS TO A DISBARRED LAWYER. After opening with a restrained, even sympathetic, account of the killings as "an act of love, a way to spare his family the humiliation of poverty," Margolick articulated the legal issue exactly as Bob had hoped:

> For those who can get past its horrific facts, Mr. Rowe's case raises profound questions about mental illness, punishment and the legal profession. How high a price must someone pay for conduct for which he is found not culpable? When psychiatrists vouch for a patient's recovery, does anyone believe it? And should public perceptions of insanity—and the courts' fear of those perceptions—govern who is deemed fit to practice law?

Bob was inundated by calls from friends, and from acquaintances who had known nothing of his past. They offered their support and sympathy.

The man who framed Bob's paintings broke into tears on the telephone. The *Times* piece wasn't the redemption Bob Rowe had been looking for, but it was an endorsement from the establishment, a public statement that he wasn't a terrible person and a complete disgrace.

In his journal, he wrote: "Excellent article. We finally won one."

—

A couple of months after Bob's disbarment, on January 17, 1993, Colleen came home after midnight from a case. (After graduating from law school, she'd gone to work as an assistant district attorney.) As she went upstairs to their apartment, she noticed her landlady sitting at the kitchen table smoking a cigarette with her nephew.

Colleen fell almost immediately into a deep sleep and could barely wake up, even though she realized that Bob was shaking her and shouting. An alarm was ringing; the house was full of smoke. "There's a fire, get the baby! Get out of the house!" Colleen heard Bob yell.

Confused and exhausted, Colleen stumbled to the baby's room and was stopped by a wall of smoke. The baby must be dead! she thought. When she returned to her bedroom without the little one, Bob sent her back into the baby's room. This time Colleen persisted, screaming the baby's name. Her head popped up and Colleen grabbed her. Bob told them to get out of the house while he tried to break down the front door to help the landlady.

That's what Colleen would remember when the terror subsided: By the time she was fully awake, Bob was standing next to her holding the baby, who was thirteen months old. The landlady and her nephew were dead.

The fire destroyed most of the Rowes' belongings, including their cats and guinea pigs, thirty-five or forty of Bob's paintings, and most of his books, except the ones on the lower shelves, where the photo albums were. Colleen was certain that she and the baby would have gone up in smoke if not for Bob.

After the fire, Colleen was deeply disturbed. She refused to return to the apartment to help Bob salvage what the fire had spared. She had nightmares filled with flames. In the middle of this difficult period, her father died.

She was a mess, angry at the world, angry at Bob. Yet he didn't explode. He didn't leave. He helped her. He forced her to take a leave of absence from work. He took her to a psychiatrist. He was the one who made her well, but it wasn't easy for him. "I finally reached Colleen's brain and her emotions," he wrote in his journal. "Very difficult. She is very negative, surly, very insulting. I am determined to cut out to Hawaii for an extended visit (two months) to find out who I am and why 2–22–78 happened."

He didn't "cut out" for Hawaii on his own. He waited until Colleen was better and then they all took the trip together, as a family. When Colleen continued to mourn her father's death, he sympathized with her as if she were still a child. "She has not accepted that people die," he wrote in his journal. "She will realize that the world is a dangerous place, but it is beautiful."

PART III

When one man dies, one chapter is not

torn out of the book, but translated into a

better language; and every chapter

must be so translated.

—

from "Devotions Upon Emergent Occasions"

JOHN DONNE

CHAPTER 22

The Meeting

O n September 23, 1997, Bob Rowe died at the age of sixty-eight, of cancer. A month after his death, I met Colleen for the first time—in the New York Supreme Court, Kings County, in downtown Brooklyn.

During the first two years that I spent researching the case, I'd put off contacting Rowe, telling myself that I wanted to be fully informed first.

The truth is, I was afraid. Theoretically, I understood the difference between mental illness and evil, but I felt an irrational fear of this man, who was by then in his late sixties. I sympathized with the mothers and their feelings of having been betrayed by him and society—and with their indeterminate desire for redress. By the time I approached Rowe, he was quite ill, and then he died. I never met him.

Now I was trying to review his court records, which had been sealed under a New York law designed to protect defendants whose guilt hadn't been proved, and Colleen was trying to stop me. I knew little about her except that she was an assistant district attorney. I had heard that she was a religious person and that she was fiercely protective of her husband.

Though I had no real expectations—since I couldn't imagine what kind of person could marry someone with Rowe's history and then have a child with him—Colleen wasn't what I expected. By that I mean her appearance was unremarkable. She was an attractive woman in her thirties, of medium height and build, with stylishly cut light brown hair. Her eyes, however, were an arresting shade of blue.

When we met, her eyes were piercing. She was angry with me, because I'd just convinced a judge to unseal Bob's records (the case is filed in Kings County Supreme Court as *Matter of Anonymous,* Indictment No. 538/78). Colleen had discharged the lawyer representing her family, and now, acting as her own attorney, she had come to ask the judge if she could reargue the case. She'd asked to meet in his chambers to protect her privacy.

Both of us were wary. I had been so nervous about Rowe that months earlier, when I began sending requests for interviews, I'd rented a mailbox so that he couldn't trace me through my return address. The letters had gone unanswered, and it was clear that Colleen regarded me as a predator. Still, I noticed that we dressed almost identically, in the uniform of New York professional women: black pants suit. For some reason, this gave me hope.

At the meeting with the judge, she argued calmly but with evident passion about her desire to keep her husband's file hidden from public scrutiny. She spoke about her desire to protect her little girl. I spoke briefly and carefully, wanting to sway Colleen as much as the judge. Without her input, the gaps in Bob Rowe's history seemed insurmountable, no matter how many official records I would have at my disposal.

The judge listened politely and told us he would give his decision soon. As we left his chambers, Colleen surprised me by agreeing to have a cup of coffee with me.

I didn't record the conversation or take notes, because we were in the early stages of the relationship between journalist and subject, when a notebook can seem like a weapon. But I remember explaining what had drawn me to this story: the fragility of ordinary expectations, the fine line between happy families and tragic ones. Does the introduction of a disabled child automatically vault a family across the line? How does society, including the institutions designed to help them, treat these children and their families?

I told Colleen that I had become preoccupied by the stories of the mothers from the Industrial Home for the Blind and the lodestars of their friendship—the birth of their damaged children, the killing of their friend and her children. The sustenance they gave one another, and even their success as mothers, seemed sadly shadowed by Bob Rowe's very existence. He was no Gary Gilmore, who had accepted responsibility for the murders he committed and then asked to die. The mothers felt there was something suspect—no, grossly impenitent—about Bob's desire to live again, and to live fully, with his professional status intact and with a new family.

It seemed incongruous to talk about these matters while sipping cappuccino at Starbucks, but in small matters as well as large we adapt the scenario to circumstance. I was careful not to use words like *bludgeon* or *murder* or *evil,* even though in my mind I had hot-linked them to *Robert Rowe,* about whom I still knew relatively little. Instead, I continued my philosophical barrage: Can the criminal justice system adequately deal with shocking mental illness? Do conventional notions of punishment and rehabilitation apply in cases like this? Can we reconcile our desire for retribution with our humanity—and does our humanity necessarily require forgiveness?

Colleen was tense and tired. Her husband had just died and now I was, in my elliptical but determined fashion, asking her to justify his life while answering questions that could keep a theological task force in business for years.

But she didn't tell me to shut up or to go away. Indeed, she decided to help me. Over the next few months, I spent hours interviewing her, and then the interviews continued by E-mail correspondence. Colleen also provided a trove of material, written and recalled, and opened the door to many of her husband's friends—colleagues, doctors, and lawyers—many of whom had refused my earlier requests for interviews.

Shortly after I met her, I realized that Colleen had her own reasons for wanting to get involved in the exploration I had begun with the mothers. Her entire adult life had been consumed with Bob Rowe. She had a young daughter, who would eventually find out what her father had done, and Colleen wanted to be able to explain it to her. She felt she knew his story inside and out, but the very existence of the mothers' group revealed unsettling gaps in her understanding. She wanted to hear from these friends of Mary's, not least because she felt compelled to try to make them stop hating Bob. After our very first taped session, which took place at her home, she asked if she could meet the mothers. I told her I would see what I could do. To my surprise, they were eager to meet Colleen. A date and time were set: November 21, 1997, at Geri Smith's house in Belle Harbor, in the Rockaways.

—

The weather that day was rotten—and Geri was glad. She told me later that she appreciated the mean gray chill, an atmospheric corroboration of her mood. The mothers were coming for dinner, and Geri had been cooking all day. Somewhere along the way, a big meal with lots of wine had become an essential part of their ritual. She couldn't remember a get-together when they served something light, just salad and a hunk of bread. These women liked to eat.

Usually, she would get a lift just thinking about the group, but that day she dreaded the meeting. Bob Rowe had died two months earlier, and his widow, Colleen, had asked to meet them. The request wasn't entirely unexpected. Even though none of the women had seen Bob for more than twenty years—since shortly before the killings—they had been revisiting the past for two years, as part of the research for this book, which they'd been eager to have written. After Bob died, Colleen had decided to participate. Geri didn't know more than that, since it was Ellen Alboher who had volunteered to make the arrangements.

Geri's nature was to accommodate, to be understanding, so she felt inclined to be fair to Colleen. But twenty years of anger had been uncorked, and now she was struggling to keep in mind that it was Bob, not Colleen, who did away with Mary and the kids. So Geri had asked that Colleen wait until after the meal was finished to join them. She didn't want to feed the woman who had taken it upon herself to give a new life to Bob Rowe. More than once the thought crossed her mind that Mary, not Colleen, should be at this meeting instead of lying in a grave somewhere.

The day had begun badly, with an infusion of guilt, when Geri discussed with her husband, Billy—her second husband—the logistics of keeping Eric out of the house while the women were there. When Eric was around, it was impossible to concentrate on anything but him. He had the ecstatic energy of a three-year-old but now was twenty-eight. He shouted rather than spoke and often introduced a word or a thought with a loud *Nyehh*. He seemed to be forcing his language past a barrier, with only partial success. He sputtered. His eyes narrowed and fluttered behind pink-tinted glasses; his skin was very fair. Sometimes Geri heard herself speaking to him very carefully, as though he were still a toddler, and she cringed at the singsong sound of her own voice, because she had always urged people to treat Eric like everyone else. Above all, she encouraged him to be independent. She would repeat it over and over—"Be independent"—though of course she knew that independence was an illusion for both of them.

As she knew he would, Billy had agreed to take Eric. Billy was a good man—she knew that, although she could no longer disappear into the dizzy heat that had brought them together, two escapees from bad marriages, who could make believe that there was such a thing as a clean slate. Still, they looked great together—a handsome Irish couple. She was small and still sexy in her early fifties. Billy was trim and handsome, with a weathered face, nice blue eyes, and a carefully tended mustache. But all of it weighed on him: the responsibility for Eric, who wasn't his son, the bitterness from his ex-wife and twin daughters, the middle-age blahs after the excitement and brotherhood of being a fireman all those years. So she hated to impose on him, but she did, because who else was there?

She always gave him plenty of advance warning when the mothers were coming so he could make plans for Eric. Not that Eric wasn't capable of behaving—he had even begun to work recently, in the kitchen at a local nursing home. He just wasn't reliable. She glanced tenderly at her son, who was with her in the kitchen, tearing lettuce for the salad, humming happily—and loudly. Eric had a habit of yelling unexpectedly, and also frequently, with logic that was uniquely his. *"How does it shake, Ray?"* he might scream. *"Big Bird! Big Bird!"* Not even the thick catalogue of Eric's ailments fully explained these sudden bursts, though some doctors thought they might be related to autism or perhaps Tourette's syndrome. But whatever the cause, the effect was clear: Only a few public places were appropriate for Eric, and he and Billy could spend only so much time driving around in the car.

"Hi, Mom! What's going on here?"

Eric put his face close to hers, sensing that something was wrong. "You are my good helper, Eric," she said, making sure her voice was even, thinking it would be nice to go up to the veranda on the second floor and stare out at the ocean. She tried to swim every afternoon, as soon as she came home from work, right through October, when her only companions were seagulls. She was an administrator for special-education programs in the public schools, and, yes, she realized her job fell into the coals-to-Newcastle category, but she'd gone into the field because of Eric, to learn what she could to help him.

As she chopped vegetables, she let Eric's running commentary wash over her and waited for the warm, calming feeling she associated with the mothers to settle her nerves. They were nothing like her tennis group, who provided a different kind of relief. She'd never told any of those women, a regular foursome with whom she'd played tennis week after week for years, that her only son had so many problems she couldn't recite them from memory. For that hour she could simply be Geri, an attractive middle-aged Board of Education employee, a scrappy tennis player who lived by the beach with her handsome ex-fireman husband and a grown son who worked in the neighborhood.

But her heart was with the women who knew the truth. She was often surprised at the fierceness of her attachment to the mothers, who were so different from her, spanning generations and cultures. They could be characters in a situation comedy, chosen for demographic appeal, a motley crew tossed onto a stage for laughs—though she wasn't sure how their particular brand of humor would play outside the group. Not many other people were likely to start giggling when Mady Gaskin told about the time her son's fake eye popped out at a family Easter gathering and ended up in a basket of jelly beans.

———

It was dark when the mothers began to arrive, shortly after six, dripping from the rain, another layer of theatrical portent. The air filled with the smells of wet wool and creams and makeup and perfume, the fragrance of women. I was among the first, and watched Geri begin to relax a little, helped along by the nice red wine she'd opened for the group.

Shrieks of laughter pierced the friendly chatter, indicating that Ellen Alboher must have arrived. Like a stand-up comic, Ellen knew the value of a good opening monologue and tended to walk in the door talking loudly, as though projecting for a distant table in a crowded room, even when she was standing right next to you. Life provided her material. The last time the group had met, Ellen did a five-minute riff on the trip she took to the Copenhagen pornography museum with Elyse, now twenty-seven, who, of course, couldn't see.

Ellen was fifty-three and had recently had a little nip-and-tuck around the eyes. She insisted that the procedure wasn't for vanity. "I was reading a newspaper and my eyes would start running and tearing," she would tell anyone who noticed her new look. "I thought it was an allergy, but my lids were drooping so much the tears would well up. I stopped reading almost entirely. So I didn't do it for cosmetic reasons." Then she would smile and toss her head for effect. "But you know what? My eyes look great!" That night she was dressed in black from head to toe and was reporting the latest development in her ongoing battle to control her weight—four pounds gone; thank you, Weight Watchers—and the fact that she was still taking algae for her allergies.

Soon we had settled around the table, set festively with brightly patterned dishes. Rose Mauro pulled out pictures that her daughter Anne had sent her from Louisiana, where she was spending a year at a special school for the blind.

As Rose passed around the photographs, she explained the school's philosophy, which was that the blind *could* lead the blind. Students were taught to cook and iron and even to cross the street by teachers who were also blind. It seemed crazy to Rose, but Anne wanted to do it.

The "miracle baby" had grown up to be a slight young woman with close-cropped dark hair who was always weighted down by a large backpack as she climbed rocky hills. Rose reported that Anne had told her, "If I can do this rock climbing, there isn't anything I can't do."

At first Rose thought this rugged test just might instill "self-confidence and trust," as her daughter claimed it would, especially when Anne assured her that someone would be waiting at the bottom to make sure she got down safely.

Rose pressed her lips together, and it was hard to tell if she was holding back tears or laughter as she continued. "So I'm presuming the person at the bottom is sighted, and then I find out that he's blind, too!" She sat back, looking satisfied at the round of gasps and giggles her story elicited.

"I went to visit that place," said Ellen. "While I was there, one of the blind mobility instructors got hit by a car." She paused expertly, and then added, "I decided it wasn't for Elyse."

All of them were laughing by then, none more vigorously than Mady Gaskin. At seventy, she was part of the older generation, honey-voiced and elegantly unadorned, her hair short and gray, her eyes dark and lively. She sat across from Silvia White, with whom she had recently gone on a cruise to Alaska. Silvia, crisp and authoritative-looking in a tailored suit, remained the sardonic one, always on the alert for unseemly softness toward wayward children and husbands. Like all the mothers, Mady and Silvia had first met a quarter-century before at the IHB, and then Mady had become Silvia's mentor at the Board of Education, where both of them had worked for years. The two of them, along with Geri Smith, would always attribute a large part of their will to go back to school and earn degrees and graduate degrees to the encouragement they had gotten from the other women at the table.

Edith Patt, sitting at my left, was now a fragile-looking elderly woman, following the conversation carefully as she sipped wine, her shrewd eyes making various calculations as the others spoke. She hadn't fully recovered from an accident two years earlier. She'd been wheeling her shopping cart up Henry Street in Brooklyn Heights to buy vegetables for crudités—her assignment for Thanksgiving dinner, which she and her husband, Ray, were planning to spend as usual with two old friends in New Jersey. The front wheels had wedged into a crack in the sidewalk, causing the cart to stop so abruptly that Edith flew over it and landed hard on her temple. Completely conscious, she lay on the cement, her left eye bleeding, her arm and wrist broken.

She heard an ambulance siren, and then someone told her a car had sideswiped the ambulance and she would have to wait. What choice did she have? Edith waited. And when the next ambulance came, she carefully instructed the attendants to take her to St. Vincent's Hospital, in Manhattan, not to a Brooklyn hospital, and to contact her cataract specialist immediately. Cool and competent as always, she revealed nothing of the terror she felt as the blood drained from her eye. She'd had cataract surgery followed by two implants, and she knew that her vision in that eye must be at enormous risk—a catastrophe for a woman who, for most of her seventy-five years, began conversations by talking about a book she had just read. After the accident, she told me, "It ruined mý life. I went from being totally independent to being scared of my shadow. When we go to the theater district, I'm afraid of being pushed, of falling. I won't go out without a cane. I feel like an old woman. I never felt my age, but now I feel my age and yours put together."

When the mothers had first met her, Edith was in her forties, tall and self-assured, the kind of woman who considered what kind of brooch to wear with a dress, who liked to stare at her own hands, admiring their loveliness. Now she was shriveled and bent from osteoporosis and wore only slacks and loose sweaters, though her conversation still crackled with wit and intelligence and the occasional obscenity. The *fuck*s seemed calculated to startle, and they did, being so incongruous with her frail gentility.

For almost an hour, the mothers avoided the subject at hand. They drank and ate and praised Geri's cooking, then amused one another and me with family stories. Rose, usually the quietest of the bunch but stoked by wine and fellowship and anticipation, recounted the saga of her son's recidivist borrowing. Silvia played imaginary violin strings and raised her eyebrows. "We've heard this one before!" she said, groaning. "How old is he?"

"He'll be thirty-four in January," Rose said, and then continued.

When she was finished, Ellen offered a moral for the story. "The normal children are the real problems," she declared. "The handicapped ones at least are limited in the trouble they can cause."

They continued in this manner until, inevitably, they began talking about Bob Rowe.

"We saw him as a really nice guy who was a chauvinistic pig who was very interested in his family, a good husband and a good provider," said Ellen, as though giving a speech.

Edith leaned forward, looking puzzled. "Why do you say he was a male chauvinist pig?"

Ellen reddened, like a schoolgirl caught in a fib. "Because Mary always said it."

Edith shook her head and looked at me. "We didn't know him as that."

For years they had vacillated between the temptation to distort their memories of Bob and the desire for accuracy. Their earlier impression—the glowing portrait—explained why they thought so highly of him, but it provided no explanation for the killings. Denouncing him as a monster was satisfying but incongruous with the man they had once admired.

It was Silvia's turn: "His involvement, or his pseudoinvolvement, which made us think he was a pretty nice person, was all part of his being a controlling man."

Edith, a stickler, was shaking her head again, forbidding them to succumb to the temptation to revise history. "He was a participating father, and that was advanced at the time."

Geri had begun to clear the dishes, to relieve the tension that had knotted her stomach all day and to make sure that everything was put away before Eric returned home. When he helped clean up—and he always insisted on helping—breakage was not inevitable, but chaos was. She paused from her cleaning frenzy to acknowledge Edith's point. "That's why I admired him so much. He was so involved in the care of the children, especially Christopher."

Wistfully, Rose said, "I remember walking away from somebody's house after a party and thinking he was so great—he and Mary had the communication we didn't have with our husbands."

"They talked to each other," Edith agreed.

None of them had met Rowe's widow, Colleen, but Ellen had spoken to her on the telephone to formally invite her to the meeting. "According to Colleen, Bob didn't reach out to anyone, because he was afraid. He only remained friends with people who reached out to him. I didn't say the reason he didn't reach out to us was that he couldn't deal with us."

Edith shrugged and took a sip of wine. "We were angry at him."

The talk turned to Colleen.

"Does she resemble Mary?" Rose asked me.

Until that point I had kept quiet, hoping to maintain the illusion that I was simply an observer, though by then I had known them for two years and had listened to their most intimate stories. But this question was clearly mine to answer. Only I had met Colleen, and I had seen photographs of Mary. Still, I held back. I had done enough playing God by arranging this meeting.

"She's thirty-four," I said, noncommittally.

Silvia snorted. "The age of my twins! The age Bobby Rowe would have been."

Diverted, they began to speculate on Colleen's motives for wanting to meet them, and tried to imagine what kind of person would marry a man who had killed his family and then have a child with him. It was all the more mysterious because they knew she was an assistant district attorney. Her job was to put away the bad guys, not to marry them.

"She sounds like a nun on the phone," said Ellen, not coincidentally, because I had told her that Colleen had once briefly enrolled in the novitiate.

Silvia, a parochial-school graduate, raised her eyebrows again. "How many nuns have you known?" she asked Ellen, who was Jewish.

From the burst of laughter emerged the name of the actress Julie Andrews, who was immediately identified as the nun-turned-governess in *The Sound of Music*. The women began singing from the musical's theme song: "The hills are alive, with the sound of music . . ."

Geri opened another bottle of wine, and the room became quiet. "Mary had a wonderful sense of humor," she said soberly, invoking Mary's name as if to remind all of them how Bob became single again.

"Colleen said they talked about them every single day," said Ellen. "Mary and the children."

Silvia straightened up in her chair, frowning. "I'm sorry, I can't buy this."

Mady said little. Though she and Edith and Silvia had been friends for years and she had known the other mothers a very long time, she was a relative latecomer to the group and would have been hesitant to offer her opinion even if she was sure what it was.

There was a brief silence and then Rose said, "Before we forget— Silvia, what is the date for the mass for Mary? February twenty-fourth?"

Silvia had kept the holy card from the funeral and had recently reminded the group that the twentieth anniversary of the killings was approaching. She was arranging to have the names of Mary and the children read at the mass closest to the date, and wanted the mothers to be there.

It was getting close to eight o'clock, the time set for Colleen's arrival. Rose began to talk again, but now she seemed self-conscious, and Geri cleared the remaining dishes from the table. Though her anger had settled during dinner, it was rising again as she rattled back and forth between the kitchen and the dining area.

When the doorbell rang, the room fell eerily silent, as though on cue. Geri remained in the kitchen and no one else moved, so I took it upon myself to answer the door. As I stood up, I could see Edith gripping the arms of her chair, and I wondered if any of us were prepared for what lay ahead.

CHAPTER 23

The Other Side of the Door

Colleen was dead tired. She'd never thought of sleep as a luxury; it was one thing that came easily to her. But during the final sickness that led to Bob's death, she'd had to wake up often in the night to tend to him. She slept so little that she began to daydream about sleep, but she couldn't succumb, not even for a nap. There was no time. She was an assistant district attorney and a mother and the wife of an invalid. Their daughter had just turned six.

She had thought Bob's death would bring relief. He would be at rest with his family—with Mary, Bobby, Christopher, and Jennifer—and Colleen would no longer have to bear witness to his suffering. She could move on. But when he died and she began to contemplate her future, she was even more exhausted than before. Bob had been her constant companion throughout her adult life, and her Pygmalion. What was she without him? Why would she want to live without him? One question led to another, and never to sleep.

When Ellen Alboher had called her about the meeting, her harsh words took the wind out of Colleen as surely as a punch. "We don't know why you want to meet us," Ellen told her, "but we want to meet you. We have a big open wound. How could Bob just go on with his life? How could you marry him?" Then Ellen landed a knockout blow. "I think he was sick," Ellen said, "but he was also a monster."

Colleen had read the tabloid accounts of the tragedy. She knew there were people who hated Bob for what he had done, but her knowledge was secondhand. Everyone she had met from Bob's past felt compassion for him, as she did, because those who didn't had disappeared. This cruel assessment—"He was a monster!"—was crushing, coming from a woman who had once been a friend of Bob's.

Colleen tried to explain what she was feeling: She was a lover acting with loyalty to her beloved. She was the Rowe family guardian acting to preserve her family's dignity. She was a Christian, a fellow earthly traveler, hoping to ease the suffering her husband had caused this group of women. She was a mother defending the father of her daughter.

Ellen softened when Colleen talked about the little one, especially when she wondered how she was going to explain what Bob had done.

"Tell her in your own words when she is a little older," Ellen said.

Her voice was gentle then, giving Colleen some hope for reconciliation. But that horrible word—*monster*—had triggered other, terrifying, thoughts.

A day or two before Ellen called, Colleen had been rummaging through Bob's papers, as she had done often since he died, hoping to find a piece of him. She found a poem he had written in 1993 about Christopher, mysteriously titled "Only Fourteen," though Christopher was twelve when he died.

> Only Fourteen
> but could not see or hear
> Mute and uncertain.
> He had felt the fear.
> Surely he felt the fear.
>
> I was his sun, his wind, his moon
> and his mother all the rest.
> He grew, grew, he changed each day
> but still was in the nest.

Uncertain fear of the blackness
The sudden blow, the pain
He felt the fear of this wind.

"My poor Bob," Colleen wrote in her journal that night. "What sadness. What sorrow. All is restored in heaven." Colleen's growing sophistication hadn't shaken her faith. She was a Catholic, a believer. But then Ellen had called and inserted a doubt. Would Bob find peace after death, or was he doomed to struggle into eternity?

As she prepared to meet the mothers, however, her worries were more down-to-earth. She couldn't decide what to wear. Over the years, both she and Bob had gotten heavy. Their refrigerator was covered with friendly exhortations about dieting, all failed efforts. Yet during the awful months he was slowly dying, they didn't have to try to lose weight anymore. Sickness ate at his flesh, sorrow at hers. Now her clothes all hung on her.

She tried to imagine how Bob would want her to look. She put on her makeup as he had showed her and picked out a pair of black corduroy slacks and a patterned corduroy blouse, stylishly layered, with a blue T-shirt underneath. For a minute she worried that she looked too much like a kid, but it was the nicest outfit she had.

On her wrists she wore the bracelets she always wore, both of them gifts from Bob—one made of gold links, the other a brass Celtic bracelet with a design from the Book of Kells, the illustrated manuscript of the four Gospels of the New Testament, the vellum marvel created by Irish monks in the ninth century. On their honeymoon, she and Bob had gone to see the original book together, at Dublin's Trinity College, where a new page was displayed every day. They felt embraced by its beauty, which fulfilled historian Will Durant's description in *A History of Medieval Civilization—Christian, Islamic, and Judaic—from Constantine to Dante: A.D. 325–1300* (which they had read together in preparation for the trip): "The spirit of this art lay in taking a letter, or a single ornamental motive, out of a background of blue or gold, and drawing it out with fanciful humor and delight til it almost covered the page with its labyrinthine web. Nothing in Christian illuminated manuscripts surpasses the Book of Kells. Gerald of Wales, though always jealous of Ireland, called it the work of angels masquerading as men."

Before dropping off her daughter at her mother's house, Colleen finished her preparations for the meeting. She packed her black nylon briefcase (it had been Bob's) with photographs and her tape recorder; carrying the recorder had become a habit since she began wiretapping drug dealers for the D.A.'s office. She also took along photocopies of "A New Person," the poem that had encouraged Bob to keep living and which they'd framed and hung on their living room wall.

Colleen took a few bites of the dinner her mother had prepared and then left for Geri's house, driving slowly through the cold drizzle. Even so, she arrived fifteen minutes early.

Since Ellen had made it clear that the mothers didn't want to break bread with her, she pulled over to the curb and waited for the time to pass. Bob always used to say, "Everything passes into eternity," but that fifteen minutes seemed reluctant to budge. She turned the radio on and then shut it off. She prayed for strength, and had a chat with Bob and tried to remember how he had prodded her before her first trial: He'd made her practice her opening statement, first in front of him and then in front of a mirror. Before she walked into the courthouse, he gave her a pep talk, and then he watched her throughout the entire trial. That day she'd felt his eyes on her, and his confidence had turned her uncertainty into strength.

On her way up the steps to Geri's, she tried to goad herself as Bob might have: "Colleen, you have been through fire, flood, labor, trials, your husband's open-heart surgery, sexual abuse, and death! What can hurt you?" With that, she pressed the doorbell. On the other side of the door she could hear the happy, boisterous voices fall silent.

Two chairs at the table were unoccupied and she settled into one of them. As soon as she sat down, she realized she had chosen the wrong chair. Her back had been giving her problems again, and the antique chair with the lion-paws' feet had looked solid and comfortable. She didn't realize that it was also very low to the ground. She was looking up at a group of strange women and they were all looking down at her. No way, from this vantage, could she forget that she was on the hot seat, chief and only witness for the defense. Her crime was loving Bob. His crime, as far as she could tell from her brief conversation with Ellen, was living instead of dying after the tragedy.

She worked hard to keep her face from showing how scared she was, just as she would if she were trying a case. Her hands were shaking and her cheeks were flushed. But then all the women seated around the table had high color, even the older ones. She noticed that all of them had wineglasses in front of them. More than a couple of bottles had already gone down.

Geri Smith, her hostess, called out a terse greeting from the kitchen, where she remained while the others worked on their desserts and tried awkwardly to adjust to the new person in their midst. "Boy, is this cake good!" said Mady Gaskin, with a few extra decibels of enthusiasm.

One of the women offered Colleen a glass of wine.

"It might help," said Edith, openly acknowledging the tension.

Colleen accepted the wine and then clutched her glass as if it were the only thing that would keep her from sinking. She looked gratefully at Edith, whom she saw as terra firma in otherwise treacherous ground. When she first learned about the mothers' group, she'd recognized Edith's name immediately. Bob had wanted to write about her. Colleen knew this from the outline he'd made for the book he was always beginning. *"So many undedicated social workers just holding down a job,"* he'd written. *"She was much more than that. A true professional."* Though he hadn't talked to Colleen about the mothers' group, she knew that the Industrial Home for the Blind had been a beneficiary in the will Bob wrote before he married her.

Edith's voice was warm as she asked Colleen, "How are you doing?"

"I'm hanging in there," she said with a weak smile.

Edith continued to address Colleen directly and sympathetically, as though assuring her that the group recognized that whatever else she represented to them, she was also a recent widow. She politely asked after Colleen's daughter and whether Bob had been sick for long. In this context these questions—the usual questions—seemed unusually empathetic.

Colleen launched into a hurried cataloguing of the illnesses that had ravaged Bob during the last five years: the open-heart surgery after their daughter was born in 1991, which caused the liver damage from which he never really recovered; the cancer that developed from his liver problems; the dementia that came and went.

She was speaking to a partial audience. Mady had gone into the kitchen to help Geri, who had not yet emerged.

"Where did you meet him?" Edith asked.

Colleen explained briefly, and then Ellen decided it was time to get down to business.

"Did Bob ever say why he did it? What made him do it? The reasoning behind it, or nonreasoning?"

Still holding on to her wineglass, Colleen said simply. "He was ill at the time."

Ellen wasn't satisfied. "But even when you're ill, you have a reason for doing things."

Colleen's voice remained even. "He thought that he was saving them."

"From what?" asked Edith with a curious, not an emotional, tone.

"From suffering—from what he perceived as their descent into poverty. Afterwards he said the reasoning was not right, but at the time he felt he was saving them. It was an act of love."

"Because Mary had to work!" said Ellen aloud, at the same time thinking, How typical this is of a man.

"The poverty," mused Rose. "Was it like an ego thing? I know he never liked her to go to work and do those things."

Hearing from Rose, who seemed gracious and nonjudgmental, helped Colleen feel calmer. She liked Ellen but was on guard every time she opened her mouth. Was she going to call Bob a monster again?

Looking at Rose, Colleen said, "What he saw in Mary was that she was working sixteen hours a day and he was useless."

Geri had finally left the kitchen. She took her place at the end of the table farthest from Colleen.

"Mary wasn't unhappy," Geri said, then paused. "With her work."

Colleen had been shaken by Geri's refusal to come out and meet her and was relieved that she had finally joined them. Colleen wanted to reassure her that she didn't mean to speak ill of Mary.

"He always said afterward that Mary was always positive, positive to the end. It had nothing to do with Mary's attitude. It had to do with his illness and what he was perceiving."

Colleen told them she had recently talked to Irene Wagner, the professor who had invited Bob, Mary, and Bobby to speak to her classes.

"Is she the one at Brooklyn College?" asked Geri. "Did she have a child with mental retardation? I took a course with her."

Another connection had been made. Colleen allowed herself to relax a little.

"Bob and Mary had been friends of hers and the husband was also a friend, and they had actually opened their home to Irene Wagner's class," she said.

Geri nodded. "I knew that's what she liked to do."

Then a silence descended, as if the women had come to the communal realization that this was incredibly weird. They were having a friendly reminiscence about Mary and her life with the woman who had married the man who destroyed that life. Colleen looked nothing like Mary. Mary was dark Irish; Colleen was fair. Before she died, at the age of forty-eight, Mary had cultivated a dramatic look—flowing auburn hair, colorful scarves. Colleen was only thirty-four, and sitting in that low chair forced her to keep her legs apart and her arms resting on her knees, which made her look like a gawky student—exactly the impression she'd been hoping to avoid.

Colleen glanced around the table to get a feel for the women, the way she would assess a panel of jurors. Ellen and Rose were sympathetic. Edith would be fair. Mady hadn't said anything, but her eyes were warm—though Colleen knew from trial experience that it was dangerous to take a reading from eyes. It was obvious that Geri was struggling to be civil and just as obvious that Silvia didn't care if she was or wasn't. She would say what was on her mind, and it wasn't likely to be gentle.

Edith broke the silence. "I knew she had done that," she said, referring to Irene Wagner.

Geri looked dazed. "She always invited parents to speak to the class to tell students what it was like to cope." Then she abruptly changed the subject, as though she couldn't contain what was on her mind an instant longer. Looking directly at Colleen, she said harshly, "I don't mean to be very blunt, but I'm just really curious as to what your purpose is, coming here, and what you expect."

Silvia exhaled dramatically. "Oh, I'm glad you said that," she said.

Colleen felt as though she were perched at the top of the Cyclone at Coney Island and there was no turning back. Her fingers tightened around her wineglass.

"It's hard for me to do this," said Geri tensely. More than anyone in the room, she felt she knew Colleen. They came from the same place: two Irish Catholic women from working-class homes who had wanted more than they had and had gotten more than they'd wanted.

Colleen's blue eyes looked directly at Geri's dark brown eyes. "It's hard for me, too."

"I don't doubt it," Geri replied.

"I have a child," said Colleen.

"We know," said Silvia matter-of-factly.

"I know you know," said Colleen. "I have a daughter who was Bob's daughter and who loved her father. And I loved my husband. For the last thirteen years I've lived this story. I've lived with Bob's grief. I shared in his grief through the years. I heard there was a sense in this group that Mary had been erased, forgotten."

Silvia said coolly, "Certainly not by us."

"And not by Bob," said Colleen, determined not to let Silvia see how scared she was. Silvia could do her in if she wasn't careful.

Geri was trembling. "But, you see, that was not our feeling, that Mary was erased. She lives in our memory. So that was not our concern. She was robbed of her life and so were her children."

"By Bob," Silvia said, just in case anyone had forgotten.

Geri continued, "And that's our grief. She's never been erased. We never thought about whether Bob forgot her."

Ellen said, "He physically erased her."

Colleen looked distressed. "One of my reasons for coming was to tell you she was never forgotten. By Bob."

Geri was working to keep her voice in control. "I hate to say it, Colleen, but that's not a consolation at all to us."

Silvia made no effort to hide her feelings. Her voice was iron. "That's right, yeah," she said.

"I don't mean to direct any anger at you, Colleen," said Geri. "I know you have your own grief and everything, but this was never an issue or not with us, whether he remembered her or not."

The room felt claustrophobic, with too many emotions crowding in. Edith tried to clear the air with her calm, reflective voice. "Actually, it was a feeling of anger that was throughout the group," she said to Colleen. "It was something that didn't happen naturally. It was an act he did. And for this the group was angry, because she was our friend."

Rose picked up Edith's cue. They could explain their position without attacking. "So was Bob. Bob was with us a lot of times and we all looked up to him."

"It was something we wouldn't have expected," said Edith.

Geri re-entered the discussion, calmer now. "There was no sense that this was final and there was no hope and that her children had no hope. That she was depressed. He was depressed. They weren't. They were survivors."

"Had they been allowed to survive," said Ellen sadly. "Why didn't he kill himself and why did he kill them? And if he killed them, why didn't he kill himself? He still survived twenty years."

"I know he meant to die," said Colleen.

Ellen shook her head. "No. He didn't. He would have killed himself if he meant to."

Geri was upset again. Much as she wanted to compose herself, it was impossible to politely dismiss the questions that had eaten at all of them for so many years. "The truth of the matter is, if he had enough guilt, he wouldn't have gone on to start a whole new life with you and another baby. How can you bring another child into the world when you've taken away so many? This is just very hard to understand. And it's hard for us to understand how you could be a part of it, truthfully. That's hard for us to understand."

Colleen saw they needed to know that Bob had suffered.

They needed to know that their lives, his and hers together, were so calamitous that their friends began referring to them as Mr. and Mrs. Job.

She could recite a litany of plagues if they wanted to hear them, starting with the constant fear of what the doctors referred to politely as "recurrence"—meaning that they didn't want to test Bob's capacity for stress again. Every day was a test for Bob, and for her, but no one knew what the right answers were. Where was the threshold point for recurrence? He had jobs—working as an investigator for other lawyers, teaching—but nothing worked out very well. He had ambition, almost to the end. His futile pursuit of his law license had gone on for eight years.

What would satisfy them? Should she tell them about finding him the night their daughter was born, crying, "How could I have killed my family?" Or about the agony of the triple bypass, when their daughter was only eight months old? Maybe the fire that destroyed their apartment would suffice, when combined with the rejection by court after court. Where did they want her to begin?

Maybe she should elaborate on the sketch she'd given them of the last years, when Bob fell apart and suffered from periodic bouts of dementia that went unexplained until they found a doctor who realized that Bob's liver was filling him with toxins. Bob would simply disappear when the pressure started to build, and he became afraid that the old illness had returned. Once he called her from a ukulele factory in Pennsylvania. Another time he went kayaking in Jamaica Bay and couldn't find his way back, though he'd been boating on those waters thirty years or more. The coast guard found him marooned on Yellow Bar Hassock, a marsh near Kennedy Airport.

If they needed stories about punishment—about how Bob suffered—she had plenty to offer, concluding with the last eighteen months of his life, when he had become totally incapacitated, requiring care twenty-four hours a day. When his body had weakened before, he had fallen back on his intellect, but then that failed him, too. He couldn't read, he couldn't write, he couldn't paint. He would look at their little one and ask if she was Jennifer. "Did I hurt the children?" he'd ask her.

Instead of telling them all that, Colleen simply said, "It was difficult—in the end he needed care twenty-four hours a day. I had a home attendant twelve hours a day, and I took care of him the rest of the time over the last year and a half."

Geri's face was sympathetic, but her voice was still strained. "For your age, this was like taking care of your father," she said.

Colleen spoke firmly. "I was taking care of my husband, something he would have done for me, and he did."

That reminded Rose of something. "Isn't that funny," she said. "That's a quote I remember, the last time after seeing Mary, the last meeting we had, we kept saying, 'She knew that he was off his medication and that he was going to have a problem.' We had a meeting and she was very worried and we said to her, 'Why don't you commit him to the institution?' I mean, she did it once. He begged her to do it. She said, 'I know Bob would take care of me if this happened to me, and I have to take care of him.' So you're quoting almost to the word what she said."

Ellen jumped in. "I remember that. 'I love Bob . . .' "

Rose was nodding. "These are the words she said before all of this took place. 'I can't do that to him.' "

"He helped me tremendously," Colleen said. "When I met him. It's a long story . . ."

She didn't know where to go next. These were Mary's friends. Was it a good thing or a bad thing that she had echoed Mary's words?

"It would help us to understand," Edith said.

Colleen wanted to ask them, Are you people of faith? She knew that would make it easier for them to understand her story. Hesitantly, she began, "I wanted to meet with Bob. I wanted to offer my support and prayer. It's hard to understand, but this is where I come from."

Silvia's deep, dry voice cut into the conversation. "A lot of us come from that, too—okay, we don't have a problem."

"The Jewish contingent doesn't come from that," said Ellen, her voice teasing, trying to blunt Silvia's edge.

Silvia shrugged. "More than half of us do," she said.

Geri understood very well. Thinking that prayer is going to heal someone who has experienced a pain, a disease, a mental illness. Thinking that spiritually you can go and do something to aid this person. She'd been down that road. But it was one thing to help someone out, something else to get married, have a child with that person. She was working hard to keep herself under control.

"Some of us here had very similar backgrounds, so this is not a problem for us to understand on an intellectual level," she said, trying unsuccessfully to keep emotion out of her voice. "Beyond this, I'm having difficulty. The next step: When did you become attracted to him and what attracted you to him?"

Colleen had been in court often enough to sense where a line of questioning was leading. Geri was putting together the elements of the crime.

Tell me, madam, when, exactly, did you first start to notice that your feelings for Mr. Rowe were more, shall we say, than merely friendly?

And what, madam assistant district attorney, were your thoughts, if any, about Mr. Rowe's first family? The wife, the children, the baseball bat?

And tell me, madam prosecutor, how could you fall in love with a man like that?

She had to make them understand her background. Her love for Bob wasn't a whim or some perverted notion of glamour. She wasn't the kind of woman who became pen pals with convicts for the thrill of it.

"My experience was in the church," Colleen said. "I grew up around priests. I didn't have a normal teenage life. I think I was at the church because my family was in turmoil."

"Running away," muttered Silvia.

"Not running away," Colleen said.

"Salvation," said Ellen.

"This was your only hope," said Geri.

How to interpret this cacophony. Peace? Solace? What?

Colleen looked at the women, one by one. "I've never told most people any of this, and I don't know why I'm telling you . . ."

Silvia interrupted. "Oh well, this is a very good group for this."

The mood had shifted again. Even Geri seemed to relax. "Just get used to it, because this is what we are," she said. "That's why we ask you frank questions."

"We don't judge," said Ellen.

"Neither do we judge or talk about you," said Edith.

Rose recognized the specific nature of Colleen's discomfort. "You feel like you're on the witness stand?"

Colleen laughed. She couldn't believe what was happening. These women were starting to open their arms to her. Was this possible?

"I've been on the witness stand, but this is the worst," she said, relieved. "The worst in my life, I have to tell you."

It all spilled out then. She had no choice.

CHAPTER 24

Another Mother

As Colleen finished telling the mothers her story, she concluded, "I had a tragedy, he had a tragedy." But the comparison didn't fly.

"The paradox is you were a victim," Geri cried. She repeated herself, evangelically. "You were a victim!"

"I don't understand it myself," Colleen said. "But I didn't see Bob as someone who—" she ended that sentence abruptly. "I saw Bob as a victim."

Geri exhaled loudly. "Of what?" she asked. "Of whom?"

Colleen didn't hesitate. "Of mental illness," she answered. "Of tremendous tragedy."

Geri shook her head. "Did you feel that for the people who hurt you? Did you excuse them?"

An easy fly ball, no problem for Colleen, who had been fielding hard questions since childhood. "I found forgiveness for them because I had to," she said calmly. "I couldn't carry that bitterness through life."

But she didn't stop there. Geri had given her an opening for rebuttal.

"That's not what I am, just a victim," she said to Geri. "That's not where I stopped. I'm more. And that's what Bob gave me. 'You're more than that, Colleen,' he'd tell me. 'If you carry scars, it never stops,' he would say. 'You're not that person, the person that those people tried to make you. That's not you.' That's what Bob did for me. Throughout my life."

Silvia wasn't buying it. "Almost anyone who would have been sympathetic toward your history would have made you feel that way," she said dismissively. "It could have been almost anyone."

Colleen looked up. "Yes, it could have, but it was Bob."

She reached most of them with that. She saw that. But Silvia's sarcasm was unflinching.

"Yeah, but it *was* Bob," she said, openly mocking. "Did you have anybody you could tell Bob's history to who might have said, 'Think about this.' Or, 'Are you crazy?' I'm talking about during the five or six years you were together before getting married—did anybody, or many people, try to dissuade you?"

Colleen tried to explain. They'd talked to priests, to Bob's therapist. Nobody objected.

"What about your family?" asked Geri.

"My sister knew, and she was concerned," said Colleen. "Actually, she wouldn't share why she was concerned—she just talked about the age difference."

Silvia hooted. "We'd have told you why we were concerned if you'd talked to us!"

Colleen was willing to interpret Silvia's wisecrack as an olive branch, and began talking about Bob's psychiatric history, giving the women an opportunity to fill in gaps in their memories of Bob and Mary.

In the middle of this conversation, Geri glanced at her watch and started picking up everything left on the table, but not the wineglasses. As she began carting them to the kitchen, she said in a low voice, "I just want to get this off the table before Eric comes home."

While the women at the table added and subtracted from their communal narrative of Bob's illness, Geri yelled in her contributions from the kitchen area, just a few feet away. When she returned to grab a few more dishes, she apologized. "I'm sorry to be like this, but my son is coming home and he's very compulsive and he will tear everything apart. I don't mean to be rude, but when he comes, he has an obsession about cleaning up."

She told them to hang on to their wineglasses and brought another bottle and some cookies to the table.

Colleen took a cookie and even allowed herself to smile.

"Why did you put me in a small chair?" she asked. "This is a courtroom trick, you know."

Ellen laughed. "It makes you feel small?"

"Yeah," said Colleen.

"I moved out of that chair for that reason," confessed Edith.

"I love that chair," said Ellen. "It's gorgeous."

Geri looked pleased. "It's an antique," she said.

After a few minutes of pleasantly inconsequential chatter had passed, Edith asked Colleen, "What kind of a wedding did you have?"

The air seemed free of the humid emotionality that had greeted Colleen. She was eager to float some happy memories.

"In a Chinese catering hall, with an Irish band, with Hawaiian flowers on the table," she said, smiling proudly at the deliberate incongruities. The women rewarded her with a round of appreciative laughter.

But Silvia quickly reminded Colleen that the incongruities in this meeting went far beyond her Irish-Hawaiian-Chinese wedding. She wasn't going to let Colleen forget that her happiness with Bob was built on a foundation of blood.

She began with a deceptively casual question. "Did you get married in church?"

"That was another thing," Colleen began.

"Well," Silvia said coolly, "he wasn't divorced"—meaning that their marriage wouldn't violate the Catholic prohibition against remarriage by divorcés.

Colleen nodded. "He was widowed."

"We understand that," said Ellen helpfully.

Silvia groaned. "Oh please," she said, reminding Ellen that Bob wasn't just another widower. "But he was widowed by his own hand," she added. "Doesn't that make a difference to the Church?"

Edith remarked, "But he wasn't Catholic," just as Geri said, "It's interesting to use the expression *widowed.*"

Colleen hunched down in Geri's antique chair, which now didn't seem low enough. She looked pale and very young.

Pitying her, Mady tried to slow down the barrage. She asked quietly, "He was a Protestant, right?"

Colleen looked around helplessly. "I'm sorry," she said. "I'm not here to offend you."

Geri succumbed to the distress in Colleen's voice. "I know you're not," she said gently.

Silvia, however, wasn't ready to back off. "We just don't know how you can use that term."

Geri couldn't help herself. She naturally gravitated to the underdog, and sturdy as she was, Colleen seemed like a waif at that moment.

"It was unintentional," Geri said, her voice smooth and comforting, as if she were talking to Eric. "I understand."

Colleen shook her head. "I want you to express yourselves," she said gamely. "I don't want you to feel hampered."

Geri said reassuringly, "We don't."

Mady nodded. "You don't know this group. They say anything."

There would be lulls but no respite that night from gusts of sorrow and anger as the women searched for logic and reason, with no better success than Job.

"Sure you can forgive him, but I'm not going to forget it," Silvia said to Colleen. "There's a lot I don't understand. I don't know that you've clarified a lot for me, frankly. I know you've tried, so as a retired teacher, I give you a big A for effort." With that, she folded her arms as though to say, Case closed.

"I was the only one out of the group who said for years that he was sick. However, the one thing I hate to this day is the fact that he was never incarcerated and kept incarcerated, and that he was allowed to live a life. This is not fair," said Ellen. "He was allowed to love you, to have a child."

"That's right," Rose agreed.

A kind of litany arose spontaneously.

Edith: "The fact that he was allowed to have a life . . ."

Ellen: ". . . and pleasure and a child and all those wonderful things that he destroyed . . ."

Geri: ". . . and deprived the rest of them."

Ellen: "And aside from everything else, killing Mary and the two children that were his, but to kill Jennifer, that was an adopted child . . ."

Silvia: ". . . whom they wanted so much . . ."

And Edith said, "You see, this is the thing about which I have the greatest guilt, and that's Jennifer. I don't know if you have copies of the letter of reference that I wrote."

Colleen shook her head. "That, I never saw. We have pictures."

"I kept it for a long time, but I don't have it," said Edith.

Silvia's powerful voice was surprisingly gentle now. "They were the ideal couple, Edith. You can't beat your head against the wall."

Defensively, on Edith's behalf, Geri said, "She's not."

"Recessive guilt," said Ellen.

Edith explained to Colleen. "My child is adopted, too."

Colleen nodded. "Bob felt terrible for you for that reason. He wondered about Jennifer's real parents, whoever they were."

"They may never know," Edith said sadly.

Reflectively, Colleen said, "They turned this child over so she might have a life and—"

Silvia interrupted: "He killed them."

Colleen ignored her. "Bob had so much regret. He felt he deprived Mary of a life."

"Yes," said Silvia. "He did."

Colleen continued, "And the children! He killed everybody in the world that he loved. That was tremendous. That was the grief. I don't know if you understand the grief in this. This man, he knew he was mentally ill, he knew he wasn't responsible, but how do you view the cause of this horror, taking everything in life that you love? Every person in life that you love?"

As Colleen talked, Silvia walked over to Edith, pretending to give her something. She leaned over and whispered, "I'm sick of this crap," then went back to her chair.

Edith blinked, then responded aloud to Colleen's questions. "How do you justify that?" she asked.

"How do you live with that?" asked Geri. "How do you reward yourself with another life? This is the part that I don't understand, Colleen. I can understand what you're saying, that he felt this grief. I'm sure he had to have felt this grief. But how do you reward yourself with bringing a new child into the world and sharing it with another person?"

Edith turned the question around. "Is it a reward or the fact that if you're going to go on living you have to do something to make yourself—"

Silvia finished the sentence: "—want to go on living."

"To have something to live for," said Edith.

"Or to make yourself whole," added Mady.

Geri pulled back. "If you did something like that, would you want to go on living?"

Edith said quietly, "I really can't answer that."

"Bob had that struggle," said Colleen. "He had to make a choice."

Silvia groaned, frustrated. "But he never really did anything about it. He could have killed himself the day that this happened!"

"He contemplated it," said Colleen, her voice rising now.

"Big deal," grunted Silvia. "Sorry."

"No, he tried," cried Colleen. "Seriously."

Dramatically, Silvia waved her hand. "Ah, ah, Colleen. Hello! Sitting in front of an open stove? Hardly."

Colleen offered a correction. "With plastic tented over your head and sealing off all the doorways and airways?"

Sounding surprised, Rose asked, "Is that what happened?"

Geri came back. "When you are so violent with everybody else in your life, when you call your wife and say, 'Come home, I have a surprise for you.' And you bludgeon her. You would put your head in an oven and go away so sweetly? Take a gun and blow your brains out! I don't mean to be like that, but really, if you're going to be so violent with these people you love, innocent children, you're going to go so passively? I don't understand that. I can't imagine you can say that's a serious attempt."

"And also—" said Silvia.

Rose interrupted: "—I don't think anyone will ever understand."

Silvia tried again. "And also, also—"

Now Geri interrupted. "This is the part that we have a hard time with. It's not that we're striking out at you. We're trying to put closure to this. We're trying to understand how this person could say that to you, that he would have liked to have taken his life. We don't mean to be so flippant, but to say this, really, tell me the truth now."

"Also," said Silvia, "the order in which he killed the children was something he really thought out. Bobby would be the first one to kill, because he would be the one to argue with him . . . thinking about pre-meditation. And, well, as we said before, just the mere fact of using a baseball bat—anybody in this city—and you know this working as an ADA—why didn't he just get a gun and shoot them? Any moron can get a gun."

Ellen said, "And many morons are walking around with them."

"You're not kidding," said Mady.

Colleen seemed to have sunk even lower into her chair. She looked exhausted, as though her defenses were depleted.

Rose took pity on her. "Like I said, certain answers you can't give," she said.

Even Silvia relented. "We're not asking you for answers."

"I think we wanted to meet you because we wanted to know the kind of woman who would marry a man with this history. I think that was important to us," said Edith reassuringly. "You don't fit the mold of what we may have thought." Then she smiled. "You may have wanted to know what we were like."

"Yeah," said Colleen weakly.

Edith continued, "We wanted to know what kind of a woman you are, and now we've seen you're flesh and blood and human. That kind of puts it in a different light."

Ellen joined in, and there was no mistaking her compassion now. "And loving and caring and kind and forgiving."

"We didn't expect that," said Edith.

Ellen added, "And maybe a little naive."

Geri said softly, "And you have an innocent child who's here that you have to somehow protect."

Colleen spoke. "I can't change what you've gone through over the years and how you felt, but I know my husband and I know it's going to be hard for you. Bob loved Mary and the children to the day he died. He loved me, he loved our daughter, and I saw him do tremendous things with his life throughout the years. The Bob I met was working with dying children in a hospice. He took me there, to their funerals."

Silvia couldn't resist. "We went to his kids' funeral, too."

"I'm sorry," said Colleen.

"Sorry?" said Silvia. "That was not easy."

"Believe me, I know," said Colleen, and then she corrected herself. "I don't know."

"No," said Silvia coldly. "You don't know."

By now Colleen had grown accustomed to Silvia's prodding. "I don't know what you went through. But what I know is that everybody touched by this story is affected terribly. I am. I go to the graves and it's horrible."

"Where is he buried?" asked Geri.

"In National Cemetery in Calverton."

"Where are they buried, by the way?" asked Silvia. "Mary and the kids."

"In Pinelawn. Bob and Mary had bought the grave in Pinelawn."

Ellen remembered something. "Mary had a relative who was a nun. Did Bobby"—she corrected herself—"Bob ever mention her?"

"Bobby," said Colleen tenderly, relieved to hear the familiarity. "Bobby, yes, Bobby!" She laughed. "Yeah, he did, but I don't know what happened to her. I heard that she died."

"Was she Mary's only family?" asked Rose.

"Mary was an only child," said Colleen. "Her parents were directly from County Cork, Ireland. The father was a furniture restorer, polisher, a very gentle man."

"Did you know him?" Silvia asked.

"No," said Colleen. "That was Bob's description of him."

Remembering the endless conversations with Bob restored Colleen's sense of humor. "Bob said Mary's mother was quite a trip," she said. "She was very loud, boisterous, and had sayings like *Work while it's work time. Play while it's play.*"

For the moment, Mary was bringing them together. Several of the mothers called out, "Mary used to do that! Mary said that!"

Ellen's voice rose above the clamor. "Mary used to quote her mother all the time!"

"The mother was this character," Colleen said enthusiastically.

"Mary was this character, too," said Rose. "She was a character. She always used to wear these pretty scarves around her neck. And quote her mother's jokes and stories."

Didn't they know? Colleen wanted to say. *Didn't they know she wore those lovely scarves because Bob taught her to wear them, just as he had taught me about my clothing and my makeup? Bob gave Mary a makeover. He got her out of unflattering Catholic-school dresses and helped her find a style. Bob was an artist in everything he did.* But she said nothing. And she was too loyal to consider that maybe Bob was a controlling man.

It was almost eleven o'clock. The inquiry had been going on for three hours.

"Are you glad you came, or sorry?" Edith asked.

"I feel better talking with you people now," Colleen said.

"You do?" asked Ellen.

"You do?" asked Rose.

Colleen confessed, "I was scared when I first came in." Then she laughed out loud. "And you put me in a little chair here! I'm a trial lawyer, and I hate trials—they're always an effort for me. When I do them, I say to myself, 'God, you went through a fire, you lived with Bob, you were abused as a child, there's nothing else.' "

Silvia responded to that. "You're a survivor!" she said.

"You're going to get beyond this—that's what I tell myself," said Colleen.

"And you do," Silvia agreed.

As though concluding a religious service, Rose said, "This too shall end."

Colleen joined in. "Everything passes into eternity."

"And eventually that's where we pass, too," said Rose.

Colleen looked pleased. "Those were Bob's words."

Silvia recovered from her momentary softness. "Ah, please—I don't think we want to quote Bob."

Edith stepped in. "I'm glad we met you," she told Colleen. The rest of the women made affirmative noises, though Silvia's "Yeah" was open to interpretation.

"It's better than wondering what you're like," Edith said. "You acquitted yourself very well."

The term threw Colleen. So she *had* been on trial!

"Acquitted myself," she said slowly.

Edith saw what she was thinking and made a joke. "Yes, for somebody sitting in the witness chair."

Mady helped her out: "In a little witness chair."

A trial needs a recess, and this one began by tacit agreement between witness and interrogators. For several minutes, they chatted like any group of women who had friends in common until there was a noise at the front door.

"Hold on to your glasses," said Mady.

Eric and Geri's husband, Billy, had arrived.

"Hey! What's the news!" shouted Eric.

"Come say hello to Mommy," Geri called out to her twenty-eight-year-old son.

"How does it shake, Ray?" Eric replied.

Billy gave a brief, cheerful report on their evening and then quickly ushered Eric out of the room.

Colleen was frozen. She wanted to greet Eric, to let Geri know she realized how difficult life must be for her. But she couldn't respond quickly enough. The ghosts Eric had dragged into the room with him numbed her reflexes. She had been given an unexpected glimpse into the future that Bob had taken from his children, and her sympathy for Geri was accompanied by a stinging sense of loss. For, even with his oddities, even being the burden he clearly was, Eric was indisputably human.

Eric's entrance simply reminded the other mothers that they hadn't had a chance to talk about their children. There was Silvia's daughter Liz, with two graduate degrees, who couldn't get a job because she was blind, though she had been living (proudly and defiantly) on her own since she was eighteen—and was engaged to be married. Elyse, Ellen's daughter, was employed by a workshop for the handicapped, earning seventy-four dollars a week counting the plastic casings for telephone cards and placing them in boxes. She, too, had recently moved into her own apartment, with a roommate—a blind girl who was devoutly Jewish and had piqued Elyse's interest in Orthodoxy. Rose was hoping that when her daughter Anne returned from the Louisiana school she might finally leave home, though Rose had her doubts. Mady's son, Leonard, Jr., now in his forties, was living in his own apartment just across the street from Prospect Park. He had become a neighborhood character, the nice man with the sunken eye who ran errands for everyone and was always grateful for tips. He had recently shocked and pleased his mother by taking a trip by himself to Nashville.

"How did they get so old?" Ellen asked, the way mothers do. "It seems as though Elyse was a baby in the carriage a minute ago."

It seemed only natural to inquire after Colleen's daughter.

"When Bob passed away, how was she?" Rose asked.

"I had prepared her for months that Daddy wasn't going to get better," Colleen said. "He was only 143 pounds when he died. When the doctor said, 'We're talking about days or a couple of weeks,' I brought my daughter to the hospital. I didn't know if he was going to die that night.

" 'Daddy's dying—you have to say good-bye to him.' She was hyper, very hyper. She brought a picture she had made for him, a flower, and she kissed him.

"He knew he was dying. He said to me, 'Colleen, I'm dying,' and I told him, 'Yes, you're dying.' "

Geri asked, "Do you think she understands?"

"Yeah, I think so," said Colleen. "Every once in a while she'll say to her friend, 'Oh, my daddy died,' or, 'My daddy's not going to be here for my birthday.' "

Geri sighed. "You're awfully young to have gone through so much."

Colleen shrugged. "I was young when I went through so much."

"But why repeat it?" Geri asked.

Rose shook her head and murmured, as if speaking to herself. "I don't think she looked at it that way."

"I don't have any regrets," Colleen said. "I know you find it hard to be-lieve, but I loved my life with Bob."

Edith said quietly, "It's not hard to believe."

"Mary loved her life with Bob," said Ellen, but as supporting evidence, not an accusation.

Geri was trying to understand. "It seems as if your earlier life was so tragic you really had no joy and then you were attached to somebody who had a history like his . . ."

"You knew his humor," said Colleen. "He was a man who painted pic-tures and played the guitar and the ukulele. That's the man I knew, and in between, in all of this, was the grief."

Mady spoke. "It seems as though he made your life better."

"I would not have become an assistant D.A., I would not have gone to law school. I would not have had intimacy in my life," said Colleen.

Mady repeated, "He made your life better."

"And," said Colleen, "he gave me a treasure." She offered to show them pictures of the little one and of Bob.

"I'd like to see the little girl," said Mady.

"Just of her," said Ellen quickly.

Silvia studied the picture of the child, whose eyes were a startling blue, like her mother's—and her father's. "She's lovely," she said, and then added, "You know, you're not going to be able to keep this from her."

"I know," said Colleen.

"It's not us," said Silvia. "It's not that we're going to chase your daughter down."

"I know," said Colleen. "We always knew we had to tell—we just didn't know how or when."

"It's like that conversation we had on the phone," said Ellen, remind-ing Colleen. "I said, 'Make sure it comes from you.' "

"The younger she is, the less it will mean to her," said Mady. "If you wait until she gets older, it will mean something."

"You better start now—she's six years old," said Silvia.

Colleen replied, "She knows he was married before."

Silvia shook her head. "You'll have to embellish on that."

"Do it as simply as possible," said Mady. "If you had told her when she was three, it would have been fine."

Edith shook her head. "She wouldn't have understood it."

"But she would have grown up with it," said Silvia.

"You don't want to tell her when she's ten and starting puberty," said Ellen.

"She's six, and she does ask questions—she knows Bob was married, and we've always had a picture of Mary hanging on the wall of his studio," Colleen said.

"At some point she'll ask what happened," said Edith.

"I skirted the question 'Did Daddy ever have children?' I didn't say anything, just kind of changed the subject. I don't know what to say yet."

Edith said, "She's not going to ask you everything at one time."

"So you answer what she asks and don't elaborate," said Mady.

"She's going to ask you, 'How did they die?' " said Edith. "Kids ask that."

"How would you handle that?" Colleen asked.

"They were killed," said Edith. "I don't think she'll take it from there until she's older. I wouldn't rush into that."

"She keeps asking me these questions, 'How old was Daddy?' Sixty-eight. 'How old are you?' Thirty-four. 'Well, how much older is that?' 'A lot older,' I say."

"Right," said Silvia.

"The reality of life is, I could die—and I don't want to leave her with the impression that I'm going to be with her the rest of her life," said Colleen.

Mady said softly, "But she has to feel you're going to be here a long, long time."

Matter-of-factly, Silvia said, "Just tell her, 'I'm going to be here forever.' "

"I don't know about that," said Colleen.

Silvia said, "You can get away with that now."

"And what if I die tomorrow?"

"Then you won't have to worry about it," said Mady.

"Nobody lives forever," Edith said.

"It could be twenty-four hours or twenty-four years," said Silvia.

Geri looked pained. She had never had to worry about answering Eric's questions. She would never know what his questions were. What would happen to him if she died?

Edith was saying, "It's like telling your kid he's adopted from day one."

"Before someone else says it," said Ellen.

"Before the teacher says it to him in a wild moment," said Edith, whose thoughts had turned to her own son, " 'You don't deserve to have parents!' "

"Show her a picture of the children," Silvia advised.

"It's such a paradox, my connection to Mary and the children," said Colleen. "This is my daughter's family, but she would have never been born—"

Rose finished her sentence: "—if they weren't killed."

"I know you don't like to hear a lot of things Bob said," said Colleen, "but he would say he would never have had Jennifer if he hadn't had Christopher. They didn't want Bobby to be alone. They wanted him to have a sibling he could communicate with throughout life. They were afraid to have a child on their own after Christopher."

"I thought Christopher was a rubella child," said Rose.

"But the fear is there," said Geri.

Colleen nodded. "The fear was there for our little one, too."

"Tell *me* about the fear," said Ellen. "We all know about the fear."

There was a hum of assent all around the table, followed by silence.

"My son is handicapped," Mady said to Colleen, "and when my daughter was born, I tore all the covers off, pulled all her clothes off to see if she was all right. You always live with this fear. You want to see that everything is all right."

Ellen murmured, "You were brave enough to have another one."

It was pushing toward midnight when Colleen asked for another glass of wine.

"Are you driving?" Edith asked, a gentle warning in her voice.

"I am," Colleen said, "but this is it. I'm generally a teetotaler."

"We want you to get home in one piece," said Ellen. "We don't want to worry about you."

Colleen looked at her gratefully. "I'm going to be fine."

She listened to the mothers reminisce about the dances at the Industrial Home for the Blind and the arguments they'd have with their husbands over who was sober enough to drive home. She had a sip or two of wine and then, just after midnight, she said it was time for her to go.

———

CHAPTER 25

The Cycle of Life

A month after the meeting, Colleen went to her first confession in fourteen years. She had stopped after she left the convent and had come home to face the fury of her childhood priest and protector, thereby losing her confessor, whom she'd trusted with the greatest hurts of her life. After that, she kept her secrets to herself, until she met Bob.

Now it was time to go back—not to her old priest, but to the one who had helped with Bob's conversion to Catholicism and who had married them. She told him her fears: that Bob would not be saved and that she was not worthy of God's mercy. He gave her what she was looking for.

"F. said that forgiveness is a gift from God," Colleen wrote in her diary. "It is not earned. That is the most wonderful thing about it. No matter how much we don't deserve it, God gives it. F. said that Bob was not responsible when he killed Mary and the children. He did no wrong.

"As to hell," she continued, "F. spoke of Dante's *Inferno*. Dante described hell not by flame but by cold and ice. F. described hell as not a punishment from God but as a self-made isolation. It's chosen. It is a choice to turn totally away from others."

When the new year began, 1998, she removed her wedding ring from her finger—not because she was leaving Bob behind, but because she felt it was time to look forward. She soon realized that it wouldn't be simple, because in the spring her daughter wanted to know everything about Bob's first family. What were their names? How old were they? How had they died? Colleen remembered the advice she had gotten from Ellen and the other IHB mothers: *Tell her when she asks.* Though she hadn't spoken to the mothers again, she believed something valuable had passed between her and this group of women who were linked to her—whether they liked it or not—by Bob's troubled fate. While she realized they would never forgive Bob, she thought she'd persuaded them to acknowledge that maybe he wasn't a monster and that she wasn't crazy for loving him. She valued their advice, because they'd gained wisdom from their troubles—and because she couldn't imagine posing the question to her own mother.

So Colleen told the girl that her father's other children had been killed. When she asked who killed them, Colleen told her, "By someone who was mentally ill."

Why? the child asked.

"Because mentally ill people sometimes do things that they don't realize are wrong because of their illness," Colleen explained.

How? the child asked.

"They were hit," Colleen told her.

"Was it a bat or a hockey stick?"

The intuitive accuracy unnerved Colleen. In her diary she wrote, "I wimped out. I did not tell her that Bob was the mentally ill person. There will be another opportunity. She will ask."

Colleen frequently took their daughter to visit Bob's grave. He hadn't wanted to be buried with his family, because he was afraid his disgrace might somehow infect them, so his body was interred at the Calverton military cemetery, on the north shore of Long Island. Colleen picked the inscription for his headstone, a traditional white military marker: *Robert T. Rowe, Corporal U.S. Army, World War II, Korea, April 17, 1929–Sept. 23, 1997. Beloved husband, Loving father, "Aloha Bobby."*

She'd had to fight for the *aloha.* The woman in charge of tombstones had told her, "We usually don't put slang on tombstones." But she relented when Colleen explained, "*Aloha* is a sign of affection and it means, 'I love you,' and within that, 'I'm going to see you again.' "

After Colleen told her child that the "mentally ill person" who had killed Bob's first family had died, they added a stop on their trips to Calverton. They went to Pinelawn Memorial Park, where Mary and the children were buried. When they knelt together at the graves, Colleen would marvel at the paradox. Should I be at their graves? she would ask herself. No! They should be living. But had the tragedy not occurred, I would never have had Bob. I wouldn't have had my child. I have a connection to these people lying here. They're my daughter's family, yet my daughter would never have known them. She wouldn't have been their sister, yet she is.

Colleen had always known when Bob had been to visit Mary and the kids, because he'd bring home yet another map of Pinelawn. He always got lost, because dementia was part of his illness—and because it was easy to get lost at Pinelawn; there were no headstones, only bronze plaques laid flat into the ground. Bob and Mary had planned to be buried there. Instead, Christopher and Mary shared one grave; Bobby and Jennifer, the other. For years the graves had remained unmarked, and Colleen had urged Bob to take care of it. He kept bringing home brochures for the plaques, whose size and shape were strictly regulated. But finally Colleen realized that Bob was incapable of placing the order and she sent away for the plaques herself, choosing the floral-bouquet pattern, said to represent the cycle of life.

The last morning of Bob's life, Colleen saw that he was going. As she had told the mothers, she'd taken him out of the hospital so he could die at home. The little one seemed to know he was going, too. When Colleen came out of the shower that morning, her daughter was standing on a stool, reading a book to her father. Before she left for school, she combed his hair and kissed him a couple of times.

He was yellow. The cancer had closed off his bile duct and he was jaundiced. "Am I dying, Colleen?" he asked.

"Yes, Bob, you are," she told him. "It's okay. You can go. It's okay."

"Thank you," he said. "I tried so hard."

"Your struggles are over," Colleen said. "You can go to your family. Mary is waiting for you. Your children are waiting for you. Bobby. Christopher. Jennifer."

Until the end, she always acknowledged and accepted the primacy and inaccessibility of Bob's first life, yet after he died, she wanted to find out exactly what she had accepted. She wanted to know everything about the man she had loved. So she was floored—and gratified—when Kenneth and his wife and two of his sons showed up at Bob's wake. She'd thought Ken might come. He and Bob had talked on the phone not long before Bob died, and she heard Bob say, "I love you, Kenny." But Pat had kept her distance until the end, even though she always sent Christmas cards, which made Colleen believe she was a good person who was just watching out for her own.

At the wake, her sister-in-law offered an olive branch. "Bob was like a magnet for people," she told Colleen. "If you walked into a room, people were around Bob. He captured you. I'm sorry my oldest boy couldn't come—he's living somewhere else."

Colleen couldn't remember much of what Ken said, only the sadness on his face. "He had that boy," he said to her. "He was so disabled."

They didn't go to the funeral, though. They said they were going to, and then they didn't.

The summer before the first anniversary of Bob's death, Colleen and the little one, who hadn't yet turned seven, were snuggling together on a Saturday morning.

"Where was my dad when his family was killed?" the girl asked.

Colleen decided it was time. She said, "Daddy killed them. He was the mentally ill person who needed help. He tried to kill himself, too."

She studied her child's face and saw curiosity and amazement but no horror. When she finally spoke, she asked excitedly if she could tell her cousin right away. Colleen told her that many people knew what had happened and that it was fine to ask any of them questions. The conversation lasted only a few minutes, and then the little one asked if she could go out and play.

SOURCE NOTES
AND ACKNOWLEDGMENTS

Because Bob Rowe died before I had a chance to interview him, my reporting about his life and his perspective had to differ from the rest of the reporting in this book. I didn't hear directly from him; he couldn't respond to stories other people had told about him.

But he left behind a voluminous record. Because of his insanity plea and subsequent installation in the state mental health system, he was extensively interviewed by psychiatrists, social workers, physicians, and lawyers. Each of his many court proceedings produced insight into his memories, his perceptions, and his personality. (These proceedings include the murder trial, the many applications for release from state custody, and his attempt to be reinstated to the bar.) The public record also provided police reports, the prosecutor's file, and the Brooklyn assistant district attorney's report from the night of the killings.

Bob Rowe was a diligent diarist, letter writer, and author. His writing reveals much about a man at once trying to come to grips with the horrible act he'd committed—and to deny responsibility for it.

In my attempt to tell this story thoroughly, I have studied these documents and supplemented them with interviews wherever possible. There are gaps. After many requests, Kenneth Rowe, Bob Rowe's brother, had finally agreed to talk to me. The morning of our interview, however, he called to cancel. After listening politely to my attempts to change his mind, he said with clear finality: "The nightmare is over."

In the end, I feel I have given an honest and comprehensive account. However, I confess that I never will understand fully these sad, strange events. I'm not sure anyone could.

I do know with absolute certainty that I couldn't have written this book without the generous cooperation of the participants and witnesses—above all, the women in the mothers' group (Edith Patt, Mady Gaskin, Ellen Alboher, Geri

Smith, Rose Mauro, and Silvia White) and Colleen Rowe. Their forthrightness and bravery constantly amazed me, and so has their patience, during the five years it has taken to complete this book.

Their husbands, children, friends, and colleagues, and former members of the mothers' group, were willing to sit for hours of interviews, and then later to answer follow-up questions as new information came into play. Friends of Bob and Mary Rowe explored with me painful memories (as well as happy ones), most valuably the late Donald Cassidy, and Silvio Caso, Alvin Kahn, Jack O'Shaughnessy, Harvey Sackstein, Barbara Sapolsky, and Irene Wagner.

While the court records provided much information about the killings, interviews were invaluable in providing context and illuminating details. I thank especially Michael Gary, Jeffrey Mond, Natalie Mond, Alan Sapolsky, and Stephen Scaring.

For guidance on legal matters, I turned to William Brooks, Mark DeWan, Bob Kaye, Lesley Oelsner, Virginia Modest, Rick Pappas, Robert Sach, Sol Wachtler, Moses Weinstein, and Leonard Yoswein. More help came from Fred Miller at the Lawyers Fund for Client Protection, Carol M. Langford, and Lisa Rosenzweig.

Dr. Stephen Teich, Bob Rowe's psychiatrist for many years, provided helpful insight, as did Dr. Daniel Schwartz, Dr. Henry Pinsker, and Dr. David Yamins.

I was guided in my research into blindness generally and into the specific problems of the children I've written about here by the American Foundation for the Blind, Ellen Trief at the Jewish Guild for the Blind, Betty Maloney, Ligia Monzon, Santiago Monzon, Claudelina Oralio, and Walter Johnson, the ocularist.

When I was faced with corralling and confirming a multitude of details, Anne Fadiman came to my rescue. She introduced me to Patricia O'Toole and the Hertog Foundation at Columbia University, and from this connection I became the beneficiary of Elizabeth Gold's resourcefulness as a researcher.

For good counsel and much needed cheerleading, I thank Trish Hall and Patti Gregory, as well as Debbie Abrams, Marjorie Abrams, Megan Barnett, Rosalind Baronio, David Blum, Brian De Palma, Alan Einhorn, Conny Frisch, Caryn James, Barry Kramer, Sara Krulwich, David Halpern, Joan Malin, Judy McClintick, Terri Minsky, Suzanne Salamon, Arthur Salcman, and Lilly Salcman.

Pam Schwartz set this project in motion and then provided tremendous assistance from two important perspectives: as the mother of children with impaired vision and as a psychologist who works with mentally ill prisoners. She has been a wonderful friend and teacher.

At Random House I would like to thank Ann Godoff for having faith, Christen Kidd for handling so many pesky details with grace and intelligence, and Veronica Windholz for going well beyond conventional copyediting with her valuable suggestions, always aimed at clarity.

As for Dan Menaker, he has been everything an editor should be: demanding, encouraging, and unwavering. I am forever grateful.

Finally, without Kathy Robbins and Bill Abrams, this book wouldn't exist. Kathy is my agent, friend, and chief nudge, who is endlessly sympathetic but tolerates no whining.

Bill Abrams, my husband, put the nagging "Get Back to Work" screen saver on my computer, but he also knows exactly when and how to yank me away from my desk. Throughout this difficult project—and in every other part of life—I have been able to manage because of him and our children, Roxie and Eli, and their bountiful love and laughter.

BIBLIOGRAPHY

The research for this book took me down many unexpected paths. I had to familiarize myself with the insanity defense, with blindness and other physical and mental impairments, and with the special problems of families with disabled children. The following books and articles helped me deepen my understanding of those areas—as well as New York City geography and baseball history, ocularists, the constellations, the Book of Job, Hawaiian history and mythology, opera, and Catholicism.

BOOKS

Bettelheim, Bruno. *A Good Enough Parent.* New York: Vintage, 1988.

Bulfinch, Thomas. *Bulfinch's Mythology.* New York: The Modern Library, 1993.

Burlingham, Dorothy. *Psychoanalytic Studies of the Sighted and the Blind.* New York: International Universities Press, 1972.

Daws, Gavan. *Holy Man: Father Damien of Molokai.* Honolulu: University of Hawaii Press, 1984.

Eisenberg, Arlene, Heidi E. Murkoff, and Sandee E. Hathaway. *What to Expect When You Are Expecting.* New York: Workman, 1991.

Fraiberg, Louis, ed. *Selected Writings of Selma Fraiberg.* Columbus: Ohio State University Press, 1987.

Fraiberg, Selma H. *The Magic Years: Understanding and Handling the Problems of Early Childhood.* New York: Scribner, 1959.

Frith, Uta. *Autism: Explaining the Enigma.* Oxford: Blackwell, 1989.

Fukurai, Shiro. Margaret Haas and Fusako Kobayashi, translators. *How Can I Make What I Cannot See.* New York: Van Nostrand Reinhold, 1974.

Ginzberg, Louis. *Legends of the Bible.* Philadelphia, Jerusalem: The Jewish Publication Society, 1992.

Grandin, Temple, and Margaret M. Scariano. *Emergence: Labeled Autistic.* Novato, California: Arena Press, 1993.

Heffner, Elaine. *Mothering.* New York: Doubleday, 1978.

Herrmann, Dorothy. *Helen Keller: A Life.* New York: Knopf, 1998.

Hull, John M. *Touching the Rock.* New York: Vintage, 1992.

Jackson, Kenneth T., ed. *The Encyclopedia of New York City.* New Haven: Yale University Press, 1995.

Keller, Helen. *The Story of My Life.* Mineola, New York: Dover Publications, 1996 ed.

Kiple, Kenneth F., ed. *The Cambridge World History of Human Disease.* Cambridge: Cambridge University Press, 1993.

Kipling, Rudyard. *The Light That Failed.* New York: Penguin, 1992 ed.

Kirwin, Barbara P. *The Mad, the Bad and the Innocent: The Criminal Mind on Trial.* Boston: Little, Brown, 1997.

Kübler-Ross, Elisabeth. *On Death and Dying.* New York: Touchstone, 1983.

Kupfer, Fern. *Before and After Zachariah: A Family Story About a Different Kind of Courage.* New York: Delacorte, 1982.

Kushner, Harold S. *When Bad Things Happen to Good People.* New York: Avon, 1981.

Kuusisto, Stephen. *Planet of the Blind: A Memoir.* New York: Dial, 1998.

Lash, Joseph P. *Helen and Teacher.* New York: Delacorte, 1980.

Leahy, Mike, ed. *If You're Thinking of Living In: All About 110 Great Neighborhoods in and Around New York.* New York: Times, 1999.

Lewis, Dorothy Otnow. *Guilty by Reason of Insanity: A Psychiatrist Explores the Minds of Killers.* New York: Ballantine, 1998.

Magee, Bryan, and Martin Milligan. *On Blindness.* New York: Oxford University Press, 1995.

Magee, James Edmund. *Your Place in the Cosmos.* Northfield, Illinois: Mosele & Associates, Inc., 1985.

Merlis, Brian, and Oscar Israelowitz. *Welcome Back to Brooklyn.* Brooklyn: Israelowitz Publishing, 1993.

Moran, Richard. *Knowing Right from Wrong: The Insanity Defense of Daniel McNaughtan.* New York: Free Press, 1981.

Nilsen, Robert, and J. D. Bisignani. *Big Island of Hawaii Handbook: Including Hawaii Volcanoes National Park, the Kona Coast, and Waipio Valley (3rd Edition).* Moon Handbooks, Avalon Travel Publishing, 1998.

Powell, Thomas H., and Peggy Ahrenhold Ogle. *Brothers & Sisters—A Special Part of Exceptional Families.* Baltimore, London: Paul H. Brookes, 1985.

Preiser, Peter. *Practice Commentaries, McKinney's Consolidated Laws of New York, Annotated: Book 11A CPL 330 to 469.* St. Paul, Minnesota: West Publishing, 1997.

Rivera, Geraldo. *Willowbrook: A Report on How It Is and Why It Doesn't Have to Be That Way.* New York: Vintage, 1972.

Rothman, David J., and Sheila M. Rothman. *The Willowbrook Wars.* New York: Harper & Row, 1984.

Rubin, Theodore Isaac. *One to One: Understanding Personal Relationships.* New York: Viking, 1983.

Sacks, Oliver. *An Anthropologist on Mars.* New York: Vintage, 1996.

————. *The Island of the Colorblind.* New York: Knopf, 1997.

Seligman, Milton, ed. *The Family with a Handicapped Child: Understanding and Treatment.* New York: Grune & Stratton, 1983.

Sheehan, Susan. *Is There No Place on Earth for Me?* New York: Vintage, 1983.

Simon, Henry W. *100 Great Operas and Their Stories.* New York: Doubleday, 1989.

Simons, Robin. *After the Tears: Parents Talk About Raising a Child with a Disability.* New York: Harcourt Brace Jovanovich, 1987.

Simos, Bertha G. *A Time to Grieve: Loss as a Universal Human Experience.* New York: Family Service Association of America, 1979.

Snyder-Grenier, Ellen M. *Brooklyn: An Illustrated History.* Philadelphia: Temple University Press, 1996.

Spock, Benjamin, and Michael B. Rothenberg. *Baby and Child Care.* New York: Pocket, 1985 ed.

Sulloway, Frank J. *Born to Rebel: Birth Order, Family Dynamics and Creative Lives.* New York: Pantheon, 1996.

Turnbull, Ann P., and H. Rutherford Turnbull III. *Parents Speak Out: Growing with a Handicapped Child.* Columbus, Ohio: Charles E. Merrill Publishing Company, 1979.

Wachtler, Sol. *After the Madness.* New York: Random House, 1997.

Wells, H. G. *The Country of the Blind.* Mineola, New York: Dover Publications, 1997.

Willensky, Elliot, with Norval White. *The A.I.A. Guide to New York City.* New York: Harmony Books, 1986.

Wills, Garry. *Saint Augustine.* New York: Viking Penguin, 1999.

Woychuk, Denis. *Attorney for the Damned: A Lawyer's Life with the Criminally Insane.* New York: Free Press, 1996.

Wybar, Kenneth, and David Taylor, eds. *Pediatric Ophthalmology: Current Aspects.* New York: Marcel Dekker, 1983.

Zitrin, Richard A., and Carol M. Langford. *Legal Ethics in the Practice of Law.* Charlottesville, Virginia: The Michie Company, 1995.

PERIODICALS

Blakeslee, Alton. "Defending Preemies' Eyes from O_2." *Sightsaving,* vol. 51, no. 2, 1982.

Devine, Edward T., ed. *Charities and the Commons*. Vol. XV, February 3, 1906.

Doman G., and C. H. Delacato. "Train Your Baby to Be a Genius." *McCall's*, March 1965.

Fjeld, Harriett Anderson, and Kathryn Erroll Maxfield. "Why a Program of Research on Preschool Blind Children?" *The Journal of Psychology*, 6, 1938.

Glaberson, William. "Brother Asserts Prosecutor Misled Him in Unabom Case." *New York Times*, November 23, 1997.

———. "Unabom Trial May Prove Landmark on Illness Plea." *New York Times*, December 9, 1997.

Gupte, Pranay B. "Hyman Barshay, 77; Former Justice Served 30 Years on the Bench." *New York Times*, May 22, 1979.

Hamill, John, and Cass Yanzi. "Say Dad Killed Wife and 3 Kids." *Daily News*, February 23, 1978.

Ingalls, Theodore H. "The Strange Case of the Blind Babies." *Scientific American*, vol. 193, no. 6, December 1955.

Kihss, Peter. "A Brooklyn Family's Long Struggle Ends in Tragedy." *New York Times*, February 24, 1978.

Levy, Lawrence C. "Mother, 3 Children Found Slain," *Newsday*, February 23, 1978.

Margolick, David. "Horror's Stigma Still Clings to a Disbarred Lawyer." *New York Times*, May 15, 1993.

McKenna, Chris, Paul Schwartzman, and Esther Pessin. "Family Killer Fit to Practice Law Again." *New York Post*, April 7, 1989.

Nissel, G. "The Mullers of Wiesbaden." *The Optician*, December 10, 1965.

Ozick, Cynthia. "The Impious Impatience of Job." *American Scholar*, autumn 1998.

Palmer, Eber L., ed. "The Teachers' Forum for Instructors of Blind Children." Vol. VIII, September 1935.

Patt, Edith. "Preschool Children with Visual Impairment and Who Can Serve Them." Unpublished lecture given at St. Paul Technical-Vocational Institute, May 4, 1973.

———. "The Challenge of Educating the Preschool Blind Child with Multiple Handicaps." Unpublished lecture given at the University of the State of New York, April 1970.

Pessin, Esther. "Sequel to Slaughter," *New York Post*, April 16, 1989.

Raftery, Thomas, and Owen Moritz. "Despair Led to Slaying of His Family of Four." *Daily News*, February 24, 1978.

Roberts, Sam. "1977, Summer of Paranoia." *New York Times*, July 1, 1999.

Schanberg, Sydney H. "German Measles at Epidemic Rate." *New York Times*, February 8, 1964.

Schmenck, Jr., Harold M. "German Measles Yielding to Study." *New York Times,* May 4, 1964.

———. "Women Advised on Measles Care." *New York Times,* September 13, 1964.

Schumach, Murray. "It Was an Exciting Day for New York: Yankee Fever." *New York Times,* October 11, 1977.

Silverman, William A. "The Lesson of Retrolental Fibroplasia." *Scientific American,* vol. 236, no. 6, June 1977.

Smith, Red. "Hemingway Wouldn't Have Dared," *New York Times,* October 21, 1977.

Sullivan, Ronald. "Psychiatrist Whose Testimony Led to Acquittal." *New York Times,* December 1, 1977.

Toobin, Jeffrey. "From Park Avenue to Death Row," *New Yorker,* September 22, 1997.

Trester, Wolfgang. "History of Artificial Eyes and the Evolution of the Ocularistic Profession." Cologne: August 2, 1981. Lecture reprinted in *The Journal of the American Society of Ocularists,* 12th Edition, 1982.

Trief, E. and R. Duckman, A. R. Morse, and R. K. Silberman. "Retinopathy of Prematurity." *Journal of Visual Impairment & Blindness.* December 1989.

Walsh, Elsa. "Strange Love." *New Yorker,* April 5, 1999.

West, Debra. "Murder Suspect Accused of Faking Mental Illness." *New York Times,* November 25, 1995.

(No byline) "German Measles Hits 200 Daily Here." *New York Times,* March 31, 1964.

(No byline) "Spreading Across U.S.: German Measles." *U.S. News & World Report,* May 11, 1964.

(No byline) "Infectious Diseases." *Time,* April 24, 1964.

(No byline) "The IHB Way: An Approach to the Rehabilitation of Blind Persons." A publication of the Industrial Home for the Blind, 1961.

(No byline) "Slayer of Family Wins Hearing For Reinstatement as Lawyer," *N.Y. Law Journal,* April 7, 1989.

INTERNET ARTICLES

"Abnormal Development of the Penis and Male Urethra," David Hatch, M.D.
http://www.meddean.luc.edu/lumen/meded/urology/abnpendv.htm

"Anterior Impingement of the Femoral Head in Perthes' Disease," Masafumi Homma, M.D., and J. Richard Brown, M.D., 1996.
http://gait.aidi.udel.edu/res695/homepage/pb_ortho/educate/clincase/perth.htm

Ask NOAH About: Pregnancy/Rubella.
> http://www.noah.cuny.edu/pregnancy/march_of_dimes/pregnancy.illness/
> rubella.html

"Belle Harbor," compiled by Yoon Kim and Tina Morales.
> http://www.newsday.com/azq/bellehar.htm

"Dialogues de Carmelite [*sic*]: Synopsis," Cara Leheny, 1996.
> http://www.orc.soton.ac.uk/ngb/ddc.html

Encyclopedia Mythica.
> http://www.pantheon.org/mythica

"Hypospadias," University of Michigan Medical Center Section of Urology.
> http://www.um~urology.com/clinic/pediatric/hypospadias.html

Kamehameha I.
> http://www.kohala.net/historic/kbirthplace

"Legg-Calvé-Perthes Disease," Geofrey Nochimson, M.D., author, and Eric
> Kardon, M.D., ed., 1998.
> http://www.emedicine.com/emerg/topic294.htm

Mamalahoe (Law of the Splintered Paddle).
> http://www.ksbe.edu/history/paddle.html

The Mission Statement of the Order of Ecumenical Franciscans.
> http://www.franciscans.com/docs/basics/docs_basics_bluebook.html

Opera synopses, 1997.
> http://www.classicalmus.com, by Mediapolis.inc.

"Psychomotor Patterning," Steven Novella, M.D. *The Connecticut Skeptic.* Vol. 1,
> Issue 4 (Fall 1996), p. 6.
> http://www.theness.com/pattern.html

St. Charles Borromeo Catholic Church: Organizations: Secular Franciscan Order.
> http://www.scborromeo.org/org/sfo.htm

FACING THE WIND

JULIE SALAMON

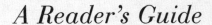

A Reader's Guide

*To print out copies of this or other
Random House Reader's Guides, visit us at
www.atrandom.com/rgg*

QUESTIONS FOR DISCUSSION

1. In *Facing the Wind,* Julie Salamon addresses the very nature of guilt and innocence. "It was a monstrous story," she writes, "but Edith Patt assured me that [Bob Rowe] was not a monstrous man." Do you think Rowe was a victim of mental illness and bad luck or a man who refused to take responsibility for his actions? Do you think there should be a distinction between moral culpability and legal culpability? Where does justice lie?

2. Salamon spent years researching, reporting, and writing this book and must have strong feelings about the case, yet she never passes judgment on Bob Rowe. Did her impartiality disturb you? Why do you think she chose to remain neutral? Do you think Salamon's impartiality strengthens or weakens the narrative? Does an author's passionate advocacy of a given person or issue get in the way of readers' ability to judge for themselves?

3. The tragedy that befell the Rowes had enormous repercussions beyond their immediate family. Apart from paying respect to the mothers, why do you think Salamon included their stories? Does reading about their ongoing struggles distract from or illuminate the issues in the Rowe case? The chapter called "The Ocularist" appears to digress into an example of how fate alters lives and perspectives. Is the chapter really a digression, or does it offer additional insight?

4. After declaring Bob Rowe not guilty by reason of insanity, Judge Hyman Barshay concluded that "if this defendant had been more competently exam-

ined and treated, I am sure this would have been avoided." But couldn't this argument be made in many criminal cases—that if a defendant's life had gone differently, no crime would have been committed? Does the insanity defense seem more valid or less valid to you after reading the Rowes' story? Do you think there's a distinction between "guilty but insane" and "not guilty by reason of insanity"?

5. *Facing the Wind* tells of many struggles for faith and endurance and of great longing for a sense of completion. Bob Rowe seemed to be a source of strength for both the mothers and Colleen. Were they unrealistic in their reliance on him? The mothers admired and looked up to Rowe before the killings. Do you think they were wrong about him? If so, why do you think Colleen came to lean on him so heavily after the killings? Was he a different man before the killings than afterward, or did circumstances determine their perceptions of him?

6. The subtitle of the book refers to reconciliation. Do you feel that the participants in this tragedy really did achieve a sense of reconciliation? What does that mean after terrible events such as the ones described here? Is forgiveness an element of reconciliation, or is it something apart?

7. Why do you think the mothers and Colleen wanted to meet one another? What were your feelings as you read about their encounter? What, if anything, do you think was achieved by this confrontation between Bob Rowe's first life and his second?

SUGGESTED READING

The Executioner's Song, by Norman Mailer

The Adversary, by Emmanuel Carrère

Touching the Rock, by John M. Hull

Planet of the Blind, by Stephen Kuusisto

Is There No Place on Earth for Me?, by Susan Sheehan

A Good Enough Parent, by Bruno Bettelheim

A Cold Case, by Philip Gourevitch

In Cold Blood, by Truman Capote